AMMUNITION

ESSENTIALS OF LEADERSHIP

Alexander Pelaez

Graphic Design by Janet Sarah Allison

Geolatin Publishing
Baldwin, New York

Additional copies may also be obtained from BookSurge

BookSurge
www.booksurge.com
1-866-308-6235
orders@booksurge.com

Publisher's Cataloging-in-Publication Data

Pelaez, Alexander
        Ammunition: essentials of leadership / Alexander Pelaez
        Baldwin, NY: Geolatin Publishing, 2009
           p. cm.
        ISBN 978-0-9840951-7-9

PS616.E357 A58 2009

Library of Congress Control Number: 2009905570

This book is dedicated to the six most important people in my life.

My wife Kelly

Mom & Dad

Cherise, Alex, and Andrew

About the Author

Alexander Pelaez

Mr. Pelaez possesses a unique and diverse set of expertise blending strategy, management and technology. He has a successful track record of leading groups through complex issues, developing strategies for organizations, and counseling managers and executives at all levels on strategy and leadership development.

His research interests focus primarily on strategic concepts, strategy development, leadership and organizational behavior. He lectures, both academically and professionally, on strategic thinking, management organization, and leading edge technologies.

He has over 20 years Information Technology experience holding senior level technology positions with companies in the financial, retail, media/entertainment, and health care industries. In addition, for the past 10 years, he has been an Adjunct Professor of Information Technology at the Zarb School of Business at Hofstra University.

Mr. Pelaez holds a B.A. Degree in Mathematics and Computer Science from New York University, an M.S. Degree in Computer Science from New York University, and an M.B.A. in Marketing from the Zarb School of Business at Hofstra University.

CONTENTS

Chapter 1

INTEGRITY

Opening day in any league always had a special aura unmatched for sports fans. The feeling of a new season, new players, and a whole new start always had that appeal to Ryan Sheridan, an avid baseball enthusiast. It was always comforting that no matter how disappointing any season was, baseball would always return and start anew, and anything was possible the next year. It was the circle of life for baseball; it was as true as the hands on the clock or the days on the calendar. This year would be no different. He knew even though he was watching a peewee league baseball game, everything about it was generally the same. The diamond, the ball, and the bat were all basically the same, and to Ryan, this was very comforting, even if everything on the field was pint size.

Ryan enjoyed watching his five-year-old son, A. J., play baseball in the backyard. He was a very shy little boy, a bit tall for his age, but very thin. He enjoyed tossing the ball with his father every chance he could, and his excitement only grew as the thought of playing on a real team drew closer. This was A. J.'s first year playing but with patience and focus his son would learn the same rules of life he had learned through his many years of playing baseball. Lessons like teamwork, patience, persistence, perseverance, and qualities of leadership remained with Ryan to this very day.

Playing baseball was one of his fondest memories of growing up. He remembered his coaches, specifically his father, who coached him for many years. The fundamentals and attitudes of players were important lessons that children don't realize until they are much older. It was a great feeling to watch the other children play, laugh, and have fun, except when other parents would ridicule their children for simple errors creating uneasiness for every child on the field.

Time was a precious commodity and it was important to balance the discipline and fundamentals of baseball with a healthy dose of mud-filled, dirt-covered fun. All boys love to play in the dirt and mud, and baseball was the perfect way to get dirty, although his wife, Lisa, did not welcome the tracks of mud and dirt in the home. Although she wasn't very athletic, she loved to share in the sports experience with Ryan and A.J.

As he watched the game, he saw how the children interacted with each other. They would run around, sometimes lost and seemingly without purpose. The major challenge for the coach was keeping the children in their assigned areas when the ball was hit. The children were so lost at that age that in one instance, the first baseman ran all the way to the third baseman so he could take the ball and run it back to first. The concept of throwing was something that would eventually need more work, as is every new concept.

The coach had a unique skill of dealing with children. First, he taught them how to throw and catch, then how to field, and finally how to hit. The coach needed time and patience to work with children this age, and he always appreciated it when parents would chip in and assist. Some parents wanted their kids to be superstar homerun hitters, and it was easy to tell who they were since they were usually the most vocal adversaries of the coach's methods.

Hitting was a skill that Ryan didn't think needed to be mastered at this age, but he sure found it a lot of fun and so did the children. Who doesn't like the sound of the ball hitting the bat? Being a purist, Ryan never really liked the "ping" sound of the aluminum bat, but it was better than the sound of wind after missing the ball entirely.

Ryan recognized defense as the most fundamental aspect to baseball. At a very early age, he understood its importance, and spent a lot of time practicing fielding and throwing, and later blocking as a catcher. He found that people who focused on the hitting aspect of the game were looking for glory, while the defensive-minded players focused on every aspect of the game in detail. That summed up Ryan in a nutshell. He wanted to learn more about what he was doing. It was never enough to play; it meant everything to learn more and do it better.

In college, he was a good catcher with a strong arm. He loved the position because he commanded the field, enabling him to be in every play coordinating the team and their movements. Some believed he liked the position because it was a source of power. But Ryan always contended that he loved the position, because he wanted to be the last person between the out and the run, the lightning rod of activity, which meant standing firm and blocking the plate with a well built 225-pound third baseman running full speed, ready to knock him down. For Ryan, holding on to the ball after a major collision was exhilarating, albeit painful, to which Ryan's knees would attest.

Watching his son and his son's friends hit the ball was a lot of fun though; he fully enjoyed watching them try to then run the bases. It took some time for the kids to understand that you have to run to first base as opposed to third. It's easy once you learn, but very funny watching the kids as they run from base to base trying to figure out where to go to next. For the kids it's a bit harrowing not knowing exactly where to go. When children can't figure it out, and every parent is screaming to run the other way, it could be a bit frightening. In the chaos of everyone moving, it is important for anyone, especially children, to know where to go. Clarity is always comforting at any age.

It was time to start a new season—a great time to begin learning new things while practicing the fundamentals. Baseball is a metaphor for life, as so eloquently stated by sportscasters. It represents all that is good in life and the obstacles one faces. It is a representation of who we are and the challenges that life presents us. As long as we practice, persevere, and focus on the fundamentals, we will succeed.

This spring was much more than the start of baseball season, it was the beginning of a new job, or what he hoped would be a long career with his new employer. He had left a media company at a low-level grade and salary, and could now focus on what he believed would be his destiny. The job was a team lead role, in which he was responsible for a small group of developers at a major retail sporting goods company, Paltz. He had waited awhile for this opportunity, realizing his success was dependent on some level of risk taking. It was important to grow as an individual, and growth was achievable only by taking risks. He didn't want to be a lifer like so many of his colleagues at his old job, doing things the same old way, never really getting anywhere, and always afraid to try anything new. These middle managers were complacent to receive their bonuses, and move up the pay scale in increments of 3 percent per year. Although many seemed happy, inside, they just never fully achieved their true potential.

Ryan spent eight years at his former employer, a small, 150-employee, family-run media company, where he was originally hired as an application developer, programming and maintaining systems. While he had a good college education, much of his technology knowledge was self-taught, since the company had used systems that colleges don't teach. The company was known for hiring students directly from college and requiring them to be self-sufficient and entrepreneurial in spirit.

The curriculum at State was archaic and left students unprepared for the real world; therefore, it was difficult to appreciate the value of the education. The programming classes he attended, focused on languages that hadn't been widely used in over ten years, but were "academically useful for teaching concepts," he recalled one professor saying when Ryan had challenged him on its use. He was developing cutting-edge Web site applications that utilized the latest technologies, which he never learned in school. Thus, he focused on developing his own skills, believing that his path to success was learning more technology on his own, increasing his overall marketability.

After a series of spats with his boss, however, it was time to leave. Ryan's immaturity was evident, as these confrontations always left him with a bitter feeling. He never really handled these situations well, which was most likely a sign of a bruised ego. These arguments had increased as his responsibilities expanded and had intensified over the past year. In the six years, he felt he never won an argument and his frustration level had built up like a volcano on the verge of exploding.

He started with the company when he was twenty-two, after completing his bachelor's degree, and immediately thought he could begin conquering the world. This would have been typical of a hotshot programmer who had been designing applications since high school. He intensely desired to be right all the time, and although it took time, he would learn how to play *the game*. Unfortunately, he wasn't really sure what the game was or how to play it. His education in school didn't prepare him for any of these problems, nor did anyone ever tell him about *the game*. His classes, as designed, always stressed basic programming techniques; nothing he learned could help him deal with his current situation, causing him to question the value of his $80,000 education.

"What good is European Art Appreciation?" was Ryan's favorite question at the bar with his friends, referring to a class for his liberal arts requirement. He complained constantly about all the problems with State—how they should transform the school—which simply revealed manifestations of his own professional frustrations. He had good ideas, and many of his friends in similar positions shared the same sentiments. It was a good talking point, but nobody ever really believed it would amount to anything.

The final straw for Ryan at his job came when he was asked to write a program to sort a series of records, a straightforward task. He could most expeditiously complete it with an algorithm called a Merge Sort; however, when asked, his boss, Jeff, directed him to use a simpler algorithm, Insertion Sort, which was not as efficient. Ryan became increasingly agitated as the two discussed the merits of their respective algorithms, and even though he was technically correct, Jeff would not allow him to use his idea. He demanded an explanation, but received none; Jeff simply walked away.

Jeff was the kind of manager everyone loved to hate. In his mid forties, Jeff was short tempered and lacked technical prowess, leaving many to question how he landed the position of leading this department. The founder of the company, who wasn't very technical, always relied on Jeff, his cousin, for technical decisions. It was nepotism at its finest. Jeff wasn't stupid; he understood application development but he simply had an archaic view of how programs should be written, how programmers should work, and how to manage a team. His own ego would blind him many times to the issues surrounding him.

Refusing to be wrong, Ryan wrote three programs to sort the same set of records and demonstrated the performance of each, clearly showing the superiority of his method. Technically speaking, it was the better way, and any academic could clearly prove it. Jeff instead chose the simpler algorithm and never gave Ryan an explanation, leaving him bewildered at his boss's obstinate position.

After briefly reviewing the results of Ryan's work, Jeff abruptly dismissed Ryan from his office by flicking his hand toward the door and refusing to speak. The two were like rams at the top of a mountain banging heads for territory, only Jeff had the bigger horns. Ryan believed that if there was a better way to accomplish a task it should be done, and he couldn't understand why Jeff would dismiss him so blatantly and in such a condescending manner. It affected him more personally than any other confrontation between them. Ryan, dejected and angry, not only exited Jeff's office but also stormed out of the building and left for the day.

Later that night, Ryan met up with John, his friend and colleague from the office, and explained what had happened. John was Jeff's softball buddy and a friend for the past ten years. He had a very pleasant smile which stood out from the mustache and goatee, and while John loved to horse around with a fraternal shove, he couldn't match Ryan's broad physique, even though he stood a few inches taller.

John explained that Ryan needed to learn how to deal with Jeff. Jeff wasn't an academic and fostered a great disdain for academics. Ryan quietly felt the same way, and although at times he enjoyed the school environment and some classes, he never developed an appreciation for academics, believing many of the professors were high-in-the-sky theorists who couldn't get out of a paper bag, but could easily calculate the optimal path of escape under certain conditions in time and space.

What puzzled Ryan was why, if a solution were proven to be superior, wouldn't Jeff accept that solution? John responded and remarked that Jeff's ego was larger than Ryan's, which Ryan didn't find amusing.

"To understand Jeff, you really need to understand the way he thinks," John said.

"A few years ago we were playing softball and Jeff was the manager. He played third base, and honestly, he sucked. He could barely reach first base, but since he was the manager, he played third base. Although there were some private gripes, no one argued since we were just out to have some fun."

"How could you stand for that?" Ryan asked.

"Simple," John replied, "he's the boss and we don't want to take anything from the diamond to the office. We just let it go."

John pulled his glasses off and continued with his story, "Anyway, we were tied in the last inning, and the opposing team had a runner on first with no outs. A ground ball was hit directly at him, and he came up with it cleanly. Now fundamentally, he should have thrown the ball to second base to try for the double play or at least get the lead runner. That's basic baseball, any Little League coach would stress that point. Not Jeff, he threw the ball to first base," John said as he rolled his eyes, recalling the game.

"Well, Jeff argued intensely that he'd made the right play. Even to this day, he doesn't admit it was wrong. Unfortunately for us, that run scored on a base hit and we lost the game two batters later," John said with a sigh as he finished.

"Oddly enough, he still blames the pitcher for not pitching effectively in that inning. Ryan, you could have heard a pin drop. No one would speak with him; they just went back to their cars, drove home, and prepared for work the next morning."

"What does this have to do with my situation?" Ryan asked.

"Simple. Jeff thinks he is right; he doesn't know any better and won't acknowledge any alternative way. In your case, you may be right, but Jeff's disdain of academics comes from the fact that he never went to college. He puts down academia because he couldn't handle college and thought he knew better himself."

"I'm confused. If he hates academia, why does he write Ph.D. on his business card?" Ryan asked.

John answered, "It's because he wants to be important, he likes the title and the respect it brings, but he doesn't want to earn it. Jeff feels threatened by you. He isn't aware of those other algorithms you wrote and won't take time to learn."

"So is that my problem?" Ryan asked.

"Actually, yes, it *is* your problem, because you work for him. You need to learn to play *the game.*"

Ryan realized something had to change. Was he just going to capitulate to someone who he felt was inferior and had a Napoleon complex? Jeff's physical appearance, with a five-foot six-inch frame, fit the mold of Napoleon Bonaparte very well. Jeff would have even declared himself emperor of the floor if he had the opportunity.

He believed this situation was so abnormal that it had to be unique to this company, or maybe just his department. He wondered how he could learn to deal with this situation and if it was possible to endure this predicament. Fundamentally, his problems weren't technical, but rather political. If this was the game that John was referring to then he needed to figure out whether to play the game, and if his success was tied to learning the game, he would need to consider whether he could afford not to play the game.

In his mini quest to find out more about office politics, he spoke to some friends who provided him with many different answers. Generally, he concluded, there was no real consensus on how to play. He had received advice such as stay below the radar, basically kiss ass, and never go out on limbs. None of the advice received seemed to fit his personality. Ryan wasn't going to kiss anyone's ass, and he wasn't afraid to go out on limbs. There needed to be a different avenue to find the answer.

Returning to his favorite place, the bookstore, he wanted to see if he could find something that would give him an idea of dealing with office politics. Unsure of what he would find, he roamed the various sections of the bookstore to get ideas, starting with the areas of political science and philosophy.

As time progressed, he walked through the store and focused his attention on the business section, specifically management. A few of the more intriguing books presented organizational structures and theories on behavior within organizations; however, his negative bias toward academics prevented him from absorbing any of the material he perused. These theories seemed too abstract with no real practical application.

Biographies and success stories about people like Sam Walton, Herb Kelleher, and Andrew Carnegie were always great sources for learning. These books provided real examples of success and overcoming adversity. However, as good as they were, he wasn't looking for a biography, but he still couldn't find what he thought he needed.

As Ryan continued through the bookstore, he spotted a few books about the importance of MBAs. It wasn't an isolated one or two; there were at least four shelves of books on MBAs. Ryan wondered if he would learn more on office politics in an MBA program. The thought had crossed his mind in the past, and he figured an MBA was a way to learn more about general business. At the very least, it would look good on a resume, but he was afraid that after investing the time and money he would still be in the same spot, so he never seriously considered it. After an hour of browsing through the bookstore, he decided to leave and resume his search another time.

The next morning, riding the train on his way to work, Ryan was reading an article in *Time* magazine. The article presented an interesting analysis of the keys to successful businesses and business practices. There were a few quotes from Harvard University Business School professors and additional references to articles published in *Harvard Business Review*. Once again though, his disdain for academia somewhat blinded him to the intent of the article. However, as he continued to read, the theories of leadership and management presented in the article were too intriguing to simply ignore. The article, "Examination of Leadership Styles of Distinct Periods in History," focused on different types of leaders from various eras. What was different about this particular article was its analysis of leadership styles using historical figures and its application to a contemporary business environment.

Ryan loved history, although, not every period. This passion would consume countless hours reading books and watching television documentaries on historic military battles, strategies, and campaigns.

The causes and effects of wars and conflicts intrigued him, and while sometimes the horrific nature of battles and wars saddened him, he hoped that future leaders would learn lessons from history to ensure those events would never be repeated—although he wasn't naïve enough to believe that would happen.

The article spoke of key military people in history such as Patton and Eisenhower and their contributions to leadership as well as their differing styles. He particularly noticed that although Patton was a brazen and crass general who some considered a renegade and difficult to control, he earned the respect of his men, but not out of fear. Ryan knew this story very well. He understood that respect for a leader must come from somewhere, and though there may be no unique character attribute that would be a litmus test for a good leader, there might be a key to leadership. If behavior wasn't a clear determining factor for a good leader, what was? His inquiry led to two relevant personal questions: "Was his boss, Jeff, a good leader?" and "Did **Ryan** himself have the attributes of a good leader?"

Ryan continued struggling with Jeff and had a difficult time putting the incident behind him even though it had occurred last month. The best course of action was to speak to Jeff, who coincidentally requested a private meeting, but never gave any indication of the subject. Ryan thought he could use the opportunity to see if there was something that could be learned from the experience, instead of letting it continue to fester and allowing the animosity to brew. At a subconscious level though, Ryan was really looking for vindication and he fooled himself into thinking that he sought a real dialogue.

As he went into Jeff's office and sat down, he was surprised when Jeff opened the conversation about the very same topic. They hadn't spoken much since the incident and this was the first private meeting between the two since their altercation. Ryan was pleasantly surprised that Jeff had decided revisit the incident. Jeff offered a seemingly humble opening of how he respected Ryan's intellect, which was promising. Jeff might now realize how good Ryan's talents were and it would be his stepping-stone to a promotion, if not now, then at least when the next opportunity presented itself, he thought. It was a pleasant surprise that Jeff had finally come to his senses and had realized that there were better ways of doing things.

"Are you with me, Ryan?" Jeff asked.

"Yes, sir," Ryan responded. "Why do you ask?"

"It seemed for a second you may have been daydreaming," Jeff said.

"No, sir, I was listening to what you said, I may seem a little off. I've had a head cold for the past two days and today it is killing me."

Ryan was suffering from a head cold and his sinuses were definitely adding pressure as though two fingers were pressing on the each side of his nose. But, in reality, he was daydreaming. He was a very quick thinker and could come up with an explanation quickly. His friends had always complimented him on his quick thinking, although they knew they were sometimes on the receiving end of his quick thinking.

"Ryan, your sorting code from the other day was good." Jeff had no sense of time, it had already been over four weeks since Ryan submitted that code, but without flinching he continued, "But you really should have just listened to me and programmed the one algorithm I wanted. You didn't have to try to show me up. It's lucky for you that you were wrong," Jeff said.

Ryan went through about ten emotions in a single second. He paused and was about to ask a question, when Jeff continued.

"I know you have some-top notch education. But you need to realize that just because you have a degree doesn't make you any better than anyone else."

Ryan silently agreed with that point.

"In fact, people like me, who don't have a degree, really learn the hard way about what works and what doesn't work. It's the school of hard of knocks, guy, that's where the real learning is done."

Ryan, still completely dumfounded, was speechless, an event that could have been recorded in the Guinness Book of World Records. If many of his friends could witness this event, they would probably be lining up for a ticker tape parade. Ryan was not amused by the conversation and was more confused than ever before.

Jeff continued, "See, Ryan, the algorithm that I wanted is simpler and easier to implement. Although some of the work you did on the other programs may appear faster, according to the book and the stats you ran, I completely disagree. Let me explain.

"The algorithm that you wrote is based on academic research in algorithm design, specifically sorting, and only works in certain cases that are determined by..."

At this point, Ryan completely tuned out and heard nothing more of what Jeff had to say. Ryan had already begun his exit strategy. It was time to leave. This conversation was going nowhere and he couldn't wait until it finished. Unfortunately, it would be another twenty minutes of uninterrupted self-serving conversation for Jeff who, at this point, apparently didn't notice Ryan was completely tuned out and focused on the window where he could see a baseball field in the distance behind the parking lot.

When Ryan left Jeff's office, he immediately decided to update his resume. He couldn't stand working for Jeff anymore, and refused to tolerate Jeff's arrogance and pompous attitude. Although it was part of Jeff's personality, this was the last straw. He was getting out.

Over the next few weeks, the work Ryan was doing came to an almost complete standstill. He wondered how long it would be before someone actually noticed that he wasn't producing anything. Every day he quietly worked at his desk, and gave halfhearted efforts, which would last until the day he finally resigned.

Ryan's search for a new job was a challenge, and the prospect of starting a new job was a bit daunting. It was exciting to wonder what challenges a new job would present. He had been advised to just stick it out at his current job because things always get better and "the grass isn't always greener on the other side," but his decision was final and there was no turning back. If he remained in this position, he would be dealing with a boss who was just a boss. There was nothing more to be learned from Jeff since there were no more real challenges.

What would be the ideal job? He looked at all the requirements and in many cases, he had sufficient technical expertise but lacked some of the key nontechnical items. In some cases, he didn't apply to jobs that he would have loved, because they required significant management experience or certifications he didn't have.

Since the economy was in a downturn, companies were offering drastically lower pay for jobs, and it was frightening to contemplate a reduction in salary. A pay cut was such a strong possibility that he stopped his search for a week, until he revisited the bookstore.

On a table near the self-help section, a motivational book caught his eye and while leaning on the table, he inconspicuously began thumbing thought the book. These motivational books are a bunch of "hooey," as he liked to say. Until it came to a sentence that read, "If you change the way you look at life, your life will change." It was a measure of serendipity opening to that page and the sentence that was as captivating as the brightest star in the heavens.

The sentence interested him so much that he kept reading and ultimately decided to buy the small 150-page book. That simple sentence and the message it conveyed revitalized his entire outlook on his job search but its impact would go far beyond. His focus changed from getting a new job to becoming the head of large group he could lead and make successful. He would be the driving force for success and in the process make a lot of money. Jeff would look completely stupid once Ryan became a boss with a successful team.

Ryan continued his job search and reminded himself to change the way he looked at things. This more positive attitude along with the prospect of a meaningful career reinvigorated him. As he closely looked at the job postings, a pattern began to emerge. The higher-paying jobs and the leaders of the applications groups were not necessarily technical positions. These jobs required more management expertise, including experience in managing budgets and time lines, experience he didn't have. Discouraging at first, he remembered the article he had read in *Time* magazine that focused on leadership qualities and general responsibilities, which he was seeing as a requisite for the jobs he found, leading him to revisit the question of getting an MBA.

An MBA would mean three to four years of work with long nights and weekends of research, homework, and projects. Going back to school wasn't very appealing, but he seemed to run out of options at every turn. For every excuse about applying for the MBA there were twice as many higher-level management positions saying "MBA preferred." In a competition between two candidates, how much of a difference would it make? It was a well-accepted principle that generally, MBAs were higher paid and more sought after for senior management roles. All of the senior executives at his company had MBAs; some from prestigious schools and others from mid-tier local schools. A majority of the midlevel line mangers also had plenty of experience but quite a few also had their degrees. The information surged at him like a tidal wave confirming his need to get back to school and earn an advanced business degree.

So now Ryan had two dilemmas, one was to get a new job and the other was to go to school. He wondered what a new employer would think about his choice to pursue an MBA. Should he wait and finish the degree before he looked for a new job, or just go for broke and get a job and while completing the course work simultaneously? Staying in his current position, dealing with Jeff, was no longer an option; therefore, the job search would take precedence.

Sure enough, Ryan interviewed within two weeks for two positions for which he was highly qualified. At the first interview, the technical portion posed no significant challenges, and his interviewer was very impressed with the score he received. The face-to-face interview progressed better than expected, until questions arose about his desire to leave his current job. Believing that honesty is the best policy, he explained, in detail to the human resources manager, the horror story of his boss. In spite of his obvious displeasure with Ryan's response, the HR manager brought him to the hiring manager who also listened intently to the same story. At the end of the interview, the hiring manager stood up from his chair, walked over to his office door to ensure the door was completely closed, and said, "Ryan, just a quick critique. It's never a good practice to tell a horror story about your last employer."

"But you asked me what happened. I answered truthfully," responded Ryan.

The employer said, "Yes, and I commend you for it, but no one wants to work with someone who has a negative attitude and no one wants to hire "a problem." I'm not saying you're a problem," he said as he recognized the complete and total deflation of Ryan's demeanor.

"I'm saying there's a way to tell your story without all the negativity. I'll call you if there is a second interview, but I really doubt HR will recommend you, if you told HR the same story."

At that point, the supervisor thanked Ryan for coming and shook his hand. Ryan turned and walked away very slowly, as if he had been diagnosed with a terminal disease.

Sitting in the lobby of the building, he slowly sipped his coffee from Starbucks as he stared into space. Thoughts raced through his mind. What happened? Why can't I tell the truth about what really happened? What are they looking for? I can't be a yes-man. It was forty-five minutes of reflection before he realized he needed to rush to get to his next interview.

On his arrival at the next interview, he ran to the bathroom to wipe the sweat off his forehead. He had taken so much time reflecting after the previous interview that he drove like Dale Earnhardt Jr. at Daytona, and ran through the parking lot for what seemed like two miles, moving between cars and dodging traffic, having a few minutes to spare.

At the preliminary human resources interview, the seemingly disastrous interview he had just completed weighed heavily. The scene just replayed in his head as he stared at his interviewer trying his best to remain focused. He anxiously waited for the question he knew was coming. Luckily, there was a written technical test once again that measured his technical aptitude. Since he could take the test almost instinctively, his mind focused on a new answer to the dreaded question of why he was leaving. Using the time wisely, he crafted a new response that would create a positive spin, and focus on the opportunities as well as the work he felt most proud of, remembering the passage in the book he had read earlier in the month, "If you change the way you look at life, your life will change."

Upon his completion of the written test, he signaled the interviewer back to the conference room. After she marked the test with the answer key—Ryan scored perfectly—she began her portion of the interview. She was very nice and professional and understood that many people are generally nervous when they come in for interviews; therefore, she provided guidance and comfort in an attempt to relax candidates. She could easily have been a nurse or a teacher with her demeanor.

She laughed and joked at the company and explained what they were looking for technically, but never really focused on the position as much as she focused on character and personality. It was a very comfortable and friendly interview until she hit him with the dreaded question. Every word of the next question appeared to approach him in slow motion.

"WHY...ARE...YOU...LEAVING...YOUR...CURRENT...JOB," she asked.

Ryan took a deep breath, and said, "Well, it's actually disappointing that I have chosen to leave. I enjoy the people there and I have made some great friends, including one who was in my wedding party. I play softball with them and we generally have a good time," Ryan said as he paused, believing that he had a good start.

"However, as I look at my career, I noticed that there is limited opportunity for growth, and I am really hoping that I can take my experience and make positive contributions in a new environment as well as learn new things. My boss is generally content with our team's performance, but I think I need more of a challenge."

For a split second, Ryan thought he had just blown it, but immediately followed up, "He has been very successful in his position, and I am grateful for the opportunity. However, given my desire to be challenged to a greater extent, I decided it was time for a change."

She gave him a big smile and said, "That's great. This place is definitely a challenge, and by looking at your technical expertise, I'm sure they can use your talents. Let me see if your next interview is ready."

The rest of the interviews went very well and the two other managers he met commended him on his experience and provided positive feedback. Ryan spoke with confidence and optimism as he discussed his work experience and career goals. The conversations with his prospective boss were very enjoyable and informative, including a discussion on Ryan's decision to pursue an MBA for which the interviewer was supportive and persuasive. During the discussion, Ryan asked him many questions about an MBA program, and the interviewer, who never missed an opportunity to talk, gladly answered until he had to leave.

At the conclusion of the interview, he said to Ryan, "When you go for your MBA don't think of it as school, think of it as an experience to meet other students and professors. Learn new ways of solving problems. Don't be afraid to go outside of your area, and try to excel in areas like marketing, management, or finance. You have enough technology background; go out of your comfort zone. Do the MBA because you want to learn, not because you think it will make you a lot of money. The more you learn and apply the better manager you will become, and the more effective you will be."

Ryan thanked him immensely before leaving the interview—it was the greatest interview he'd ever had. More importantly, he was sure he would get the job.

Ryan replayed the interview in his head multiple times thinking how great it went. He began to notice things that seemed to work very well and he fully intended to use them again. He was hoping for more interviews to try the techniques again. The focus changed from being technical and knowing how to program systems, toward a better understanding of how to communicate more effectively. He was no expert, but he had a lot of fun doing it. Waiting for the outcome would be torturous, especially because he had to go back to work the next day and deal with Jeff.

Ryan heard nothing for four days, and then his cell phone rang with the number he wanted to see appearing on the caller ID display. He thought to himself, "This is it."

He had to let it go to voice mail because he couldn't answer the phone in his office. So he calmly walked outside the building and went to his car with his cup of coffee. When he got to his car, he listened to the voice mail message. It was from the nice human resources woman from the second job interview who had asked that he return her call. He was certain they were going to make an offer.

He called the number. Each ring seemed to take an eternity. Finally, she answered.

"Good afternoon, Ms. Ramirez speaking."

Ryan replied, "Hello, Ms. Ramirez, this is Ryan Sheridan returning your call."

"Oh, hello, Ryan, thank you for your quick response," she said.

After a pause and some shuffling of papers in the background, she continued, "The reason I was calling, was to inform you that the director has made his decision and he has chosen another candidate. He indicated that he was very impressed by you, and we wanted to wish you luck on your job search."

The silence on the phone was deafening, but Ryan mustered the courage and thanked her, after he felt his throat clog up, which must have sounded like a muted grunt. Stunned, he uttered a pleasant good-bye, hung up, and dropped his head against the steering wheel, sick to his stomach. He was completely annihilated. He hadn't felt this way since his baseball team lost the championship conference game in college.

Ryan had always viewed that one game, above all other games he played, as a watershed mark in his life. It was the most depressing moment he had ever faced, and left an indelible memory. After losing by three runs in the seventh inning, he came up and hit a grand slam homerun to take a one-run lead against their bitter conference rival. There were high fives in the dugout as everyone was ecstatic. The victory they had fought for all year was closer than ever. Their rival, however, wouldn't be undone, and responded with two runs in the top of the ninth inning to retake the lead. Full of confidence, his team knew they could stage a comeback. Scheduled to bat third in the inning, he would have an opportunity for heroics again, and he was pumped. Unfortunately, his team made two quick outs, and then pinned their hopes on Ryan.

Energized as he walked up to the plate, he focused on simply getting into scoring position with a simple hit. It was all about fundamentals. He visualized the swing over and over, focusing on a nice level smooth swing, elbow up, good hip turn, arm extension. A perfect swing with perfect timing on the second pitch resulted in the unmistakably loud pinging sound of the bat hitting the ball. He had sized up the pitcher perfectly and sat on a fastball driving a perfect hit into the right center gap, between the center fielder and right fielder. As he was running and approached first base, he thought he could stretch the hit into a double. His right foot landed on the inside corner of the base as he turned toward second base and accelerated. The center fielder raced to the ball, perfectly picked it off the ground, and threw it to second base to make a play at second.

Midway between first and second Ryan's cleat gave way, and he lost his footing. He stumbled briefly and lost a step, but recovered quickly and dove headfirst into second base at the exact same moment the ball arrived. His outstretched right arm reached for the bag and he knew his fingers were there before the tag was made.

"You're out!" the umpire exclaimed.

In a split second, the game was over and the umpires were trotting off the field, with the opposing team pouring out of the dugout toward the pitcher's mound to celebrate. Ryan's coach, who was coaching at third base, ran to argue but couldn't catch up to the umpire as the celebration was commencing on the mound for the other team. Ryan's heart sank. He had done everything perfectly, the hit and the turn at first base. If he just hadn't slipped, things would have been different.

He stayed on the ground at second base with his head in the dirt for a good thirty seconds. The coach who had now started to run off the field, made a U-turn near the first base line when he looked back and saw Ryan still on the ground. He quickly made his way over to second as Ryan slowly rose, dusting himself off, and obviously killing time to avoid seeing his teammates.

Coach C was a humble man who knew his role in life was a mentor to his team. He had been coaching college level baseball for over twenty eight years. He knew he had the responsibility of counseling these young men and preparing them for life as they exited the relative safety of college. Through his thick black rimmed glasses were the eyes of old school baseball coach who stressed the fundamentals, but never raised his voice in anger.

Coach C finally approached Ryan, put his hand out, and said in a very stern voice, "Get up, son. You did nothing wrong."

Ryan had finally gotten up and with his head down jogged with the coach back to the dugout. He couldn't help but notice the celebration going on, putting him on the verge of tears. Coach C, still next to him, ran between the celebration and Ryan in order to briskly move him off the field. He wanted Ryan to get off as quickly as possible to keep Ryan from getting too upset.

He said to Ryan, "It's OK to be upset. You will learn in life you can do everything perfectly, but circumstances will dictate whether it works perfectly. Look at their celebration not as a disappointment for you, but rather as an opportunity for you to aspire."

They moved closer to the dugout, when the coach said, "One more thing, it's not the end result that counts, it's the journey that really counts."

Ryan really had no clue what he was talking about. The other team was jubilant while his team was hunched over the bench or walking away from the field as though they had lost a loved one. It just didn't make sense and no philosophical statements were going to make it better. At that point, Coach C had called the entire team together. Coach C, who was also very religious, opened his statement with a prayer thanking God for allowing his team to participate in the championship game and thanking Him for all the players' determination and perseverance. Every member of the team, with one knee on the ground, nodded and replied, "Amen."

Coach C then went on to say, "Team, you fought hard, and today was not your day. One day it will be your day, and when that day comes, you will remember this day more than the day you win. Because it was here that you believed in yourself, and in each other, and that you never let each other down. It was here that you played as a team and fell together until the last possible moment. You will remember this moment, not because of the outcome, but because of the work you put in and the effort you gave until the last out. Take away from this game the specific lesson, that no matter what the outcome, what you put in to the effort is what you will remember, the trophy will never matter."

Ryan thought he felt a bit better; actually, he was praying it would be true, because he felt horrible.

When Coach died two years ago, every member of the team for the past twenty years, or so it seemed, attended his funeral. He was a wonderful character, and everyone remembered the words of wisdom this one man had preached. Some of the team members were senior executives who said that they always remembered what Coach C had preached and incorporated his words into their management style. They never hesitated to give him credit, and, to a man, there were only words of fondness and kindness. Ryan was no different; he had always remembered that day, and he often thought about what Coach said.

Ryan was disappointed that he didn't get the job, but he took away from the experience the valuable lesson that he had made an impression, and the interview made an impression on him. He also still felt invigorated at the prospect of going on more interviews. Sooner or later, he would get another job, because he knew persistence and perseverance would pay off.

A week later, Ryan received a call from the first interviewer. He immediately assumed this was a rejection call. The HR representative wasn't as nice as Ms. Ramirez, but he was very professional.

"Hello Mr. Stenz, happy to hear from you," Ryan said, knowing this call was a lost cause.

Mr. Stenz replied, "Your interview with Mr. Depardeau went very well and he would like you to come back for a second interview with some other people."

Almost speechless, he replied, "Sure, I would be happy to come back, and I appreciate you having me back."

"That's great, let's set up an interview for Monday at 10:00 a.m. is that OK?"

"Excellent," Ryan replied, "I'll be there."

Ryan got off the phone and was perplexed. The interview that he thought was horrific turned out to be good. He wondered how it happened, especially in light of what Mr. Depardeau had said in his earlier interview. There would be no second-guessing though, he was ready to go.

On Monday's interview, he showed up quite early at the company, Paltz, a retail firm whose strategy increasingly focused on online sales. The position would be a great step in a young aspiring manager's career, based on the detailed information Mr. Stenz provided about the position during the phone call.

They were looking for a person to lead a small team of developers within a larger group, utilizing new technologies, and they needed an individual that could meet the challenge of incorporating it into the mainstream. The online strategic initiative was a major endeavor for the company and the proposed budget was over $5 million in infrastructure and personnel, including consultants. He had plenty of ideas and thoughts on how he could be an asset to the project and how he could help transform the company. While the role would be a small part of the entire initiative, the prospect was very exciting.

Gradually backing off his enthusiasm, it was possible that he was just the "second" guy, part of a process to interview the final two candidates, even though one had already been selected. It was a definite possibility that they made up their minds on someone else, making him just a formality. Although he was generally an optimist, sometimes he had a very pessimistic view of the world.

Ryan met with Mr. Stenz, who proceeded to explain with whom he would be meeting and what to expect. He desperately wanted to ask why they invited him back after the last interview seemed so horrific, but his senses got the better of him. Toward the end of the interview, Mr. Stenz said, "One more thing, it would be a good idea if you didn't speak so negatively of your previous employer, just some friendly advice."

Ryan replied, "Mr. Depardeau mentioned that to me on my interview last time. I certainly appreciate it and I've heeded his advice."

Mr. Stenz walked him to the interview room. He had a slight limp since having knee surgery recently, so their progress was slow and it gave them time to speak. He mentioned that Mr. Depardeau enjoyed speaking with him; Mr. Depardieu had seen some similarities of his younger days in Ryan. He thought Ryan was an extremely talented individual and had never seen a candidate with the technical prowess he had demonstrated. Those qualities prompted him to invite Ryan back. Mr. Stenz, who seemed a very formal person by his well pressed three-piece suit, also mentioned subtly that Ryan's honesty was appreciated, even if the delivery was not prudent.

After the interviews were completed, he left the building fairly confident, but had no inkling of what direction they were going to take. Since he avoided repeating the same mistake, everything generally went well. His answers were very deliberate and focused on his delivery and work product. There wasn't a sign of nervousness, only a calm confidence as he answered the questions from all interviewers. He even reflected afterward on how much fun he had speaking with everyone.

On his way back home from the interview, he remembered Coach C saying, "It's about the journey and the people you meet along the way." This statement rang true since his focus wasn't his rejection by the other company, but rather how he felt after that interview, which helped him in his latest interviews. Something had changed inside of him, but he didn't know exactly what it was, and he didn't mind at all.

Two days later, he received another phone call from Paltz. They were extending him an offer to come work for them. Elation would have been an understatement to describe his emotion, and without hesitation, he accepted. Faced with the task of leaving his current employer, he relished the thought of walking into Jeff's office and saying, "I quit!" and, although it was unprofessional, it sure summed up his feelings.

Ryan spent the evening writing a few letters of resignation, using different styles and different words, until he finally settled on one that he thought would work. The chosen letter was a very simple two-paragraph letter thanking Jeff for the opportunity and stating how much he would miss his colleagues. It concluded with praise for Jeff on his leadership and tutelage. He almost gagged on that last line, but it was a prudent thing to say.

He would submit the letter the following Monday, so as not to drop a bomb on a Friday. There were a few critical projects in which he was engaged, and the extra time would give him a chance to develop a transition plan.

He was a pivotal member of the team and felt a tremendous responsibility to his teammates for those projects. These attitudes of teamwork and responsibility came from his baseball days coupled with his admiration of the sense of honor that came from the military, especially the United States Marine Corps, although he was never in the military. He was concerned that his departure would be viewed as a betrayal of trust, but he hoped his teammates would understand and accept his decision. Inside he believed they would understand, but he wasn't sure.

Monday morning, Ryan arrived at the office earlier than usual as he waited for Jeff. Unfortunately, Jeff wouldn't be available until 11:00 a.m., because he needed to attend a managers' meeting, called upon his arrival. Ryan, anxious to tell someone the news, decided to break the news to John, his closest friend at the office, who was taken by surprise at Ryan's imminent departure. The two had a tremendous amount of respect for each other's talents and spent many long nights working together fixing programs and meeting deadlines.

John shared Ryan's pessimistic outlook on the company, but he would be a lifer, craving the steady job content to develop systems. He had no interest in managing people, because he didn't want the responsibility of, as he would say, babysitting anyone. Many people like John believed that employees should be given tasks, do their jobs, get paid, go home, and do it again. If everyone did this, he believed, more work would get done with fewer problems and everyone would be happy.

Ryan didn't share John's "theory" on management. Contrary to John, managing a group was an exciting prospect, and he believed he could do much more than sit at a stupid terminal writing lines of code for the rest of his life. Technology also changed very quickly, which could be disastrous for an employee, left behind the technological curve.

He also didn't share John's notion that companies would always protect their best workers. He had other friends laid off by companies even though they were star performers, which seemed completely counterintuitive. With that understanding, he vowed to do everything he could to protect the best workers if he ever had the opportunity. It was not only the right thing to do ethically; it was the right thing to do for the company. "Selling out," as he referred to it, for political gain was unacceptable.

Ryan finally received the call to come up to Jeff's office. Unsure of Jeff's reaction, he cleaned off his desk and left only a few items to make it appear as though it was just a spring-cleaning. He copied all e-mails and personal files so that he could keep a copy of his work product, even though it was against company policy to do so. Although he didn't think Jeff would overreact and tell him to leave immediately, it was a distinct possibility.

He made his way to the tenth floor, taking the stairs since it was only two flights up. Although it was the healthier way to live, it was just a stall tactic. As he exited the stairs and turned right, he went through the glass doors with his electronic key and stopped for a moment to say hello to the receptionist.

She was a very nice woman with very black curly hair in her late fifties who had suffered the tragedy of losing her husband and son in a fatal car crash four years earlier. He always made it a point, whenever he could, to talk with her, strike up a casual conversation and throw in the odd joke. She really appreciated it, although she never told him, since no one ever took the time to speak with her, unless it was to ask her to get coffee, pick someone up from the lobby, or send a package.

As Ryan turned down the hall, his pace picked up as he mentally committed himself to the conversation with the letter in his green manila folder ready to present. Approaching the office, he could hear Jeff on the phone cursing a storm, obviously not in a good mood, and Ryan knew why.

The main project was behind schedule because Jeff allowed the business owners to change the requirements of the application late in the game and now they were holding him accountable for the late delivery. This was an unfortunate circumstance; however, because there was no process in place to manage "scope creep," as it is known in the industry, the users believed they could make demands without affecting the delivery date. The business community also used this tactic to add requirements to a project after the initial conception phase.

If projects seemed too difficult or time consuming, such as a two-year project, it probably would be denied, so the corporate culture figured out a way around it. A smaller request, which had a higher likelihood of approval, would be proposed and once it was approved, supplemental requests would be added, since the original request would be of little use without the additions, causing significant delays and problems for management. This caused a lot of problems for delivery times and even more problems for management. However, the urgency of fixing the process problem was less than the urgency of implementing these systems.

Ryan waited anxiously outside Jeff's office for him to get off the phone. About a minute later, Jeff, facing the window, turned, saw Ryan at the door, and waved his hand in frantic fashion to come in and sit down. Jeff was noticeably agitated and Ryan knew this was a bad time to levy the resignation, but it was too late now, and the circumstances were beyond his control. Jeff complained on the phone about a particular user who consistently made requests days after the deadline, and who would inform senior management that the product couldn't go into production without the modifications. Her favorite line was "The IT department will just have to figure it out." Management always seemed more than happy to appease her but no one was really sure why. She would become so agitated at meetings that decision makers, including Jeff's boss, felt it better to give her what she wanted to silence her tirades.

Jeff slammed down the phone, and rudely asked, "What do you want?"

Ryan was taken aback, pausing to see if there was a laugh or a joke. There was none. Ryan's plan of a nice meeting went through the window and he quickly scanned the room for two things, anything in Jeff's vicinity that Jeff could use as a projectile and a place to duck and cover. Everyone knew Jeff had a temper, Ryan especially. He had been on the butt end of Jeff's attacks numerous times, which reinforced the decision to quit.

Ryan opened up with "Is everything OK?" as he tried to diffuse the situation a bit.

Jeff replied, "That's a stupid question, but that's why you're just a programmer, you don't understand what it means to be management."

"True," Ryan replied, "I am just a programmer, but my aspirations are to lead a group someday."

Jeff laughed. "Whatever. What do you want, what is so urgent?"

"Well," at this point Ryan wanted to just get the hell out. He changed his plan from a review of his entire career, to simply being direct and forthright to save everyone a lot of trouble.

"Jeff," Ryan paused deliberately as he took a deep breath, "I have decided to pursue other interests. I think the time is right for me to move on."

Ryan noticed Jeff's ears turn red. He was pissed. Ryan went on to say, "It's been great here, and I've sincerely enjoyed my time. I have learned a lot from you and appreciate everything you taught me. Unfortunately, my last day will be in two weeks. However, I have created a transition plan that I would like to go over with you and begin implementing immediately, I think once you..."

Jeff cut him off and said, "You know, you're a piece of work. I've put up with all your shit, and you think you're better than everyone else," as his voice raised with the level of his agitation. "If you wanted to leave, you should have done it after the project was done. You're the reason the project is late and this is typical of you."

Ryan wasn't expecting this at all. He knew Jeff would be upset. Now, Jeff was challenging his work and his integrity, and that was unexpected. He was ready to battle back, but thought better of it.

Ryan calmly said, "Jeff, I know you're upset, but sometimes, opportunities and situations dictate our actions. In no way am I being disrespectful to you or the team. In fact, I put together a transition plan..."

Once again, Jeff cut him off. He picked up the phone and began dialing. Ryan's voice gradually descended as he tried to finish his sentence.

"Get in here now. I don't care what you are doing, drop it, and get in here," he said to the person on the other end.

Ryan wasn't sure who Jeff was talking to as he slammed the phone down. Jeff blurted out, "Here is what you will do—Steve is coming up here now. You will give him all the information today in the conference room. You can take your transition plan and shove it up your ass. I don't need you telling me how to transition anything. You're not that important. Tell Steve what you're working on and where the code is. You have one hour and then you get the hell out of here."

Ryan could begin to feel the blood rushing to his head, his ears getting warmer. He felt threatened and just wanted to leave. He didn't have to take any of this abuse, but then Steve entered.

Steve was a good friend of Ryan's. They had been together at the company almost the same amount of time and spent many lunch hours together.

"Hey, Jeff. Ryan. What's up?"

Ryan was about to say hello, when Jeff pointed at him and said, "You keep quiet; you have nothing to say here."

He then looked at Steve and said, "Steve, go to Conference Room G, take him with you. You have one hour to find out everything he is working on, then take him back to his desk, find some boxes, and help take his personal shit to his car. Ryan is out of here today. Understood?"

Steve nodded. He knew better than to ask Jeff any questions when he was in one of his moods.

"I expect him out of here in one hour," Jeff continued.

Ryan stood up and proceeded out the door. Just as he got to the edge of the door, Jeff yelled at him, "Don't ever use me as a reference, or use my name. If you do, I'll be sure to tell them what I think. You're a real asshole. Now get out."

Ryan took a few quick steps; he was noticeably shaken and couldn't believe what he had heard. He never expected that reaction. He knew Jeff would be upset but he never thought to that degree. After a few seconds, they heard a loud crash come from Jeff's office, but Ryan didn't turn around, remembering the story of Sodom and Gomorrah. He kept walking toward Conference Room G, which, thankfully, was on the other side of the building. If there was going be an explosion on the north side of the building, he didn't want to be within the fallout radius.

Ryan and Steve settled into Conference Room G. Both of them sat and chuckled quietly at how absurd Jeff had become. Ryan explained the transition plan to Steve, who was very familiar with the project. Steve said he was more interested in getting Ryan's stuff packed away than worrying about a transition. There was no way they could effectively transition all the work in one hour and it was just stupid for Jeff to think that would happen. Jeff frequently overreacted, managing simple tasks but never looking at the bigger picture.

By not allowing a transition, Jeff was actually shooting himself in the foot, or maybe both feet. Ryan's participation was so critical to the project that very few people could just step in and do what needed to be done. Steve told Ryan that he thought it would take the team ten weeks just to recover. Ryan asked why Steve wasn't taking as much information as he could in the hour.

Steve replied, "I don't care what happens. There will always be another project, and I can easily spin this if they ever come back at me. Personally, I have no loyalty to Jeff, and I wouldn't mind seeing him go down. But that's not up to me. I'll collect my check, do the minimum amount of work, and leave every day. It's that simple."

After about twenty minutes of bantering, Steve nodded to Ryan to head back up to his cubicle to collect his stuff. The cubicle was clean as a whistle; everything was packed and ready to go. Steve turned with an eyebrow up and said, "You were ready?"

"Yep," replied Ryan.

"I wasn't going to be taken off guard."

Steve helped Ryan carry his stuff. It was only two small boxes, which Ryan could have carried by himself one on top of the other, but Steve didn't mind getting out of the building for a few minutes. Besides, Jeff told him to walk Ryan out of the building, and that's exactly what he would do. Who was he to question Jeff, he thought sarcastically.

As they were walking out to Ryan's car, Steve asked Ryan, "If I run into a problem with your code, can I call you?"

Ryan replied, "Of course, I'll always help you out; we can always go back to my place and load up the code, order pizza, and nerd out for a while."

Steve laughed, "Thanks, it's just in case Jeff gets too much on my case. I'm going to try not to bother you at all. In fact, if I mention to Jeff that I need your help, he will go ballistic and tell me not to call you. So maybe that's what I will do."

They both laughed at the ridiculous situation.

Steve thanked Ryan for being a great team member and leader, and Ryan returned the appreciation. They shook hands and Steve turned to go back to the office knowing that his return was not going to be very pleasant. In fact, as he was walking away, Steve looked at his BlackBerry and sighed. Jeff had called a full team meeting for 12:30 p.m.; there would be no lunch hour for Steve this day.

Ryan got in his car and played the scenario over and over in his head. He couldn't believe the fury that enraged Jeff. In the hour he was eating lunch, he grabbed a napkin and started jotting down a few of Jeff's characteristics. He made a T chart of attributes and labeled it "Jeff." On one side of the chart were positive characteristics, and on the other side, negative. He began to write, as objectively as possible, positive qualities for Jeff. This was a very difficult prospect, and it took almost five minutes to write down three qualities; however, notes such as "wears expensive cufflinks: weren't going to count.

Jumping to the negative side, the opposite problem appeared with an endless stream of negative attributes He wrote down everything like "temper," "self-centered," "egotistical," "uncaring," "blamer," "no responsibility," and "know it all." The list kept going, making him wonder if he was just so biased or if everything he had written was true.

He decided to create a different list on another napkin, using another person in a leadership role. "Coach C" was a perfect candidate. He figured that leadership is leadership, and that it really didn't matter the field or the circumstances. Once again, he made his T chart and wrote Positive Qualities and Negative Qualities. He wrote things like "cares," "mentors," "takes time to work with you," "patience," and "perseverance" on the positive side, while negative qualities included "yells," "sometimes rash (but not a lot)," and "unrealistic goals," "mediocre sense of humor," and "forgets things."

At first, he did not attempt to compare the two, thinking it was a futile exercise and a waste of time; however, he stared at both T charts and it gave him an idea. Maybe he could find a magic bullet, something that would make him a better leader. Starting with these two people as a reference point, and continuing with other leaders including historical figures, there might be a way to compare everyone. The result might be the key to successful leadership.

Ryan was very serious. His passion to become a leader was fueling his intense desire to learn and understand leadership. As he left his lunch, he thought about leadership the entire way home and contemplated some of his favorite figures in history: President John Kennedy, General George Patton and President Dwight Eisenhower.

When he arrived home, he picked up the biography of Eisenhower, a book his wife had given him for Christmas the year before. He had a great respect for the man and referred to Eisenhower as the compassionate leader, the one who the troops looked to as the father figure. Here was a man, a five-star general, sending men off to die for a greater cause. It wasn't unusual for that era or even for other eras in history, but for Ryan, Eisenhower seemed to possess a different quality. He was mild mannered and even tempered, unlike some of his counterparts. These qualities were most certainly different from Jeff but very similar in many ways to Coach C. Eisenhower was quoted as saying, "The supreme quality for *leadership* is unquestionably *integrity*. Without it, no real success is possible…"

Integrity was the supreme quality. Jeff, he thought, certainly had no integrity, specifically in the way Jeff treated everyone because of his bad temper and rancorous behavior. There was always an excuse for his limitations and there was never any accountability.

Ryan most certainly knew that Jeff had no integrity; in contrast, Coach C had impeccable integrity. Every player, without exception, had always known Coach C to be an honest man, accepting responsibility for not teaching proper techniques because of poor execution. He did not allow players to take any blame for anything in which he played a part. He epitomized the notion of "we" during the team's success, and "I" when the team failed. The captain of the team, when Ryan was a freshman, had remarked, "He would take a bullet for you, and he always put himself on the line."

During his sophomore year, the team lost to the last place team from the neighboring state, an embarrassing loss. It was the worst season in the history of the program; the team won only a single game and Coach C was in the hot seat. He never allowed anyone to put the team down, and took full responsibility for every negative outcome, which almost cost him his job. If it weren't for the captain, who also showed a tremendous amount of fortitude, Coach C might have been fired.

The captain stormed into the athletic administrator's office and demanded that the AA apologize to Coach C, since it wasn't his fault that the team had lost. The captain had a bit of political capital with the AA; he was also the captain of the football team and had attended many booster events raising money for the programs.

Integrity, Ryan realized, was the key aspect to leadership. Ryan looked at the napkin he had saved from lunch earlier and transcribed it on his computer. He decided to change the makeup of the chart and instead created a spreadsheet with characteristics on the leftmost column and leaders' names across the top. He was intrigued to see where this would lead, and interested to see if he would stick to the plan.

As he contemplated the exercise more and more, he found himself drawn to this idea of studying leadership and management, and reviewed some literature he received from his alma mater regarding an MBA. He reviewed the requirements once again and spent a good hour on the course curriculum, to see if he was interested. It took less than an hour for him to decide to apply. Of course that meant the GMAT and reference letters, laughing at the thought of asking Jeff for a reference letter. It would have been funny since Jeff hated education and, of course, Ryan. The question was which Jeff despised more.

Ryan spent the next two weeks finishing the application to State and getting all his transcripts. His wife hadn't seen him this determined in years, and she gave him her full support, which he greatly appreciated.

There was a more pressing issue on the horizon. It was time to prepare for a new job and leading new team. This was his opening day of a new season, and it would be time to focus on the basics. His energy level was high and he was excited. He would lead his new team, focusing on integrity.

Chapter 2

FAILURE

A year had passed since Ryan started the job at Paltz. He'd spent a challenging year developing trust and cultivating an environment whereby his team would be successful. When he first started, he had a group of four developers, originally focusing on Web site development; however, in the past six months the group saw the addition of two developers to handle the increasing amount of work. By understanding the strengths and weaknesses of each team member, he effectively used them on projects, putting the best programmers on the more difficult projects and providing challenging, yet simpler tasks to the junior-level programmers. He couldn't just assign tasks to whomever he thought had time; assignments needed to match capabilities, a radically different approach from his previous job.

As the head of the group, he not only had to be a technical expert, whom they could rely on for advice and direction, but more importantly, he needed to guide them collectively. They were his responsibility; he had to ensure they completed their assignments, received proper training, and had the tools they needed to succeed. He listened to their problems as best he could. Unfortunately, sometimes he felt like a babysitter as he monitored their assignments. He knew that was not the right attitude, but that was how he felt.

Even though Ryan's team focused on Web site development, his successes compelled his management to assign him more responsibility. Gaining additional responsibility was a stated objective for him, and their recognition of his work product was a testament to his capabilities as a young leader, which he greatly appreciated. However, more recently, his level of frustration increased, due to the lack of direction from management on the two major initiatives assigned to his group.

First, his group was responsible for the new version of the Web site, which still required a major overhaul. Recent assessments by external parties revealed the Web site's lack of functionality and its poor appearance, which senior executives in the company from various departments cited as the cause of falling market share and eroding profits. Unfortunately, senior management's solution was to request trivial and meaningless Web site projects that didn't address the major problems. He was hoping management would finally release the promised golden pot of money, and enable his team to work with a first-rate design team to create the next-generation e-commerce site. Repeatedly, however, the project stalled and restarted as senior executives quibbled over the requisite functionality; with no real mandate, it was impossible to gain any momentum.

The second project, the implementation of an inventory management system purchased about five months ago, was a bit of a stretch for Ryan. He had no experience with an inventory management system but he did have a good foundation in the technology used to develop it. The marketing and operations departments had collectively sought out a system that would help manage inventory levels and keep track of outgoing orders and incoming deliveries. Unfortunately, the two groups purchased the system without ever consulting IT, not realizing the difficulty and expertise required to integrate this system into the existing set of systems at the company. The project was supposed to be a three-month effort using consultants retained to integrate the system. After spending over a half million dollars in software, and another three hundred thousand dollars in consulting, the company fired the consultants two months ago in cost-reduction measures. Management decided to divert in house resources toward the implementation in an attempt to salvage the system and move it into production. They selected Ryan to take over the project, because of his expertise using the base technology.

Tom Depardeau, his boss, who by this time was very impressed with Ryan, had asked him to take over the project. Tom had been with Paltz for over 15 years and the stress of the position appeared to accumulate near his waistline. Ryan's enthusiasm for the position was a welcome change for Tom, who could never seem to motivate his staff to accept any responsibility. Ryan, in contrast, accepted this responsibility willingly, without fully understanding what was required, thereby putting him in a unique and precarious situation. Not only did he not know anything about the product, he accepted the project without understanding the intense political nature of the product and its implementation.

Unfortunately, his ego jumped ahead of rationality by agreeing to the project before thinking about the consequences. His confidence in his, and his team's capabilities, blinded him to the need to review the situation carefully before accepting the challenge. Although Ryan willingly accepted it, he also wasn't sure he had a choice when the vice president came to him and asked him to take over the project. It might have been detrimental to his career if he declined the challenge. What type of message would that send? If they didn't think he could do it, he thought, why would they have asked him? The uneasy feeling about the project would gradually intensify from the moment he said yes, and he would regret not learning about the system first.

Ryan's team worked very hard on both projects and they became very comfortable with him during his first year's tenure. They adapted well to his management style, and slowly trusted him and his decision-making ability. They relied on him for technical advice and exchanged ideas freely during his many whiteboard technical sessions. Advocating an open approach to problem solving would become a trademark of his management style.

He focused his energy on the team and their well-being to make them better programmers, relying heavily on his past experiences to serve as a guide. He avoided the same mistakes Jeff made, and strived to become the leader he knew he could be—a leader who would lead his troops into battle over the hill, with the flag waving in the background under the trumpet's call. Unfortunately, for Ryan, there was no flag, no trumpet, no hill, and no battle. There was an office and a job.

Over the past year, he had spent enough time with his team to understand them and their thinking. Through his casual conversations, he learned as much as he could about them to understand the type of work they enjoyed doing. Focusing on their core strengths, he aligned tasks and projects that would take advantage of their skills, utilizing each of them as effectively as possible, which didn't always work. Since it wasn't a very large team and the projects were somewhat limited, it was occasionally analogous to fitting a round peg into a square hole.

Each member of the team had his or her own unique personality. One member, Stacy Gilfoil, was a generally jovial person who loved to joke around, but maintained a very direct and no-nonsense attitude toward her work. Her tenaciousness could be overlooked through her moderately long brown hair, and stylish large rectangular lenses, which softened her appearance. Any faults she may have exhibited were trivial because of her programming skills, which were exemplary. She could analyze a problem and quickly provide answers, which, for the most part, were right on the money. She became Ryan's right hand gal. Over the course of the year she earned many accolades from her peers for her ability to get the team working together and for solving some of the toughest issues the team had faced. Her tough-nosed attitude toward her work was an asset during crunch time.

On the other end of the spectrum, was Subbu Reddy. Subbu was a very quiet individual from Bangalore, India. He had been in the country about eight years and was a graduate of a top school in India, IIT, Indian Institute of Technology. Subbu knew his role and always performed his task as directed. He would never object to any directive and consequently never provided feedback. Ryan wondered if there was a cultural issue that he needed to understand, but never had the nerve to ask. He wasn't sure if it was politically correct to ask such questions. He genuinely liked Subbu, but he found Subbu to be a yes-man, and while it was always nice to have someone agree with him, Ryan found it a bit unsettling at times and was never confident about Subbu's responses.

Ryan knew the four other members of the team were qualified, and some had great potential. He spent time earning their trust, and for the most part had succeeded, but he could sense even after a year there was still some apprehension. Some of the team members had expressed reservations about him when he first came on board, but because of his technical capabilities and his willingness to help out, most of the team gradually showed their confidence. Ryan knew whom he could count on, and he knew where they stood even if they didn't agree with him or each other.

He applied different techniques to help effectively develop his team from both technical and management perspectives. He had his own perspective of how the team was performing and continually expressed his satisfaction with the team's performance as a morale booster. The company had introduced some key performance indicators, KPIs, to objectively measure teams' productivity. Ryan wasn't keen on these metrics because they didn't capture the reality of the situation. They were performing well and he didn't need an Excel spreadsheet from the Business Oversight Group at the other end of the building telling him that his team was successful. However, since they were in the top five of every category, he didn't complain very much.

Ryan objected to metrics that he believed were created in a vacuum, and thought that the application of general corporatewide statistics, while well intentioned, wouldn't provide an accurate view of productivity. Metrics needed to be tailored to meet the needs of the department to measure it effectively against itself and not against other departments. He knew the group didn't know anything about programming and they couldn't possibly understand the complexities of technology, and thus the metrics wouldn't be truly reflective of work effort or productivity. It was bad practice to allow people who didn't understand the actual work to judge it.

Ryan structured his group to optimize their performance, allowing him to efficiently assign tasks and monitor deliverables. The team had responded exactly as he anticipated in many cases, but there was still something missing, and the recognition for their effort was lacking. They had performed admirably on some key projects such as the new Web site and inventory; however, concerns over these projects were directed generally in his direction.

The Web site project had stalled but not for lack of effort on their part, and the inventory system was a debacle from day one. The inventory system project caused a significant amount of turmoil between Ryan and his management. While the company's metrics showed his group remaining in the top five of all major categories, they also showed the group trending downward, which raised questions about Ryan's management. If the trend continued, there would be consequences. Consequences he didn't really want to address.

Ryan called a meeting with his team early one Monday morning to address the projects that were seemingly spiraling out of control. The meeting was scheduled for 9:30 a.m., since he knew everyone would be at work by that time. He had instituted a flextime policy, which management approved, enabling the members of his team to pilot a project whereby they could work an eight-hour shift however they liked by coming in later or leaving earlier. His team was very happy about not being "on the clock," and the program was so successful it had spread to other departments. This type of initiative was a bit pioneering for the retailer used to the "old way of doing things." Ryan hoped to implement this kind of initiative in his leadership role, which now seemed so far away because of the current situation.

Prior to the 9:30 meeting, Ryan spoke to Stacy to get her input on the situation with regard to the metrics and projects.

"We have to do something; these projects aren't necessarily going well. I wanted to get your opinion," Ryan said.

"Well," Stacy replied, "I don't know what we can do, they keep changing the requirements for the Web site, and no one has a damn clue about what to do with this inventory system."

"So that's obvious, can we accomplish what we believe is being asked, at least for the Web?"

"And what the hell would that be?" Stacy asked.

"Maybe we should just do what we think is right, based on anything we've received so far, at least it's something. We can't be any worse off, can we?"

"Your call, Ryan, I really don't have any ideas." Stacy hesitantly said.

The bewilderment and urgency in Stacy's voice wasn't very reassuring to him. He had to come up with a plan, and it needed to be fast. Ryan had already broken down the problem into two main components. The first was lack of clarity and vision, and the second was lack of communication. But how could he get his management to buy into a resolution?

Five minutes before the meeting, his cell phone rang. Ryan was agitated at this point because now he had to answer the phone instead of focusing on the meeting. He looked at the phone. It was his boss.

"Hey, chief," Ryan said.

"How's it going, Ryan? You have a minute?" Tom asked.

Ryan explained that he was heading into the meeting about the Web site and the inventory system.

"That's what I wanted to talk to you about. I just got out of an 8:00 a.m. meeting regarding all the projects, not just yours. I know there is a lot of confusion, but you have to pull it together somehow. You need to focus on the projects and just get it done. Is there any reason why you think it can't be done?"

Ryan was a bit perplexed and said, "Well, the requirements are shaky, and you're right, the team is confused."

Tom replied, "It's your job to get them clear on what needs to happen. I don't need another problem right now; I'm getting beaten up at every turn. Just get these projects done."

"We'll do the best we can."

Now Ryan knew he was in a pickle. Not only were the requirements bad, it wasn't exactly clear how the team was supposed to build what the business wanted. The inventory control system just didn't work as the company had promised, and his boss told him to "just get it done." Ryan had no confidence in the application and his stomach was turning from the stress. The system wasn't working, consultants couldn't get it to work, and now he was left holding the bag.

Management was supposed to be easier than just programming, he thought. Lead the people, assign the tasks, and discuss strategies in meetings. It wasn't supposed to be a complete mess like this project. He was supposed to be able to go up the hill; charge up like Teddy Roosevelt and his Rough Riders and come back a conquering hero. He felt on top of the world aboard the Titanic. What could he tell his team?

Ryan was a few minutes late to the meeting. As he walked in, he could see the anxiety on the faces of his team, and wouldn't soon forget the perplexed look of uncertainty and confusion, which he knew was directly related to the projects. Their morale was low and they were looking to him for answers. They respected his technological prowess and his "go get 'em" style. Right now, they needed leadership, and they all look to him to provide the answers, except Stacy, who knew he was as clueless as they were. She actually knew it before he spoke to her this morning. It was evident by his body language and had intensified over the past week. She didn't blame him though; she was just as clueless.

Stacy could have had his job last year, but she didn't want it, for this exact reason. She hated politics and loved technology, preferring to step into a computer rather than into a conference room. Give her a computer and a mouse and she was off to the races. Put her in a contentious meeting and one better have a flak jacket.

She didn't envy Ryan right now; he was in a very tough spot. She would do anything to help him, because she believed he genuinely wanted to make the situation better. Ryan was different than her last manager, who was a self-absorbed egotistical jerk. Ryan came in with a calming demeanor and cultivated a sense of teamwork, which was a foreign, but welcome attitude. She wasn't about to let him down or sabotage him in any way, but she just couldn't put her finger on a solution to this problem.

Ryan didn't waste any time at the meeting. He spoke about the call he had just had with Tom. Ryan thought maybe he had explained a bit too much when Stacy blurted out, "The schmuck, he has no clue what *he* did." Ryan curtailed Stacy right away or she might have continued her tirade, which was borderline unprofessional. Unfortunately, the entire group shared her sentiment.

As Ryan continued talking, he remembered the movie *Apollo 13* when, in spite of all obstacles, the team found a way to save the lives of the crew. There was always a way to solve a problem. Ryan, without any hesitation in an effort to raise the morale, said in a stern voice,

"Team, failure is not an option. I don't want to hear any more complaints. Here is how we break down the work."

He told Stacy to take the three developers across from her, and focus on the Web site according to the original spec. He would abandon some of the smaller projects for the short term by reassigning two of the developers to Stacy. If there were any holes in the spec, he instructed her and her team to fill in the gaps and take an educated guess. He figured if the business couldn't properly write requirements, his team would do it for them. He felt they were smarter than the business users anyway.

"Subbu, you and Tim continue working on the inventory system, get hold of the vendor and if they can't help us, start writing your own programs and create workarounds. Can you do that?"

"Yes, sir."

Ryan concluded, "Any questions?"

After he answered a few trivial questions, the meeting adjourned. He felt good about himself, believing that he had motivated them enough to succeed. They just needed a bit of a pep talk.

Stacy stopped Ryan in the hallway about twenty minutes later, away from everyone.

"What's up, Stace?"

She responded, "You really don't think that bullshit worked, do you?"

"Actually, I don't think it's bullshit, but I believe they will be motivated now. We have no choice. We have to make it work."

"You know, I actually thought you were better than these other jerks in management. I really respected you for your honesty and your ability to communicate with the team, but you know damn well this won't work. If you thought it would have worked, you would have done it awhile ago. What the hell happened to you?"

Stacy walked away noticeably angry, but her expression was more than angry, it was something else. Ryan felt a sense of betrayal, but it wasn't Stacy that betrayed him, she told him exactly how she felt. Rather, he knew that *he* betrayed Stacy. He was motionless for a few seconds, as he felt hate, anger, disappointment, and bewilderment simultaneously. He wasn't sure exactly what he was feeling, but he felt as if he had been punched in the stomach.

Ryan couldn't function the entire day. He attended his meetings, checked his e-mail, and reviewed some documents, but he couldn't stop thinking about that conversation. She was usually blunt with him, but this was so different. Why would she insinuate that he wasn't honest, especially since he told the team what was happening?

Ryan fought through the paralysis and spent his evening reviewing the documentation on the inventory system. He would roll up his sleeves and help the team figure this out. He would be the extra man on the field, he told himself. He figured if there was an extra set of eyes on the project it would have a better chance at success, making the team, and him, successful.

As he sat down with a cup of coffee in his home office, he looked over pages and pages of documentation and examined various ways to hook the application into the other systems. He even downloaded a trial version onto his computer to begin playing around with the software. After four long hours of reading, he hadn't made much progress. Various elements of the application were just too difficult, and it would take awhile to decipher some basic functionality. He needed an alternative approach.

He punched up the name of the application onto Google. Google returned 1,500 entries, and he thought he was about to hit the jackpot. As he scrolled down his screen, the entries focused on the inability of the application to live up to its promises. One entry listed a lawsuit from a Florida company, claiming breach of contract. The plaintiff claimed that the sales team sold them a product that was never near completion and that a number of false statements accompanied the sale.

Ryan began to feel his heart move to his throat. He was so certain he could get the system working, based on the assumption that it was possible to get it to work. Now he was in a pickle because even though he searched through the Google entries looking for one positive article or note, he couldn't find one. Almost every entry, except for those from the company itself, was highly negative, or worse. Ryan looked at the time and saw it was 11:30 p.m. He picked up the phone and dialed.

"Stacy, sorry to bother you," Ryan said.

Stacy replied, "You know I almost didn't pick up the phone when I saw the caller ID, and what do you mean sorry to bother you? You know I'm up till 1:00 or 2:00 every morning, so I'm guessing you want something. So what is it? Oh, and by the way, I'm still pissed at you."

"Well, there's a good evening for you," he said sarcastically. He could easily brush aside Stacy's jabs, because he knew she meant what she was saying, but it wasn't malicious.

"Anyway, I was reviewing the documents regarding the inventory system, but I had no luck installing the demo copy, and when I reviewed Google, I found nothing but a horror show."

"Tell me something I don't know."

"You knew how bad this was? Why didn't Subbu say anything, especially today?"

Stacy, ready to jump through the phone, said, "Do you think we are idiots, and can't do basic work? Subbu and Tim tried to get this thing going for weeks. You haven't been listening to what's been going on for the past four months. You know Subbu will try his best to get the thing working and he isn't going to tell you no, but I told you there were major problems and that it was a piece of crap."

"Stacy, you always say things are a piece of crap, and I thought you were just using it as an expression."

"Fine," she said, realizing he was right about that, "but you should have realized if the team hasn't gotten a simple installation done in four months, then something else is wrong!"

After they exchanged some tit-for-tat comments, they agreed to discuss more on Monday. After he hung up the phone, Ryan realized he was too tired to look any further at this system or any other system. He would wait until Monday and try to figure out how he could get out of this predicament; he prayed that the Web site wouldn't end up like this.

As the weekend progressed, he felt he had made a big mistake on almost every front. Now, instead of the glorious charge up the hill, he envisioned himself halfway up the hill watching bodies fly downward past him with men running down the hill screaming for their lives, all the while oblivious to the reality of the situation as he faced upward with his sword in the direction of the top of the hill yelling "*CHARGE.*"

He said to himself, "I'm such an idiot."

He was lucky that he could get his mind off work for a brief period on Sunday with a welcome opportunity to play golf at a very well manicured course about 30 miles from his home. He loved to play, but never had much time to play due to his hectic schedule at work and home. A few of his friends occasionally convened at the public course and when they had a chance, playing a high stakes round of twenty-five cents per hole. They were a bunch of cheap bastards, including Ryan.

As the game progressed, they would discuss family and things that had happened at work. Ryan wasn't a very good golfer but he enjoyed it. He liked the strategy part of the game where you could set up the next shot, account for the wind, and avoid the traps. Although none of it ever seemed to work. He never hit the ball well enough to account for the wind, and he ended up in so many sand traps that he brought a beach towel to every round.

At the sixth hole, Ryan hit his drive onto the right side of the fairway; the ball trickled into the rough about twenty feet. Normally, this wouldn't be a problem. Ryan was such an expert at hitting out of the rough, or so he thought. Actually, he could never hit a fairway, so he was right at home playing from the rough. This shot, though, was especially tough. The hole curved to the right with low-hanging trees along its right side but directly in front of his position. Ryan figured he could take a low iron and punch the ball beneath the trees like a low-line drive all the way up to the green, which was about 175 yards away. Ryan took his club and began to take a few practice swings. He was getting ready to approach the ball, when he heard, "Hold up!"

Ryan's old friend John, a really good golfer, had stopped him and asked, "Ryan, what are you doing?"

"I'm going to punch the ball through. I have enough room to make it scoot through this path up to the green," Ryan said as he pointed to a narrow fifteen-foot clearing between the trees and saplings. "It's a clear shot if I hit it right."

Ryan mentioned to John that he saw Phil Mickleson, a professional golfer who was known for his creative ways of scrambling out of trouble, make the exact same shot two weeks ago at a tournament and he made it looked easy.

"First of all you're not Phil Mickleson; second of all you should look to play a better shot. Your drive put you in a bad spot, so allow your next shot to put you in a better position to get a better score."

Ryan laughed, "Look, when I'm on the green in two, you can give me the twenty-five cents 'cause I'll lock this hole up. Besides, you're fifteen yards in front of me and I have to be aggressive."

Ryan approached the ball, took his practice swing, and took a quick short punch shot right onto the ball. The ball sailed low, but further to the right, hitting a tree at an angle causing the ball to go deeper into the woods, giving Ryan a more difficult shot. Ryan sighed, not because the ball was farther in the woods but because his ego had suffered a major blow. It was about to get worse. John approached his ball a few feet in front of where Ryan was, took a look at the position of the ball, pointed to Ryan and motioned that he was going to put the ball softly on the fairway about twenty-five feet to his left, not toward the green. John yelled a bit with a fake Scottish accent as Ryan was walking away, "Ryan, I'm going to chip it onto the fairway and I'll be on the green before yee."

John chipped his shot onto the fairway a bit farther than he wanted but still on the fairway and his next shot was a nice 150-yard lofty 9 iron onto the green fifteen feet from the pin. John looked over to the right and could barely see Ryan's legs as he scrambled for his ball, shoveling leaves back and forth as he tried. Ryan eventually found his ball and made three more punch shots but finally got his ball out to an area where he could put it on the green.

Ryan at this point hated every minute of this situation because he knew he would hear it from John. As Ryan approached the green, now laying six, for a par four, he could hear the sarcastic quick and quiet golf clap of John and his companions as he walked up. John belted out,

"Let's hear it for 'lefty,' on in six."

Ryan couldn't help but laugh, and finished with a remarkable and jubilant eight. He knew he looked really stupid at this point.

John said, "Look on the bright side, it could have been worse."

"Yeah, I could have lost to you by five strokes instead of four."

As they were waiting at the next hole, Ryan and John sat in the golf cart and began chatting. John reminded Ryan that sometimes we have to let go of the ego.

"You made a bad shot—sometimes you have to take a step back to move forward. If you're driving a car, and arrive at a fork in the road, proceed left and find a dead end, do you go through it? No. You back up to the fork, admit it was the wrong way, even if silently, and move the other way. You could do much better if you just had a bit more patience, and a more realistic approach. It's important to be honest with yourself when you have no shot. It's not admitting defeat; it's recognizing that you can't win every shot and every hole. You can lose a hole or two and still win the match."

Ryan said, "That's easy for you, you have a six handicap."

"How do you think I became a six handicap? The reason I got better is that I got smarter. I knew when I hit a bad shot and I moved on from it. I didn't try to force every shot. You can't fit a round peg into a square hole, so don't. Find another peg or another hole."

Ryan knew John was right but didn't really want to admit it and, furthermore, he was getting tired of John. He felt John was trying to show off, even though he knew John was trying to be helpful.

Coincidentally, the next hole curved as well, only this time to the left. Ryan was determined to keep the ball on the right side away from the trees, which would not give him an angle into the hole. This was another par 4 but a bit longer at 440 yards. Ryan approached his tee shot and let it rip. Unfortunately for Ryan, he hooked the ball to the left. Even though he hit the ball 275 yards, the ball rolled into the trees once again. He was only 110 yards from the pin though. As he the golf cart approached the ball, he looked to see if he could punch it again and possibly make it to the green. Since it was shorter, he felt he didn't have as much risk. He grabbed his 3 iron ready to punch the ball once again, and began to approach to the ball.

John, who was sitting in the cart, had already hit his second shot and was just short of the green with an easy chip shot up about twenty yards. John shook his head as he saw Ryan approach the ball, planning another punch shot. He couldn't believe it, but he wasn't going to waste his breath this time.

Ryan who had already taken his practice swings was ready to address the ball, set up over the ball, then stopped. He picked up the club head off the ground, paused and walked back to the cart. Ryan had pulled another club, a nine iron, and gauged a shot backward and to the right looking at the fairway. John was amazed, he knew Ryan was about to admit defeat and try to reposition himself. Ryan addressed the ball, swung, and placed the ball 35 yards right onto the fairway and was sitting about 135 yards from the hole.

Ryan then moved to the ball with the same club and took his practice swings. At this point, John, who was amazed at Ryan's perfect shot, was holding his breath waiting for Ryan to make his next shot. He was pulling for Ryan to put it on the green. Ryan was pretty good with the 9 iron. He had much better control of that club. He addressed the ball, and swung. The ball lofted into the air straight with a slight fade to the right. The ball landed twenty feet from the pin right on the green and the ball spun back to the hole about five feet from the pin. Ryan was about to have his first par for the day. John gave a genuine clap, yelling, "Great shot, Ryan" as he walked back to the cart.

When Ryan got into the cart, John continued to praise Ryan on his shot. Ryan was very pleased with himself, he knew he had a par within reach and if he hadn't played it safe, it would be an easy six.

Ryan turned to John and said, "Thanks, John, I think I'll do that more often and give up the dream of the perfect shot."

John said, "Good for you, that's the way to play golf."

Ryan replied, "I think I've gotten something more out of this than hitting a golf shot."

John was a bit perplexed, not knowing what Ryan was talking about, but he went on with his game.

He always knew the proper way to handle those situations while playing golf, but this lesson had special meaning. Playing with his friends, he always maintained that he knew the right way to play, but never remembered to do it—in fact, he just didn't listen to reason. He continually let his ego get in the way of doing the right thing. There was a time to be aggressive and a time to play it smart. John's statement about going backward to move forward related directly to his situation at work. He wasn't sure exactly how, but intuitively he had to reevaluate his work situation.

Over the next few weeks, Ryan and Stacy barely spoke. The jovial nature of their relationship took a slightly downward, but not irreparable, turn. Both of them seemed content with staying apart; however, for different reasons. Ryan knew that Stacy harbored a bit of animosity toward him, and while he was confident it would pass, he was glad she kept her distance, because if she did speak to him, he would probably have a permanent residence at the hospital. Ryan knew he needed to earn Stacy's trust. Fixing the problems at work was secondary to repairing his team. His team would be unsuccessful if they were in disarray and, more importantly, if he were the cause. That's what his heart told him, but he was petrified of being fired.

During this time, Ryan tried many different things to help the two teams. He worked tirelessly with the team leaders resolving issues and contacting vendors. He was the first person in and the last person to leave and he bounced from each project looking for solutions, trying to be helpful, but trying not to over manage. He felt comfortable in this renewed technical role and he enjoyed getting into the code and playing with the systems. It was like riding a bike for the first time in ten years and getting a tremendous rush.

His efforts didn't go unnoticed and some on the team explicitly made their appreciation known. One member of the team thought he was meddling; however, that was an isolated comment and feeling. Everyone else could sense the sincerity of his actions. They knew he didn't have to be there with them, arrive before them, and leave after them. Stacy even confronted Phil, the doubting Thomas of the group, and said, "Would you be doing the same if you were in his position? I think not. He needs us to get this done."

As Stacy walked away, Phil's reply was muffled, but audible to Stacy, who turned back and said, "What did you say?"

Phil, a good programmer with a tendency to shoot off his mouth, replied, "Nothing."

Stacy angrily barked, "Bull, what did you say?"

Phil wouldn't reply. He was smart not to reply. Stacy, knowing better than keep it up, continued to walk away, but she had an idea what he had said, and she was pissed.

Phil was a very jealous colleague always believing he was pariah of the group, never having been given the respect he felt he deserved. Phil was a very awkward individual, whose clothes never seem to fit properly and whose general appearance was somewhat unappealing. He greatly disliked Stacy and her capabilities, dating back prior to Ryan's arrival. Phil's animosity toward Stacy was exacerbated by Stacy's increasingly prominent role in Ryan's group. As Ryan relied on Stacy more, Phil became more removed and his frustration with both of them increased.

Phil's situation was precarious at best, and Ryan had recently scolded him about work not being completed properly. He never agreed with Ryan's assessment and felt ostracized and singled out. No matter how hard Ryan tried, Phil never seemed to respond positively to Ryan's mentoring, and the situation between Stacy and Phil worsened by the day.

Ryan heard Stacy's bark from down the hall, exited his cubicle, and moved toward the programmers' area. As he walked out, Subbu caught him and explained that he needed Ryan to come with him because he had good news about the inventory system. Ryan distracted by Subbu, reversed direction and followed him to the data center, forgetting his original reason for leaving his cubicle.

Subbu explained that he had come up with a way to keep the inventory system running, alleviating one of the major problems with the system, and, while not perfect, he did exactly what he was asked to do. Ryan was ecstatic.

Subbu, very happy at Ryan's response, began to demonstrate his work and explained how he fixed it. He managed through the system and after getting past a major hurdle, the system unexpectedly crashed. He rebooted the system, executed a different set of tests, all with the same result. He explained to Ryan that this was further than anyone had expected, and that Ryan should still be happy. He thought it was good progress and, eventually, he would figure it out.

Ryan knew this wasn't going to work, but he didn't want to demoralize Subbu. He told Subbu to keep working on it, but it wasn't quite good enough to show management. Subbu couldn't understand Ryan's displeasure, and once again stated that it was further than anyone had achieved so far.

Ryan clarified the need to have the system not crash at any point, and that it wasn't good enough to just progress. He urged him to continue pressing on but he didn't know how much time they had before they would be questioned by management again.

In the cafeteria, a few members of the team, Stacy, Ryan, Tim, and Mike, gathered for a quick sandwich. Most of the time, the team went out for lunch, but now, with the time pressures, they had been eating in the cafeteria or at their desks. Ryan, who was sitting across from Stacy, asked what all the barking was about earlier. Stacy said Phil was shooting his mouth off and he wouldn't repeat what he had said that pissed her off. Ryan asked Stacy to cool it; he knew how Phil reacts, but at this point, it wasn't worth her time. Ryan was too busy to worry about petty squabbles, explaining that Phil is probably still upset about his discussion with him, where he needed Mike to finish Phil's work, which was grossly behind schedule. Ryan told the team to forget about it and move on, with or without Phil. It would be dealt with after the project was over. Ryan finished his drink and told the team he would see them later.

Tim and Mike knew she was upset, and they knew she had an idea of what Phil said. Neither dared tell her what they knew, but something was wrong. Stacy was abnormally distressed. Tim asked Stacy why she was so upset with Phil; it was unlike her to bottle up her emotions as she was doing.

Stacy said, "It's all the stress. I have some personal issues at home and this job is just ridiculous. Ryan can't get his act together, I know he's trying but there's no way this is going to work and then all Phil does is run his mouth."

Tim empathized with her, and began to change the subject. Stacy interrupted him, and said, "Tim, I know you guys know what he said. Tell me." Tim was very hesitant to tell Stacy what Phil had said, and Mike responded, "Stace, it was nothing, he just doesn't know when to shut up."

Stacy seemed detracted.

Tim blurted out, "Stacy, he made a comment about you and Ryan."

Stacy said emphatically, "Oh really?"

"Phil mumbled that you're having an affair with him, insinuating that was why you were defending him."

Stacy grumbled, and Tim motioned as if to console, "Stacy we know you're not. He is just a jerk. Ryan's like the coach of the team, and you're the captain, and it's due to your ability, nothing else. Everyone on this team knows it."

Stacy angrily picked up her tray and as she stormed away, Tim hoped he had done the right thing, but Mike wasn't so sure. Stacy, however, never brought it up again to either of them.

It was five weeks later when Ryan received a call from Tom. He wanted a status update on the progress of both projects. He had called for a special meeting early the next morning. Having less than twenty-four hours to pull together a status report, Ryan needed to pull the team together to find out where things were in order to present an accurate status report. When the team finally gathered, he asked for a status report on each project. First, he asked Stacy to give an update on the Web site. She told him they had completed the requirements as well as possible. The Web site was functioning well in testing, but the results didn't make sense, although they were functioning as requested.

She presented an example where the system indicated that inventory levels for products were negative. It was absurd for a Web site to indicate a negative number for inventory levels, but the way the requirements were written made this a possibility. This was brought up to the marketing department that brushed aside the concerns, indicating that it wouldn't matter since inventory levels would never achieve those levels. Stacy, however, told Ryan that the team had built contingency code that they could quickly activate should the users change their mind. The status of the project wasn't great, but it certainly was a far cry from where they were a few months ago. Ryan would indicate that they had completed the Web site and designed it according to specification. He would convey the concerns about some of the errant functionality and let management decide.

Next, attention turned to the inventory system. Subbu went through a series of items, and achieved very positive results, at least according to him. When Ryan asked whether the system crashed during operation, Subbu said, "Yes, but very little."

Subbu was confident that it would work well, but Ryan knew this couldn't be true. He hadn't seen anything to indicate that the system was stable. The software was junk and he knew it, but that was something that he could not write in the report. He had committed to the project and he would deliver it.

He thanked everyone, and said to keep heading toward the finish line. Management would receive their report tomorrow, and he hoped it would quell any concerns. After Ryan dismissed them, Stacy stayed back and asked him what he would report about the inventory system.

"I'm going to tell them what Subbu said, that it's working as well as he can get it to work."

"But you know the thing doesn't work."

"Yes, but Subbu believes that it's working. Maybe he can convince management of that."

"He's telling you what you want to hear!"

"What am I supposed to do?" Ryan responded.

Stacy started walking away, and said, as if exhausted, "I don't know. I really don't know."

The next day, Ryan was scheduled to discuss the situation with Tom at 8:00 in the morning. He had decided to arrive at work early to prepare for the meeting and finalize his report. Truth was he couldn't sleep, and he had no idea what the consequences would be for him or his team. He struggled with the entire situation, and went back and forth about arguments, issues, tasks, and even blame. An early-morning vanilla chai from Starbucks might have calmed him down, but even that didn't taste good today.

As Ryan walked up to the building, his mind continued to race with the thought of his status meeting. The current Web site was in a sufficient state that management would find it acceptable, and it was working; management could see it work, and provide feedback. The worst-case scenario might be changes to the site that would prove difficult. It most certainly was better than it was before, but he knew it was nowhere close to where it should have been. He was proud of Stacy, even though she wasn't really speaking to him that much, except to lambaste him, although her animosity seemed to have tempered temporarily.

The night before, Ryan had a long discussion with his wife, Lisa. Lisa would always listen to Ryan's technical discussions and problems, even though she really didn't understand much of it. They would usually talk near the kitchen where she would make herself comfortable on a bar stool, and ask him to make her coffee or snack while she listened to his boring subject.

He explained what was going on and described his apprehension about the meeting. He felt that everything was off track, but he needed to figure out a way to make it right. Stacy had pulled everything through on the Web site, and he was very grateful for that, because two catastrophes might be unbearable. It was easy to speak to Lisa about Stacy since the two had become very good friends over the past year. They were very much alike in their blunt and grounded personalities. Ryan used to joke that he had two women who weren't afraid to let him have it, one at home and one at work. He was safe nowhere.

After listening to Ryan's predicament, Lisa said, "You blew it; you should have just not taken the projects."

Ryan said, "It's not that easy to just say to your boss, no, I won't do it."

"Probably not, but you should have figured out a way, especially since that inventory system thing doesn't work. I'm sure Stacy would have told them off."

Ryan was so appreciative at the compassion and support of the "you suck" comments. Deep down, he knew she was right though, Stacy would have told them off, but then again that's why she wasn't in his position and that's why she never wanted it. None of that helped, nor did he think it would have helped him back then. It was a reminder of another mistake that he continually played in his head as he walked into the building.

Ryan finally reached his cubicle, sat down, and settled in. He decided his report would completely separate the two projects. The best chance of survival was to show the success of one and minimize the failure of the other. He would report each project's state exactly as both leads had described, allowing his boss to promote them as he saw fit.

Ryan finished up his status reports, cleaned them up, and showed the statuses as mostly green, indicating the projects were on target. Some yellows would appear, but they would be minimal and nonmaterial for a move to production. For the Web site, it was an acceptable representation, but for the inventory system it was complete spin.

Ryan printed out his report and started walking to his boss's office. Tom was OK as far as managers go, but his lack of technical expertise made working for him slightly difficult. He was very personable and well liked, though. Ryan thought he suffered from a bit of a personality disorder, since his mood could change in an instant. Ryan was warned about his personality when he came on board, but he never experienced too many problems. He hoped Tom would be in a good mood, and if he explained everything well, he could get by unscathed and Tom would be able to keep the remaining few hairs on his head.

Ryan knocked on the door to Tom's office, and he motioned for Ryan to enter. Ryan could sense Tom's demeanor was unusually tense, as he watched him drink his morning joe, which was always black with no sugar. There was no doubt he was especially wired this morning, as Ryan noticed the first empty cup on the desk.

With a sigh of exasperation, Tom opened up, "Morning, Ryan, please tell me you have good news."

"Yes, there is good news, and better news. The good news is there is no bad news, and the better news is that we have great news on the Web site and good news on the inventory system," Ryan replied.

His boss noticeably relieved, pounded his fist on the table, and said, "Wonderful. Let's go into some detail."

Ryan first went into the discussion about the Web site. He mentioned that Stacy had led the team to a great success, stating that the project was on time and the team had met all the original requirements, adding that the team had built in contingencies, since they lacked confidence in the original requirements being adequate or accurate.

Tom was noticeably pleased, and he said, "Love that Stacy, one of the best hires I ever made. Good job. I'm scheduling a demo for tomorrow afternoon with the senior team from marketing. Sorry I can't give you more time, but it's too pressing."

Ryan responded, "We're ready."

The discussion turned to the inventory system, where Subbu had been working diligently but faced a multitude of obstacles. He added, using a touch of creative license to overcome the dryness of Subbu's report, that Subbu said they had overcome many of the issues and deficiencies of the application itself.

"Subbu is very confident that this is working," Ryan said.

Ryan probably went a bit too far there; even if that was Subbu's intent, he didn't share the confidence. Then Ryan was hit with a question he wasn't expecting.

"Do you believe him, Ryan?" Tom asked.

Ryan responded quickly, "Subbu is really good, I have no reason not to believe him."

"Did you see it work?"

"I saw a limited demo, which appeared to have the functionality working. Honestly, I would like it to be better, but you know how I feel about the application anyway. Look, chief, we did what we needed to do, and Subbu has given me assurances it works."

Tom wasn't sure about the answer, but went on to say, "I'm not sure if Subbu is really stepping up to the plate. I've always had my reservations about him. I never really got a straight answer out of him on any project. We need the thing to work. And what about that pathetic guy working with Stacy, is he doing what he needs to do?"

"You mean Phil? No, I reassigned his work to make sure it got done. As for the inventory system, Tim filled in and assisted, but otherwise, it's been all Subbu."

"If someone isn't stepping up, then we need to get rid of them."

"I agree, but at this point I'm not sure it does any good except to cause more disruption. I have Phil handling some other tasks, freeing up a resource."

"Well, let's see what happens," Tom said, and then he dropped a bombshell, "Get ready for a demo at eleven."

"At eleven?" exclaimed Ryan, as he glanced at his watch.

"Yeah, eleven. I have an important meeting this afternoon with the CIO and COO, and they want an update on this project. Is there a problem?" Tom asked.

Ryan was a bit stunned, but jerked out, "No problem, but let's do it in the data center. I don't want to introduce any variables that might deviate from the demo."

"Agreed, see you there at eleven," responded Tom.

Ryan quickly exited the room, went right to his cubicle, and called Subbu. "You have to get a demo ready for eleven at you're area in the data center. Understood?" he asked.

"No problem, sir," Subbu replied.

Ryan hung up the phone quickly. He didn't feel confident that Subbu was going to be ready so he would head to the data center at 10:00 a.m. just in case Subbu needed help. Unfortunately, due to another meeting he couldn't go earlier. Before heading to his other meeting, he reviewed some of the documentation and status reports to see if there was any indication that the application would work. Every test that was executed had basically failed. Although Subbu was able to get certain parts of the application to work, he couldn't prevent the application from completely failing. At that very moment, his BlackBerry began to buzz. He looked at the miniature screen and read an e-mail that had just arrived from Tom. The e-mail read,

Ryan, one more thing I forgot to mention. I heard from a key member of your team that you really pitched in on each of the projects. I noticed all the time you had been putting in as well. I appreciate your effort, honesty, and your commitment to your team. See you at 11. Tom.

"Just shoot me now," Ryan thought.

He never explained to Tom the real state of the project. He simply skirted around the issues and tried to put a positive spin on the status. Although he never lied, it was definitely a massaged status. While not comforting, this was the consequence of the unrealistic demand.

"It had to get done!" remembering Tom's voice. What did he really expect? Ryan didn't know what Tom would think or say, and poor Subbu, who had been saying what everyone wanted to hear, was now right in the line of fire.

Ryan wondered who had spoken to Tom about the work he had done. He figured it must have been Stacy, because no one else would have spoken to him, but why would she go out of her way to tell Tom what he was doing, especially after how she felt about his handling of the situation?

Ryan glanced at his watch, which said 10:00 a.m. and unfortunately, he was still at his desk, avoiding the trip to the data center. He hustled down to the data center, sat down next to Subbu and began discussing the progress. During the conversation, Ryan told him that Tom was coming to see the inventory system and that Subbu needed to make it work.

Subbu explained the tremendous progress he had made, and insinuated that the progress was exceptional. Ryan knew that wasn't the case, but Subbu felt confident that the situation was reasonable and assured Ryan he could fix any problems that arose. Ryan knew that assurances were hollow at this point and he became fearful of the outcome of this meeting. Intuition told him this wasn't going to be a pretty sight, and he became very concerned about how much damage control he would need to do. Ryan worked with Subbu over the hour to understand the key problems in hopes that he could rationalize the problems.

A few minutes before 11:00 a.m., there was no sign of Tom, so he decided to take a quick break and head to the bathroom; with nervousness setting in, he felt very uneasy. He felt the blood rushing to his head and his ears were heating up. The beads of sweat across his forehead were readily apparent before he brushed them aside with a cold paper towel. His watch read 11:04 a.m. as he quickly dried his face, realizing that he should head back to the data center before Tom arrived.

Tom had a habit of showing up to meetings ten to fifteen minutes late, so he wasn't terribly worried. Ryan threw the paper towel away with a fifteen-foot jump shot, which naturally missed. He was trying to shed some nervousness by horsing around a bit. As he opened the bathroom door to exit, he quickly glanced down the hallway to the data center door, and his heart stopped as he noticed who had entered the data center, Tom and the CIO.

Ryan quickly bustled over to the data center, about a hundred feet from the bathroom. When he opened the data center door, he saw Subbu and his boss shaking hands.

"Glad you could join us, Ryan," his boss said as he turned to Ryan

It was obviously a joke, because Subbu had told Tom that Ryan was in the bathroom, but Ryan wasn't laughing. The CIO, who couldn't resist a quick pun said, "Hopefully everything came out OK."

Ryan smiled and thought to himself, "My God, there's going to be a lot 'coming out' very soon."

Tom indicated they could only stay for a twenty-minute demo, so it needed to be brief. Tom asked Subbu, as though Ryan didn't exist, "Subbu is this going to work?"

Subbu replied, "Of course, sir, everything will work."

Ryan stepped in and said, "Subbu has done a great job and has assured me that this works fine."

He knew that wasn't true, and he had no idea why he said what he did. Fifteen minutes after the demo started, it was over.

Ryan was at his desk a half hour later with his head resting in his hands covering his face. Subbu had come up to see him, and said, "Ryan, I think it went well. It only locked up twice, but I know I can fix those problems."

Ryan knew it wasn't OK. The CIO had walked out with Tom, and he distinctively heard, "This is unacceptable."

The remainder of the conversation was inaudible since the data center door had closed as they exited and scurried down the hallway, but Ryan could see through the windows the flailing arms and finger-pointing. Ryan wasn't sure what was going to happen, but he knew it wasn't going to be good.

Ryan told Subbu he appreciated the effort and he would find out from Tom later that day what they thought. Subbu walked away with a big grin on his face, confident he had done a good job. Ryan clearly understood the severity of the situation. It wasn't good, and there was no spin in the world that could repair the damage. Ryan dropped his head on his desk creating a big thud, loud enough for everyone within two cubicles to hear. Stacy, overhearing the conversation between Subbu and Ryan and hearing the thud from her cubicle walked over to Ryan's desk.

"What happened?" Stacy asked, as she approached his desk.

Ryan went on to explain what happened in the demo. He told her that it couldn't have been worse, and that he wasn't sure what was going to happen.

"Do you think you're going to get fired?"

"Probably." he responded.

Stacy asked what Tom and the CIO had said. He indicated most of the conversations were between Subbu and Tom, with the CIO watching intently. He deliberately left out the fact that he barely spoke. Ryan knew the demo shouldn't have taken place, but he wasn't given a choice. Stacy told him not to think about it, because there was nothing he could do. At least there was nothing that could be done at this point.

Ryan was petrified as he awaited the dreaded call from Tom. Each hour passed by, as if he were on death row awaiting either the call from the governor for a stay of execution or the clock to strike the hour of his demise. The call never came. Four o'clock rolled around, and he expected to be called into Tom's office before his big meeting in the afternoon. No calls or e-mails ever came though. Ryan left the office at 5:00 p.m. and he desperately tried not to think about what had happened. But he would have to endure an evening of uncertainty.

At home, once again, he spoke with Lisa, who found the incident ironically amusing.

"These people are stupid. If it doesn't work, it doesn't work. Just admit it and move on. It's not your fault the damn thing doesn't work," Lisa said

Ryan then went on to detail the meeting in the data center, and he agreed with Lisa's assessment that the meeting was a play by Tom to look good to the CIO. Ryan was hesitant to say what he had told Tom in front of the CIO, but relented due to the immense feeling of guilt weighing on him. "Subbu has assured me this works fine," he repeated from earlier.

"Did Subbu really say that to you? He was setting you up. He should have known better. If you get fired it will be because of him."

Ryan started to agree with her, and then backed up.

"He never said that to me. He said he could get it to work, but it wasn't his intent to say it works fine; he was just trying to do the right thing. He wanted to get it to work and would keep trying until he did. He's good, but he isn't a miracle worker. No one could get that system to work."

"I don't understand how you people operate in this world. It must be an inbred defect in technologists or management positions that makes you stupid."

Ryan smirked at the support, and while he didn't mind the sarcasm, he knew there was some truth to what she was saying. Unfortunately, it was the nature of the beast; there was politics and there was *politics*, and there was his handling of his team. Nothing seemed quite right.

The next morning, Ryan came in to a note on his desk to see Tom immediately. It was odd that it wasn't via e-mail or voice mail, but a damn Post-it note in Tom's handwriting. Ryan thought, "Here we go."

He was going to begin packing his things, just to be prepared, but decided instead to just go to Tom's office. He would go in with a positive attitude, take control of the situation, and handle it as well as he could. He was so nervous that he drank a half a bottle of water on the way to quench the dryness that had built up in his mouth and throat. Ryan knocked on the office door.

"Come in, Ryan," Tom said.

Ryan didn't get a word out before Tom went on a fairly long diatribe, which, for the most part, was palatable for him, until Tom began ranting about Subbu.

"Ryan, you can't let these guys pull the wool over your eyes. They aren't pulling their weight. The fact that they are telling you that everything is fine is unacceptable. They aren't pulling their weight; there is no other way to say it. He lied to you, he lied to me, and he lied to the CIO. He's done, today. And that other guy should go too. There was no reason to fire him back then, but now there is, he's done too."

Ryan thought very quickly of why he should fight for Subbu. Subbu was a hard worker and he did the best he could. This was wrong; he needed to right this situation. He thought for a second, but replied,

"You're right, he's done. Phil should be terminated as well?"

"Let's see how the other demo goes later today," Tom said as he backtracked from his original thought.

Tom was more confident in the Web site demo because Stacy was in charge and because the users had seen it and had given positive feedback. So he wasn't concerned. His boss concluded, "You don't have to do the dirty work, but I want you to tell Subbu to come to my office immediately when he gets in. You and Stacy coordinate packing his things and inform human resources. Make sure you don't start the process until he comes up here. I don't want him tipped off; I have to get his ID disabled so he doesn't sabotage anything. We will then talk later about the inventory system and get your thoughts on how we can proceed."

Ryan went back to his desk, and all he could do was feel a great sense of relief. He couldn't feel any sympathy; he was too relieved about his personal situation. He knew he should feel something for him, but he just couldn't. He slowly walked up to Subbu's cubicle and said to him. "Subbu, you need to go to Tom, he wants to talk about the inventory system."

Subbu acknowledged, and said, "Very good, he must have liked it. Did he like it?"

Ryan nodded, but said nothing, as Subbu said, "I will go right away."

Ryan watched him walk away, and when he was sure that he was in Tom's office, he went over to Stacy's cube.

"Stacy, I need your help."

"Sure, Ryan, what's up?" Stacy responded,

"We need to pack up Subbu's things."

"Are you kidding me?" she exclaimed.

"Shhh! I want to keep this a bit quiet, at least for now."

Stacy whispered, "What happened?"

"I've been told to have Subbu's things packed up, he is gone."

"Because of the inventory system?"

"Yep. It sucks, but let's get his stuff to HR, and then let's go out to an early lunch. I need to talk, do you mind?"

Sensing the urgency, Stacy said, "No, not at all."

Stacy had never seen the look of complete despair on Ryan's face. She quickly realized he was taking this very hard so she didn't dare make any comments.

Ryan and Stacy packed the things avoiding any questions from the other team members, but it was obvious what was happening. There was no real way to hide it. A noticeable uneasiness came over the entire team, and no one said a word. The two of them just scurried around gathering stuff, and putting some mementoes in the boxes. Neither of them could believe what was happening. Ryan was carrying more than boxes though; he was carrying a very heavy burden, one that he wasn't sure he would ever shake.

Ryan and Stacy went out to lunch as he had requested. Stacy listened to his recollection of the events, and his pain at not protecting Subbu. While he was very detailed in his description of the meeting, he did omit a few embarrassing points. Stacy could sense Ryan's disappointment at himself, about letting Subbu down, especially in the meeting with Tom. It was hard for him to reconcile the contradiction of emotions waging war within him regarding the sense of relief, and the sense of guilt.

Stacy absorbed the entire conversion, and she deduced, quite accurately, the sequence events, even with the missing pieces.

"You know, I'm not sure many people wouldn't have reacted differently. Look, you could have been fired, you tried to help Subbu out, and you worked countless hours attempting to get that system to work. You and I both know that the problem was with that damn system and they never should have purchased it. In fact, it's those jerks that should be fired," Stacy said.

"Obviously, they wanted a scapegoat, and I am just relieved that it's not me. On one hand, I'm so happy it's not me, and on the other I let Subbu down. I can't help but feel that I should have done something different," Ryan responded.

"True," Stacy said, "but remember, Subbu kept telling people, it was working, just a bit more, a bit more. That's not the way to work. If you really want to beat yourself up over something, then beat yourself up over not getting him to admit when things just wouldn't work."

"Funny you say that. I tried to tell him that, but he never did it. In fairness, we didn't give him much of a choice, especially when I told him 'failure is not an option,' when, in fact, it was the only option. There was no way it was going to work," Ryan said.

"Yeah, I hated that, but I don't need to bash that in your head again," Stacy said, completely by passing the "we" comment.

"Thanks," Ryan sarcastically said.

"Look, you tried, you don't think you tried hard enough, that's your prerogative, but don't beat yourself up over it. Things could have been worse," said Stacy.

"That's very true," Ryan said appreciatively.

As they finished their lunch, a little bit over the normal hour, Ryan said, "You know what I really got from this? It's very difficult to win. I really thought I could make a difference and do things differently, I'm not sure that I can really handle it. I'm not even sure that I really want it anymore. I hate the politics. I hate spinning things, and I hate almost everything about it. I couldn't save Subbu. I almost got myself fired. No one would listen to the truth, and if I had stood up, they would have gotten rid of me and they would still be in the same place. Maybe I should just go back to being a programmer."

"That's exactly why I didn't want your job. But you're good at it. I can tell you this. Everyone respects you, even Phil. They all trust you, almost completely. They look to you for guidance, and leadership. I can tell you that this group supports you and is very appreciative of what you do, even if your management doesn't."

"Did you tell Tom anything about me staying late and working on both projects?" Ryan asked.

Stacy responded, "Someone had to."

"You know that may have saved my job."

"Well, I didn't suspect you would lose your job. I just wanted them to know what you were doing. You deserved some credit."

Ryan nodded as if to thank her using some telepathic communication, but the more he thought about it, the more he believed her comment saved his job. Even if that wasn't the case, he was very appreciative that the team recognized he was working for them.

Over the course of the next week, there were some demos of the Web site. Most of them went well, and it performed exactly as he reported it would. There were a few minor issues, but the site was built according to design and every comment that came back was handled appropriately. They couldn't say that it wasn't delivered. It was.

Even though it was delivered, no one was happy but, most importantly, no one blamed the team or him. They all blamed each other. Ryan was actually amused and happy that they were all pointing fingers at each other. He knew that this was a political game being played by his management and marketing. The IT management stated that the system was designed the way marketing had requested, and the marketing group stated IT didn't understand what was asked. The meetings apparently became very heated, or so Ryan heard, since he wasn't part of them, and the discussions made it up all the way to the CEO and chairman, with no clear end of the blame game in sight. Ryan was fascinated at how the focus had shifted from his department to bitter infighting among senior managers. There was no doubt that serious consequences would arise for whoever lost this political battle. If that wasn't the case, why would the discussions be so intense and heated?

Ryan remembered some lectures and articles on management from his first management MBA classes, which had begun the semester before. Even though he was completing only his first year, he looked for opportunities to relate the material to his everyday work, which made the experience very rewarding. Concepts in management and leadership fascinated him, especially authors such as Peter Drucker, Jim Collins, and Irving Janis, all renowned theorists who published many books and articles on management, strategy, and organizational behavior. What fascinated Ryan most was how people and groups made decisions and interacted with each other. One such concept that intrigued him was a theory published by Irving Janis in 1972 called groupthink.

Groupthink was a theory regarding decision making, which sought to understand faulty decisions and the events leading up to them. Janis hypothesized that under certain conditions, "fiascos," decisions that in hindsight were found to be erroneous, were due to a flawed decision-making process. One of the most noted examples of groupthink was the Space Shuttle Challenger disaster. In 1986, the pressure to launch the shuttle from government officials and NASA was immense, even though the risk was very high due to the extremely cold launch day. Some engineers warned against the launch, citing various technical problems related to the cold temperatures; however, according to reports, these warnings were ignored. In some cases, engineers decided not to speak out for fear of retribution. Ryan wasn't sure which is worse; people who speak out and are retaliated against or people who don't speak out due to fear of retribution.

Groupthink is characterized by eight major symptoms, three of which include direct pressure to conform, illusion of unanimity, and self-censorship. When present, the theory suggests that the decision making is flawed and therefore the probability of success will be significantly reduced.

Ryan couldn't help but feel that the situation he had endured over the past few months was related to groupthink. He had allowed himself to become a member of the herd, saying that something could be done when he knew it couldn't. He didn't speak up, and he never pressed the issue. He ignored dissention, and forced his team to arrive at a solution that was impossible. Ryan understood the problems and only tacitly objected, due to fear of retribution. Ryan considered himself a victim of groupthink, even though he was more of a perpetrator than a victim. He knew he had fallen into a trap, and questioned whether a good leader would ever be guilty of being drawn into a herd mentality and become a victim of groupthink.

He realized that this summed up his experience. He tried to tell the truth early on, albeit not very forcefully. He was confronted with the notion of completing the task at all costs. He had then been a victim of the circumstances and forced his team to abide by this direction, even trying to motivate them with his "failure is not an option" speech. The statement echoed in his head repeatedly, deepening his disbelief that he had uttered the words.

He was disappointed mostly in himself, but he learned a valuable lesson, a lesson about himself that he despised. He wasn't sure how to change it, but he would need to come to a resolution, because the circumstance was sure to repeat itself. He refused to be dragged down like a swimmer in a riptide being pulled out to sea, if the situation every reappeared, hoping he could find such a way.

Ryan wondered what he had done right, if anything. He remembered what Stacy had said to him during that the lunch.

"You took a very bad situation, stayed calm, and put the team into solid groups, organizing them according to their capabilities. You also never let anyone down; you were there with us every step of the way. We never felt abandoned. That meant a lot to us."

Ryan realized that his relationship with his team, especially Stacy, was pretty strong. He had grouped them into a cohesive unit and they had come to appreciate him. They knew he wasn't perfect and he believed that they didn't expect him to be perfect. He would have to be content with what he had. At least he wasn't a complete failure. Although he thought Stacy might disagree on some level.

Over the next six months, Ryan noticed a change in Tom, who became a bit out of touch. He was under more stress and increasingly lashed out at everyone. No one else was terminated from the incident or anything else that had transpired, and, while it was a big plus, there was enormous tension within the entire IT group. His team, however, survived, and continued to survive.

Ryan was still searching and contemplating, not because of the events of the last six months, but rather he wondered if his career would benefit from a change of pace. He had been with the company almost two years, and had contemplated leaving the company over the past few weeks. Stacy, who was the only member of the team he told, continually urged him not to. She said he needed to get over it, and not worry so much. Stacy didn't understand that Ryan's motives for leaving were rooted in a desire to grow his career as well as grow as a person, and, although the thought of leaving was tempting, he temporarily decided against it.

One week later, Ryan heard that there were major changes coming. He had no idea what was happening or at whom the changes were directed. Later in the day, Tom called him into his office, and then spent five minutes yelling at him. Ryan listened stoically, never flinching. These tongue-lashings had become slightly commonplace and he developed immunity to the hubristic tirades. He knew that Tom had changed over the past few months, which was one of the primary reasons he was thinking of leaving.

The next day announcements came from the executive management—Tom had been fired, and the CIO was resigning to pursue personal interests. Ryan realized that was senior management code for "you're fired!" Ryan didn't expect a major shakeup across the company; however, he was wrong, the SVP of marketing and the COO, would both be gone within ninety days. This was an effort by the CEO to completely change the senior management structure and revitalize the company.

At the same time, candidates had already been selected to replace the outgoing executives, but there was no mention of the names. Ryan hoped the new management would be an exciting set of players from whom he could learn. The CEO made an announcement of a major shift for the company, which would make it a leader in retail innovation. Ryan wasn't sure what that meant, but he was becoming increasingly positive about the prospects. He felt his spirits being raised.

Over the next eight weeks, the new CIO quickly made some organizational changes, and Ryan was about to get a new a new boss. His new boss had a great background, with solid experience. Ryan couldn't wait to meet him. He was listed on Google and came with a solid background in information technology management. Ryan's role was going to be focused exclusively on delivery of Web site technologies, making his role much easier, and with his new boss's expertise, he might learn a thing or two.

Ryan's new boss, Jay Alethia, had led major implementations at other retailers and was on the leading edge of some great technology. He hoped this would be a different experience and an opportunity for him to shine and accelerate his career.

Chapter 3

TRUST

Ryan had become an avid reader since he enrolled in the MBA program two years ago, never wasting a moment to read articles on management and strategy. Although his grades were very good, they never became his primary focus; rather, he simply directed his efforts to learning the material. He became a well-known entity among the professors in various departments, and spent extra time in their offices debating and questioning the material. It was a much different and more enjoyable experience than his previous time at State.

Not all of his classmates shared the same viewpoint. They reminded him of the way he was years ago—they were just going through the motions, anticipating completing their degrees. They wanted to exit as quickly as possible and get good jobs that paid well, or they hoped their employers gave them raises; to them, MBA meant More Bucks and Advantages. Ryan didn't share that approach; he wanted more out of the experience, and it showed.

Ryan viewed his job as the experimental lab for the material he was learning. By using the issues confronting him and his coworkers at his office, he could see the application of theories that professors taught. He could never forget his firsthand experience of groupthink. The incident was deeply ingrained in his memory and he was certain that this experience led to his newly developed and expanding passion for education.

During one of his downtimes, he discussed the incident in detail with his management professor, who himself was intrigued with Ryan's situation. His professor came from an Ivy League school and specialized in organizational behavior. He shared with Ryan additional experiences and offered him advice on what to look for in certain situations when dealing with management. One particular warning sign would be the increased oversight by management, or micromanagement, to compensate for lack of direction and clarity. Ryan was lucky because he knew that Jay, who had been a great boss since his arrival earlier in the year, was not a micromanager, and allowed him to grow and make mistakes from which he could learn.

Ryan had made many connections with faculty and students, and thoroughly enjoyed the discussions. The more he opened up and engaged his colleagues the more information he received. Although it wasn't always the best information, it was information, nonetheless, that he could use. The information he was gathering enabled him to recognize patterns in human behavior, and he began to identify students' behavior in which he could determine which students would be effective and which would not. This recognition, he thought, would be critical to determining which employees or future employees would be valued members of his team.

The degree was a grueling experience with papers, readings, and presentations, but the goal would be worth it. He instinctively knew there were practical applications to the theories he was learning— quite a transformation for someone who once disdained academia.

During one of his discussions with a professor, however, he received a warning. His professor, who came from England, told him, in a sophisticated British accent, "Theories provide a strong foundation, but do not view them as a magic bullet. Sometimes it will work perfectly and other times it won't. Not because the theory is incorrect, but because some variables are not taken into account or its application to the situation is faulty."

Ryan originally had struggled with that notion, asking if the theories weren't always correct then why learn them. The professor went on to explain that in a controlled environment theoretical concepts would hold. However, it was possible that in an office environment, where conditions were not controlled, any change to the situation could change the outcome. Ryan entered school looking for magic bullets and now he was being warned against them.

If there were a magic bullet though in any of his classes it had to have been in leadership, Ryan thought and Leadership was one of the classes he enjoyed the most. During a class group discussion, the professor asked the groups to discuss among themselves two basic questions. What makes a leader and what qualities does a leader employ? This was easy for him. Being a self-proclaimed expert in leadership and history, he wholeheartedly engaged his fellow students about leadership, and great leaders. As a military buff, he spoke of great military leaders like Patton and MacArthur as being prime examples of leadership, figuring they had to be leaders since they led men into the most brutal form of conflict known, warfare. What better method of proving true leadership?

Not everyone in his group agreed or shared Ryan's sentiment. Others in his group mentioned people like Martin Luther King Jr. and Mahatma Gandhi. Still others mentioned names he hadn't heard of— Bob Geldof and Betty Williams. Ryan was perplexed that people had mentioned names he had never heard. Unsure of what he was missing, curiosity overcame his hesitancy.

"Who is Bob Geldof?" Ryan asked.

He hoped he wasn't about to be ridiculed, but the look on other students faces indicated they had no idea either.

"Bob Geldof?" the student replied. "Bob Geldof started Live Aid in 1984 to help with famine relief in Ethiopia. He saw a problem, organized a group, and took action. He raised 150 million British pounds in one day. That to me was an accomplishment."

Before Ryan could get another question out, the young woman next to him, dressed, as Ryan would politely say, in non-business attire—code for a tie-dyed shirt with a peace symbol on it, a bunch of necklaces, and a colony of earrings—said, "Betty Williams was an amazing woman. She won a 1976 Nobel Prize for organizing a march in 1974 in Northern Ireland. She had two children and one day got fed up with the violence after one incident that left three children dead. Within two days she had six thousand signatures on a petition for peace, and organized a peaceful protest with over ten thousand people marching."

Ryan jumped in and said, "That sounds impressive." Ryan obviously wasn't impressed, and the young woman knew it.

"Her protest was stopped by a bunch of rock-throwing and name-hurling jerks. She then organized another march one week later, and they had thirty-five thousand people join the march. I admire her determination. *She* is a real leader. She is someone people followed. She made a call and people answered."

Ryan was moved. He felt a bit more diminutive since he originally thought his example of leadership was *the* textbook definition of a war hero who gets the medals. He began to understand that being a leader meant more than just "leading troops into battle." All the examples his fellow students provided were very strong, but what impressed Ryan was the passion with which his classmates presented the information.

Toward the end of the class, the professor commented on the discussion and said, "As usual, this was a very spirited discussion, as I have come to expect when talking about leadership. Although this is a leadership class, you really can't teach leadership. You can lecture about leaders and their qualities but each leader possesses unique qualities that are right for the given time." The professor was walking at the front of the class with his head down as though in deep thought as he continued with his statement.

"There is one common thread among all leaders that no one could question. They were all called to action, and, in many cases, the best leaders were called to *action* for a cause greater than themselves. This isn't to say that you have to create a march of thirty-five thousand people, or lead a rebellion such as the American Revolution. It means there was a *selfless purpose.* In some instances people may have gained fame and fortune as a byproduct; however, at any given time true leadership focuses on a cause, right or wrong from a historical viewpoint, but with a moral fortitude from a subjective perspective."

The class was dismissed and Ryan was still, recalling what he had just heard. He was trying to absorb the concept that effective leadership focused on a selfless purpose. His instinct knew this was true, but he had flashbacks of Jeff, his previous manager, and *himself.* Ryan couldn't help but think what a horrible leader he was to let his team down, especially Subbu.

He quickly noticed he was the last one left as the professor was gathering his papers. The professor could see him through his spectacles as he peered upward at the stadium-like classroom.

"Is everything OK, Ryan?"

Dr. Sherlund, Ryan's professor knew Ryan well; this was his second class with him, and he liked Ryan because of his many intellectual questions. Dr. Sherlund was a highly respected faculty member for his papers on leadership and organizational behavior. His presence dominated every lecture due to his height and his very deep voice with a sophisticated British accent.

"Yes, sir," replied Ryan, "I was just thinking about this class and the comments my teammates made and your closing comments."

Dr. Sherlund responded, "Anything in particular you care to discuss?"

"Maybe we can talk while you walk back to your office?"

"Certainly," replied the professor.

Ryan went onto to explain how perplexed he was at this notion of leadership. In reality, he was dumbfounded as to how wrong he was. It was as if a spark had ignited, and every thought and memory of leadership had come back. He tried to make the connection to understand if the people he considered leaders really were leaders and if he was *that* wrong.

He explained his years on the baseball team and his movement up the corporate ladder. He was angry with himself, because he now realized some of the mistakes he made and what actions he probably should have taken. The professor sympathized with Ryan and listened intently to the story. His interest was genuine since he had written extensively on the topic of leadership and he thought he might be able to provide some more insight for Ryan or at least provide him with a better direction.

He explained to Ryan that many managers go through adversity throughout their careers and tenures, and that not every leader always does the right thing every time. In fact, they usually learn from their mistakes. Once again, he warned Ryan to avoid the magic bullet. Realizing how late it was, he began to close the conversation.

"Ryan, in a way you are lucky because your mistake, or what you considered a mistake, is a realization. You now know what *not* to do. The real issue is will you take action the next time and will it be for a purpose greater than yourself? Will you act differently in the future? It's at that point that you will learn, not leadership, but whether *you* are a leader."

Ryan thanked him, he knew it was late and he had a lot to think about. He had a lot more questions, but he was too tired and he had an early morning. He also had to begin thinking about how, when, or if he would become a leader.

The next morning, Ryan was at work reviewing the status reports. Ryan's team had produced a new version of the Web site since the restructuring six months ago, and things were moving very well. His team had focus and direction, and they were coming up with new ideas for enhancements every day. Still, Ryan knew something was missing.

The team was good, but he knew he could get them to perform better; he just didn't know how or even why he needed to do it. He could just keep going and he would get his bonus at the end of the year, and his team would do well. He didn't have to worry much. He could just let things be, but good enough wasn't good enough for Ryan.

Ryan decided to talk to Jay about what he was thinking. He knew he could talk to Jay because in the short time as his manager, he had become a mentor to Ryan. Jay was very approachable, and his management style was very similar to his college coach, rough when necessary but not overburdening. Ryan greatly respected him for both his technical ability and management style. It was the most comfortable he had been at any workplace.

Ryan sent an e-mail to Jay asking when he would be available for a discussion on "personal growth," as he labeled it. Ryan received an e-mail back within thirty seconds.

"How about lunch at 12? My day is unusually free," read the e-mail.

Ryan sent his acknowledgement back immediately and replied he would be ready at noon and wait for him in the lobby.

Jay read the e-mail and, although perplexed as to what triggered the e-mail, he was very pleased that Ryan wanted to discuss personal growth. He knew Ryan was the perfect leader for that team even though Ryan was a bit rough around the edges. He was the glue that kept the team together and made it run. He sensed that Ryan just had a knack for dealing with people and getting behind his team.

As Ryan waited in the lobby for Jay, he formulated his questions. He thought of how he wanted to approach the conversation. It was surprisingly awkward for Ryan and he wondered if he should ask Jay for his thoughts on leadership or ask how he could become a better leader.

Ryan didn't realize he was actually talking a bit louder than a whisper, when Jay tapped him on the back and said, "So you want to talk about leadership?"

Jay had snuck up behind Ryan and listened for a good thirty seconds to his whispers. Ryan's face turned a bright red, with a degree of embarrassment. Jay the joker, never letting any good pun go to waste, turned to Ryan, pointed to the parking lot and said as he chuckled, "*Lead the way!*"

He quickly put his arm around Ryan and said, "I'm busting your chops, Ryan. I'm going to answer your real question right now. You are a leader, but you will become more of a leader every day if you continue to grow and ask the questions you were asking yourself. It means you are yearning for something, and you will find it, if you keep searching. Now, let's go search for a sandwich or pasta because my stomach is leading the way."

Once again, he chuckled, and Ryan could only muster, "Oh my God, you have to stop! It's not *that* funny."

About fifteen minutes later, and after what seemed about a hundred more of his feeble attempts at dry humor, the lunch conversation focused on work. Instead of Ryan asking questions, Jay monopolized the time.

"Ryan, what would you say is the most fundamental problem of your team?" he asked.

Ryan responded, "I don't know. They handle everything pretty well. They are very good. They solve problems efficiently and professionally."

"OK, what's your goal for the team?"

Ryan, looked puzzled, it was an obvious question. He responded, "I want them to do their jobs well, and enjoy it."

"You played baseball, did you have good players?"

"Yes."

"Did you practice hard every day?"

"Of course," Ryan said, looking puzzled at this line of questioning.

He leaned back in a confident posture, knowing he had Ryan exactly where he wanted him, and asked, "Why?"

"To make sure we were on top of our game, and to get better."

"Why? You said you were already good, why would you need to practice if you were already good? Your development team is good, and they do their jobs well. The difference is your baseball team had a goal, to win a championship or some number of games. In order to do that, you had to practice fundamentals and practice situations that you might not have been ready for. You had to become masters of the game. There was a goal, there was a reason."

Ryan stopped for a moment and thought to himself, "There was a purpose."

He understood what Jay was telling him. He finished his coffee and said, "They need a purpose and a goal to strive for. It has to be something more than just a paycheck, and have more value than just that it's what someone told us to do."

"Exactly, that goal may be collective and you may have individual goals that support the team, for example a single player working on hitting better."

"The concept is very simple. How do I implement that?"

"That's the part that's not so easy. Each person gets motivated in a different way and may not respond to certain aspects of your direction. It's your job to find that and get them on the path. That's what a leader will do. A leader will get someone on the path, in some cases without them knowing they are on it, and in other cases without them knowing that you put them on it, and in still other cases because you forced them on it, for their own good."

Ryan had no clue at this point what he was going to do with the information. He literally begged Jay to give him more examples of how he could do this with his team.

"If I tell you how to do it, then you're not the leader. You're going to have to figure it out. You will need to experiment, take risks, and see what happens. Be smart about it, don't force things if they don't fit, and don't be afraid to adjust. You have to have a feel for what's going to work and what wont. Believe me, you will find a ton of things that won't work," Jay replied.

He paused for a few minutes as he cleaned up his area placing all the garbage on his tray.

"I'll give you as much guidance as I can, but I won't tell you what to do. Over time I will tell you stories of what worked for me and what didn't, but you will have to find other stories from other leaders and you will need to develop your own," he concluded.

Ryan seemed to take it in stride, and understood what Jay was trying to do. There really wasn't enough time to even go over all of the information Jay gave him. He really needed to think about what he could try, and on whom. He had to spend some time thinking about scenarios and issues, but right now, it was time to get back to work. They rode back to the office not even talking about work.

By the time Ryan got back to his cubicle, he looked at his organization chart and contemplated what goal he could make for his team. He took out a piece of paper, and began to write down what he could get the team to strive for, and what was feasible. He decided to write down anything that came to his mind. The list read:

Get the team a 20% bonus
Finish the projects under 10% of budgeted amount
Finish the projects faster by 5%
Focus on Six Sigma Quality, 3 errors in 1 million lines of code
Promote everyone
Get a parking spot of employee of the month
Free lunch for the top member of the team every six months
Whoever completes the most tasks on a project plan gets a free laptop

Ryan looked at the list and said sarcastically, "Yeah, this will work, half of these I can't do because management won't approve them, the others, like "promote everyone," are ridiculous.

Ryan chuckled at himself. He couldn't really come up with anything that he thought was feasible. He couldn't figure out what would be an incentive for the team to perform better. He paused for a moment at "perform better." Didn't this imply that they weren't performing very well? He figured out that the practice Jay was talking about when referring to baseball was to make them better players, and in some cases prepare players for life beyond college baseball. Get them ready for the next level. Ryan wondered if his team wanted to go to the next level. In fact, he really had no idea what they wanted. He then remembered something his old high school teacher had said, which was a philosophy he had always held. "If you want to know something, ask." So he decided to do exactly that.

He took the list and crumpled it up, spun in his chair and pushed back away from the desk as he took a fade-away shot toward the wastebasket. The piece of paper banked off the wall and went right in. Ryan laughed because he was such a horrible shot, and to have that one go in was just the icing on the cake. He was excited about getting the team together but couldn't explain why. He just felt like he was on the verge of something.

He came back to his computer and typed up an e-mail that said the following:

SUBJECT: Team Meeting

Team,

I am calling a meeting for tomorrow afternoon at 3:00 p.m. I am going to ask you one question based on the following.

I am looking to set a direction for our team and for each of you. In order to do that, I need you to think about your current job and your future. Then, as honestly as you can, I need you to be able to answer the following question: What do you want out of your career or what is most important to you in general?

At our meeting, I am looking for ways to make things more exciting and help you drive the direction for our group. Collectively, we can lay out a plan that will work, and you will help me understand the things that make you tick.

Ryan

Ryan was hoping that everyone would come in to the meeting tomorrow with a list of things that he could get started on. This was a sure shot. So sure, he sent the e-mail to Jay, with a note at the bottom saying, "I'm excited about this. Do you think it will work?" He had hoped Jay would read it by the end of the day so he could, maybe, invite him to the meeting. He wondered if he should prepare a presentation or something just in case, but instead decided to wing it and see what would happen.

Ryan left the office later that afternoon still upbeat. He hadn't heard anything from anyone on the team nor did he get a reply from Jay. What troubled him even more was not receiving a response from Stacy. He figured that if anyone had an opinion, it would be Stacy. As he was driving home, he thought about the meeting and what ideas his team would come up with. If he were in their shoes, what would he say? He figured that was easy for him. He wanted to be a leader and make a ton of money. He looked at his BlackBerry almost every ten minutes on his hour-long drive home. Each time he had the same result, nothing, except for one spam e-mail to enlarge his breasts.

He arrived home and began to walk up his driveway once again looking at the BlackBerry for what he hoped was the final time. As he opened the door, his son ran to the door to greet him.

His wife in the background yelling, "Is that you?"

"I'm already halfway in the house," he thought of saying, but replied instead, "Yeah," as he went into the kitchen to help finish dinner.

In the kitchen, as he chopped up onions, he told his wife about the lunch conversation and the e-mail he had written. He hoped she would provide some commentary, as she so often did, or even possibly some insight as to why no one responded. Instead, his wife kept on with the salad and continued to set the table.

As she moved between the dining room and kitchen, he wondered why she hadn't said anything. He was tempted not to ask, but curiosity got to him and he blurted out, "No comment from the peanut gallery?"

"What do you want me to say? If I were them I wouldn't say anything."

"Why not?"

"Why should they? What are you really doing about it? In fact, don't they run the possibility of being embarrassed or chastised by someone else on your team?" she countered.

She continued, "Think of what's his name... Phil. If Stacy says some offbeat comment, he's going to put it in the back of his head and it could come back to haunt her later. What about the new people you inherited after the shakeup? Do they trust you enough to understand there are no ulterior motives? I'm just not sure what they get by answering your question."

Ryan hadn't considered any of what Lisa had mentioned. Why would they tell him? They really had no reason. Maybe they were still concerned about the events earlier in the year that led to Subbu's termination. Even though they didn't know all the details, there were still rumors.

Ryan finished his dinner and, after his son went to sleep, he went into his study to begin some homework. About ten minutes into his statistics work, he put the pencil down and picked up the portable phone. He toyed with the phone, wanting to call Stacy to get her thoughts on his meeting request and question. He took one last look at his BlackBerry and, since he didn't see and e-mail from her or anyone else, he started to dial the phone.

Stacy picked up the phone. "Hello."

"Hey, Stace," replied Ryan, "got a few minutes to chat?"

Stacy was OK to talk—it wasn't that late, and she wasn't doing much anyway. Ryan began talking about his e-mail and what he was looking for; he hadn't asked the real question he wanted answered, which was why Stacy hadn't made a comment. She knew it too.

"You want to know why I haven't responded to you. Why didn't you just ask?"

Ryan said, "I was going to ask, but you didn't give me chance."

"Ryan, I just don't care. I'm tired of this. I'm tired of the comments by Phil and others. I don't even want to talk to you sometimes because I just don't want to hear anything. I want to do my job. I love programming, and I love technology. I don't like dealing with people. That is why I never wanted to move up and become a manager."

"Stacy, but everyone has to have something to strive for, and honestly, you're good and people listen to you."

"Even if I did move up, these idiots will just make some stupid comment and I don't want to deal with it. So in answer to your question of where I want my career to go and what's important, that's easy. I want to be left alone and I want to just code."

Ryan listened intently and said, "Stacy, I've heard the comments, and they don't bother me, and I'm married. I even spoke to my wife about it."

Stacy replied, "I know, so have I."

Ryan knew they talked, and probably had talked about the rumors. He just wondered how much more they talked, and what they said about him. They had become very good friends over the past two years but having his wife and Stacy talk about him made him nervous because they probably exchanged comments about all of his idiosyncrasies and he never knew when he would be the butt of a joke or which one it would come from. It was an odd pair of relationships.

Ryan continued, "Look, I've spoken to Phil and told him to cool it. I told him he needs to be more courteous to his fellow employees and that if he had proof he should produce it; otherwise, back off. I overheard Phil saying that because you talk about your boyfriends, but nobody ever sees them, it was ruse to throw them off the track. Just ignore it."

Stacy replied, "Easy for you to say. I just CAN'T TAKE IT!" she yelled as she closed her reply.

Ryan tried to calm her down, realizing something else was wrong. He allowed her to vent a bit and she calmed down and felt a bit better. She gradually eased back into the conversation about the meeting when Ryan interrupted her.

"Stacy, forget the damn meeting. I want you to feel better, and maybe you need to take some time off. Maybe that's a good idea."

Stacy replied, "Ryan, I'll be fine. I may kill Phil, but I'll be fine. Don't worry about me. Listen, I'm tired. Thanks for listening."

Ryan and Stacy hung up the phone, but Ryan wasn't really finished.

Ryan wanted to fix the problem, but he wasn't sure how. Mostly because he didn't know what the problem was. Earlier, he thought maybe Stacy just needed a bit of motivation and that the meeting tomorrow would be the spark. First, he knew now that wasn't going to work for Stacy. Second, he knew that Phil was a problem he needed to address. Third, he had to do damage control on what Phil had done. Ryan was afraid that there was a fourth, fifth, and sixth that he didn't see. He had no idea how he was going to deal with this, or even if he should. Maybe this was Stacy's problem to deal with? Maybe they just needed to get along? Maybe he should just fire Phil? No, that wouldn't work because HR would have a conniption. He still had to figure out how he was going to handle the meeting.

The next morning, Ryan walked the floor to each cubicle asking team members if they were ready for the meeting in the afternoon. He had a few upbeat responses, and a few mediocre responses. No negative ones. He wondered if that was a good sign. He wasn't enthusiastic at this point. His instinct told him he wasn't going to get much in the way of responses, so he had to come up with a reason for them to engage. In fact, he was the one who would need to do the engaging.

Stacy was in late this morning, it had become a little bit of a pattern. Prior to last night's conversation, he thought it was just a "thing," but now he was concerned. Was this type of behavior going to spiral out of control? Was she getting ready to leave? He had to find out what was going on.

He picked up a stack of metrics that were being developed to assess productivity. He noticed that for the last quarter, there had been a decline in Stacy's work. On a positive note, her team continued to show improvement. He noticed that Stacy's programming had a few more reported bugs per thousand lines of code than her counterparts'. Normally, it wouldn't be a problem, but for Stacy this was a big red flag. She was consistently the best. He always joked that Stacy could write a program from memory and it would run error free from the start. It had always seemed to be the case. There was nothing new about the technology, and the work they had been performing was just routine coding. Something else was amiss.

He wondered if what she said last night was "the root of all evil." Her work had deteriorated since Phil's subtle comments increased, even if not in public. There was very little he could do. If Phil talked in private or didn't send an e-mail, it would be a he said/she said battle and it would probably make the situation worse. He was also puzzled that Stacy hadn't decked him, although he was glad it hadn't happened, *yet.*

If he could reenergize Stacy by removing this thorn from her side, she would no longer be apprehensive about anything at work. More importantly, she would go back to being Stacy, the person he relied on to tell him the truth about anything, and everything, no matter how much it hurt. He missed that and he needed that.

By the time the meeting rolled around, Ryan was confident about what to do. He also had a plan for Stacy, which would put him a bit in the crosshairs, but that's exactly what he wanted. He rolled into the conference room, where everyone was sitting

"How is everyone?" he asked.

He was greeted with the customary grumble.

"Great!" he replied.

"The question I asked you yesterday. Forget it. I have something a bit different."

There were sighs of relief mixed with grumblings because, on one hand, his team didn't want to do this, and on the other hand, why would he have them do something and change his mind? It was a bit frustrating.

Ryan continued, "I know, I know. But I came up with a different way to ask the question. The purpose of this meeting was to set a goal for the team, and I went through a lot of data and reports and came up with no ideas. I even found myself reciting the corporate party line of increase productivity and operational efficiency," he said as he opened his mouth and placed his finger in as if he was trying to make himself gag.

"I decided to take a different approach. If we started our own company, how could we make people buy what we do? Why would a person buy software from us rather than someone else?"

Tim said, "They have no choice, they have to use us. We are the Web developers for the company."

Ryan said, "OK, that's fine, but let's say the marketing department could choose to use an outside company, instead of you, like what is currently done for the Financial System. There is no reason why they couldn't do that to the Web, is there?"

Tim shrugged and said, "I guess not."

"Good, think about that. Now, think about what you would want to do in this new software company assuming we are all part owners. What would be your personal goals for the company? Would you want to work four days a week, make enough money to retire, set your own hours, work from home full time, learn new technologies, use the money you make to get out of technology, do some presentations? What is it *you* want?"

He paused to assess the expressions on his team's faces. He could see they were thinking about it. It was a completely different idea.

"Don't think of it as a job, think of it as a stepping-stone to something greater," he added.

There was a stunned silence in the room. Even Stacy's eyes lit up a bit. Ryan had struck a chord and he could see the tiny hamster in each of their heads furiously running on the spinning wheel. They were never asked such a question. They had to think differently about their jobs.

Not much was said after that, and Ryan gave them some time to think about it. He closed the brief meeting. "Two final points—first, think about it and get back to me on Monday, either collectively or privately. Second, tomorrow evening, before the weekend starts, I'm throwing a mini party, just this group. Let's call it a Friday get-together after work, 5:30 p.m., not long, about two hours, appetizers and the first two rounds are on me."

There was a genuine cheer, the first he had heard in a long time. He said, "One more thing. I need everyone to attend, please. Is there anyone who cannot attend?" Ryan focused his eyes in Stacy's direction, but no one raised his or her hand. He had said the magic words for this group, free booze and free food.

Later that evening, at home, Ryan called Zesty's, the local watering hole, and reserved the back room for his mini party. Luckily no one had it reserved, and even though his party was too small for the room, he knew the owner, who said over the phone, "For you, Ryan, anything."

Ryan then turned to his wife, who heard him on the phone.

"What are you doing tomorrow night? Actually, never mind that. Can you have your mother watch A. J. tomorrow night? I need you to come to Zesty's."

Perplexed, she said, "I think so. Why, what's going on?"

Ryan replied, "I'm throwing a party for the team."

"Why do you want me there?"

"Actually I need you there. I don't really want to explain until tomorrow night—maybe. Can you just arrange to be there at six?"

"Sure, but I don't like the sound of this."

She really was asking out of curiosity—she would never turn down a nice cold one, especially after a long day of domestic engineering. Ryan, noticeably excited, thought, "I hope this works."

The next day, as the team was getting ready to leave the office shortly before 5:00 p.m., Ryan glanced around to see who the stragglers were. He suspected that Stacy might be one of the people staying behind. Stacy had no car for the last two days, because it was being repaired and she had been getting rides from anyone she could ask. She never asked Ryan, which was a telltale sign of what was going on.

As he walked around the area, no one was in sight until he arrived at Stacy's cubicle. She was huddled down, reading a printout of her code.

He interrupted, "Stace, you coming?"

She replied, "Nah, I can't go today, I have a lot of work, and my ride is picking me up in twenty minutes."

Ryan said, "OK, look, I'll give you a ride to Zesty's and back to your house."

Stacy said, "No I'll pass. Just go without me.

Ryan was not going to be turned down, "Look, you have to go. Call whoever is picking you up, and tell them you have a ride. Stacy, I need you to go. We are a team. I know why you don't want to go but please *trust me.*"

She wanted to go, and finally relented, but she had a genuine fear that going with Ryan or even going home with him would make things worse. She wondered if she was making a big mistake.

At Zesty's, Ryan strolled in with Stacy, who lagged a bit behind. She walked in somewhat apprehensively. Ryan greeted everyone with a few high fives, and the dialogue began for the evening.

About fifteen minutes later, Ryan noticed Stacy near the mini bar that had been set up in the back corner of the room. She hadn't moved from the spot since she arrived. This wasn't the Stacy he had come to know. The Stacy he had known was always jovial, doing shots and yelling at the top of her lungs.

He walked over to the bar and said, "Stace, you need to come out of this funk. This isn't you."

"A, you don't know what the hell you are talking about, and B, shut the hell up," Stacy replied noticeably agitated.

"Now that's better. That's the Stace I know."

She couldn't help but smile. It was pretty funny.

Ryan softly said, "Stace, you have to trust me on this."

She had no clue what he was talking about.

About ten minutes later, Ryan glanced toward the door and saw Lisa. He casually walked over, and said, "Yes, ma'am, can I help you? This is a private party for geeks and nerds."

She chuckled and said, "Jerk."

As he was making the rounds of introductions, someone asked, "Hey! I thought you said it was only us, No offense intended."

His wife smiled, but in her mind, she just pulled out a .45 and shot at point-blank range.

Ryan responded, "Hey, if I hold a party and don't invite her, I sleep on the couch. Besides, if I told you guys to invite people, I'd be broke."

Ryan kept working the room, introducing Lisa around, and moved over to the back of the room where Stacy was. No introduction necessary here. His wife pushed Ryan aside and put her arm around Stacy, and said, "Hey, girl." Stacy was relieved to see her. She had a big smile on her face, and she began to chat. Ryan slowly walked away to let them talk.

Ryan then sat down at the big table that was setup in the middle of the floor, and over a period of ten minutes motioned to everyone to come join him at the table as the appetizers were brought out. Once everyone had found a seat—and luckily, his wife sat with Stacy almost directly across from him—he began to discuss the team but just briefly. He mentioned that this was the best team he ever had the pleasure of working with and that he was honored to have a collection of skilled professionals.

Then he jokingly, but strategically, took a stab at himself, and said, "Of course me being the nerd I am, landed a very beautiful wife."

She replied, "Damn straight."

Then she began to chime in a bit, telling the story of how Ryan is such a computer geek, that he can't do an ounce of manual labor.

One member threw his two cents in and said, "The only manual labor he knows is picking up a software manual ten times." Jeers from the table came because that was a bad joke—humorous but bad.

The jokes about Ryan continued on, and he allowed them to go on. He hoped that it would remain civil and not be embarrassing, knowing that there was no chance it would stay civil, with Stacy and his wife hanging around. Sure enough, it got worse.

The two of them traded stories of Ryan, one at work and the other at home. Stacy told the group how she and Lisa would head out to the mall for some shopping, and jab at Ryan because it was just too easy.

Ryan thought, "OK, here we go, what do these two actually talk about?"

Then in the middle of the laughter, Phil turned to his left and muttered as if trying to be funny. Lisa barely heard enough of Phil's comment, but his comment was very clear to her. She sensed his intent.

Ryan never understood how the women's just "knew thing" worked, but he never contradicted it. It was usually right.

Ryan's wife turned in Phil's direction, and said, "Listen, honey, you wouldn't know what those are because you'd have to go on a date first."

The table erupted, and Phil's face turned a bright red. Lisa continued and said, "The only mistress I'm afraid Ryan would have is a computer—he talks more about those damn things than he does about me."

Once again the table erupted and she finished, "Love you, honey," as she blew a kiss to Ryan.

Ryan thought to himself, "This is supposed to be good?"

Stacy couldn't contain her laughter and neither could anyone else, including Ryan. He knew it was all true. That's what made it so funny.

This simple event became a roast and all because he started taking a few jabs at himself. He got exactly what he wanted; he wanted the attention off Stacy and onto him. It was better than he expected after looking at the expression on Phil's face, one of noticeable dejection. Phil didn't utter another word the rest of the night. As people were leaving the table ready to go home, people touched Phil on the back as if to say, "Don't you feel like a fool?"

Lisa got up and mentioned to Stacy, "I have about two hours before I have to pick up A. J. Lets blow this joint, I'll take you home and lets hit the mall before it closes. Stacy got up, and walked with her "sister" right out of the hall, waving to everyone as if she had the last laugh. She did. Phil was done and wouldn't live this down. His comments about Stacy over the past year were an attempt to demean her, and now he was the laughing stock, and he knew it.

Ryan drove home, noticeably worn, but very pleased at what had happened. A little taste of humility and a slice of humble pie never hurt anyone. He hoped that he could put Stacy's biggest fear to rest.

Monday morning, Ryan sat down at his desk and mapped out a strategy. He would focus on key individuals first. Leave Phil for last. He didn't think Phil would actually come around, but he would try. He wanted to target Tim, Mike, and Stacy, they had been with him the longest, and he knew he could get to them. Stacy in her present condition would be a challenge.

Stacy knocked on his cubicle wall, and said, "Morning, Ryan."

Ryan looked up and saw Stacy at the edge. He glanced at the clock on the wall about twenty-five feet over her left shoulder and noticed that she was in thirty minutes early for the first time in a while.

He responded, "Morning, Stacy, how was your weekend?"

"It was fine. I did some reading and caught up with some work. The party on Friday was terrific, and I had a great time with Lisa afterward."

Ryan responded, "Yeah, I know. I heard all about it, over and over. You guys are like two peas in a pod."

Stacy laughed and said, "Well, we did have a lot of laughs at your expense."

Ryan shrugged but smiled.

She paused for a moment and whispered, "Thank you. Lisa figured it out and told me. You put yourself in the firing line, knowing what would happen."

Ryan chuckled and whispered back, "Two things. First, I'm amazed she figured it out, but I guess I shouldn't be surprised. Second, I didn't *know* anything, but I sure hoped *it* would happen, and I knew Lisa would pounce like a cat."

"She did. You should have heard her go off afterward." Stacy chuckled.

As they were laughing, Phil walked by very quietly with his head down toward his desk. Stacy couldn't resist the urge and said with a bit of laughter, "Hey, Phil, have a nice weekend?"

Ryan waved his finger back and forth indicating to her to let it go. She nodded and gave the thumbs-up and walked away. But Ryan knew he got what he wanted. Stacy seemed back.

Later that morning, Mike and Tim came up to Ryan and talked about their career paths, together. Mike and Tim had a lot of energy, they were the same age as Ryan, but this was the first time they had been energized since working at Paltz. They were excited about the prospect of doing more than just simple programming. They talked about devising solutions to more complex problems.

Mike said, "If we had a business we would want it to be called Solution Providers not Programmers, Inc. We want to look at the possibility of finding more problems in the organization and see where we can help. There's one catch though."

Ryan asked, "What's that?"

"We need to figure out a way to learn the business at a more detailed level," Tim said. "We can't rely on a piece of paper with requirements that someone hands us and tells us to 'code this.' We need to understand the problem in order to be part of the solution. We have a couple of ideas that we think might work and we wanted to run them by you."

"Shoot," Ryan said with a big smile.

They went through a number of recommendations. Ryan diligently wrote them all down and asked them to document all of their recommendations and come up with the pros and cons. They told him to give them till Friday and they would formalize their ideas. Ryan was excited because he knew what they had done was provide practical solutions. They knew intuitively that in order to help the business, they needed to be part of the business. It was so simple. He was surprised no one in his management ever conveyed that approach. These were the types of initiatives that he wanted to implement. They were innovative and they could work. More importantly, these were the initiatives that the team came up with.

Later that afternoon, Ryan met with Jay for his weekly status meeting. Ryan mentioned the after-work escapade on Friday, although he didn't go into all the details. He told Jay that the members of his team came up with some very good ideas about enhancing the team. Jay was very interested in the ideas. He was not only open to new ideas, he was always willing to try things and admit when they didn't work. He specifically liked one idea, where the programmers would have a cubicle near the departments they serviced. This collocation approach would sensitize the developers to the troubles and pains that the rest of the company was having. There would need to be some controls, but he didn't think that would be a problem to implement. Other companies had done it, so this would be nothing new in the information technology industry, but it would be a first here.

After Ryan had a chance to go over the status, Jay began to describe a new initiative that came down from senior management. The task was to redesign the point of sale (POS) system. This was the system that every store used to register customer orders and accept cash and credit cards. There were some significant issues with the current POS system. It needed to be revamped. Transactions were getting lost, and it was taking too long to close the registers at the end of each day. Jay told Ryan that this was a very visible project and the estimated period was twelve months for the entire software development lifecycle.

Ryan interrupted, "Jay, have the requirements been finalized? I don't want a repeat of what happened last year."

He responded, "Not yet, your team will need to gather the requirements and understand what the business wants."

"I'd rather not commit to a date until I know the requirements. Is it acceptable to set a date for the requirements process and then determine what can be built in the appropriate time frame?" Ryan asked.

"Sounds reasonable to me," he answered.

"Then I don't see a problem. However, this sounds bigger than what my team can handle," Ryan said.

Jay responded, "You will be able to expand your team. We are figuring that you will need about eight additional people, up to four developers and four business analysts. Take a look at the project charter and then report back. Can you get back to me," he said as he looked at his desk calendar, "two weeks from Friday?"

Ryan agreed. He was excited, having received a new major project; however, he was determined not to let history repeat itself. This time he would handle things differently and his training and experience would benefit him greatly.

As Ryan was reading the requirements at his desk, he realized the magnitude of the project. This was enormous and on such a tight time frame. With the assurances that he would receive the needed people and dollars, he was confident he could pull this off. A plan would need to be created and he would need to organize his team differently to maintain its existing workload and focus a group on the new initiative. While he felt comfortable that his team could take the lead because of their ability in the past, this had to be different. He wanted them to excel.

Later that night, during a one-hour break before his class started, he read a book that provided insight on how companies become great. The book described the success of companies in relation to their leadership and not necessarily on the products that they built. As he read the book, he found that a common thread among many successful companies was their ability to hire the right talent and put them in the right roles. He remembered that even Warren Buffett made decisions on investments based on the management of companies first.

If he were to put the right people in the right spot and allow them to develop a firm but disciplined way of doing things, then he could get the most out of his team. Once again, he made the connection to his old baseball team, understanding that teams perform well when players are put in positions that exploit their strengths; they execute at their positions very well, almost intuitively, and in complete harmony. "Would it work here?" he wondered.

A thought crossed his mind to split the team into two areas. One area would work on the "business as usual" work. This was the work that came in bit by bit—maintenance work, bug fixes, etc. There was nothing spectacular about this, but it was important and required a unique skill set with highly organized and metric-driven management. The leader of this group needed to be task-oriented, methodical, and process driven. He or she also had to understand the sensitivity of the requests and be able to prioritize accordingly. Tim or Mike would be better suited for that position. Each of them had shown promise in understanding how to manage resources, and their strengths were in following a process. Their weaknesses though were in the creative nature of problem solving and long-term vision. Within a well-defined process they could fix issues and get systems and applications back up and running. He thought Tim might be better suited because he was very driven by the numbers.

Ryan then focused his attention on the special project, the POS system. He knew Stacy was perfect for this position. She was brilliant, persistent, and creative. He knew that she didn't overcome obstacles; she blew them away with dynamite. Stacy's problem, though, was that she didn't want to manage. Not only that, but until today, she had been disengaged.

He was afraid on two counts. First, if she didn't want to manage a group, it could be disastrous to put her in that spot. In addition, she wasn't the most "approachable" individual. Her style was very blunt and could turn off new employees that came in. Second, could he *trust* her? He thought about it for a while, and he knew he could trust her, but he was nervous. If he put her in that position and she disconnected at the wrong time, it would be disastrous for the team, her, and him.

Ryan wondered what she would say if he asked. He figured that if he could get through to Stacy, she could become a great manager and even a leader. She deserved it. For all the issues that she had gone through recently, and her ability to persevere through adversity, he felt she deserved a shot. Not only that, he wanted to give her a shot to prove to her that she was more than she thought and ultimately take his spot as he progressed in his career. She was the most qualified and most talented person, and there was no reason why she shouldn't accelerate her career, unless, she didn't want to. He felt he owed it to her to ask, and ultimately to persuade her.

The next morning, Ryan was immersed in his own thoughts about the organizational structure. When he saw Stacy, he approached her and said, "Stacy, let's go for a cup of coffee."

She agreed. This was a definite change from a few weeks back, where she would have declined ever so politely, in only the way Stacy could. While in the car, to the Coffee Hut, he told her about the POS project. He explained the importance, scope, and enormity of the project and what he needed to be successful. He explained to her that Jay had promised he would get what he needed in terms of resources and budget.

Stacy asked, "And do you believe him?"

"I have no reason not to. He's been very up front and accommodating at every turn. I need to believe him if this is going to work," Ryan responded

"Well then, let's see what happens."

Ryan motioned with his hands and said, "Not so fast. We have to do more than 'see what happens.' We need to do this one right."

"Ryan, remember what happened last time."

Ryan nodded. "I know, but we can't let that blind us. We have to figure out how we can do things better. I have an agreement with J that we will get the requirements from the business and, based on those requirements, we will either change the projected date or reduce the overall scope. J explained it was all about negotiation."

"Will he stick to it?" she asked.

Again, Ryan replied, "I have no reason to believe he won't. He said he will handle the negotiations."

"Well then it seems like everything is a go. However, I'm sensing there is more," said Stacy.

Ryan waited a moment trying to figure out how to approach Stacy. He wanted her to run the project. He wanted her to lead the group. She had led a couple of developers, but this was different. She would run an entire project from start to finish, liaison with the business, and her group would more than double in size. It wasn't going to be just about development.

Ryan carefully treaded, saying, "Stacy, this is going to be a large group, of around ten to twelve people and we will own the entire lifecycle of the project start to finish including analysis, requirements, design, development, testing, documentation, and implementation."

Stacy answered, "I know, it will be exciting to get to really see it work soup to nuts."

Ryan felt ecstatic, until Stacy continued, "I could be your lead developer if you want me to. Of course, I don't want to overstep my bounds. I know I've been kind of laid back lately, but I think that's behind me."

Ryan stuttered a bit, and then replied, "Stacy, you're the best developer we have, and the team respects you. Of course I want you as the lead."

Stacy smiled. Her mind started to race about how exciting this would be.

Ryan continued, "Look, Stace, you're such an integral part of this team as a developer. However, I don't think I want you as my lead developer."

Stacy exclaimed, "WHAT? You just said I was your best developer. You know you're making a big mistake, you arrogant bastard. I thought—," she paused, and then continued, "Whatever. You know, I don't understand you. Why the hell would you start saying those things? Are you toying with me? What did I do to you, is this payback for the last few weeks or something?"

Ryan looked at Stacy with a blank stare and didn't say a word. Stacy continued her diatribe and suddenly stopped.

Stacy's jaw had dropped, and after about five seconds she said, "No, no, absolutely not. Now I know you're nuts. There is no way I'm leading the entire group. I'm not qualified for that, I don't even want it. Find someone else. I'll work for anyone else even as a programmer. No way, no way, no way."

Ryan smiled and said, "Why not, Stace? You're the best person in this group, and you know it. Look how you reacted when you thought you weren't the lead developer. I told you I wanted you as the lead, you just went off the deep end for no reason."

Ryan continued, "You're better than me in many ways, I'm just playing the politics."

"We'll, that's what I want to avoid. Remember that's why I didn't want your job two years ago. I liked where I was, I like where I am. No."

Ryan, pressed on, "Stacy, you need to grow in your career. This is a normal progression. As I grow and move up, which I hope to do, I need a lieutenant. You're the person I trust the most. You call it like it is, and you provide me with the information I need to make sound decisions. I can't have a yes-man, kiss-ass, or anyone like that. I need someone who tells me when I'm drinking Draino."

Stacy responded, "I don't like this. I really don't like this. It's too much pressure and you know I can't stand up and kiss management's ass. I'm going to tell them off."

Ryan replied, "I don't want you to kiss their ass. We will work on being diplomatic. I'll help you do that."

Stacy knew Ryan was right about one thing. If she ever wanted a progressive career, she would need to move up. It made it easier that Ryan was in front. She could learn from him as well, and she knew all too well by now, that he wasn't going to throw her to the wolves. It was very risky, and she was very nervous about it.

She sighed, and said to him, "So you want me to lead the entire team from start to finish?"

Ryan nodded.

Stacy continued, "You better not hang me out to dry, or I'll cut your limbs off, all five."

Ryan laughed and said, "See what I mean, you're starting out blunt and direct. That's what I want. You have my word—I'm not going to hang you out to dry. We are going to be successful together. This will work if we work as a team. Each person has his or her own role, and we need to create a plan and stick to it. If the actors know their positions, you have a successful play."

Stacy reiterated her nervousness, and then she seemed to drift onto another thought.

"Ryan, Friday's party."

There was a long pause before Ryan interjected and said, "I know you thanked me already."

Stacy continued, "Yes. I meant that. Thank you. It really showed your character. You took a gamble that paid off. I can't tell you how I felt, and how much I appreciated what you did."

Ryan replied, "It was nothing."

She turned back and said, "It wasn't nothing, and I owe you an explanation."

Ryan questioned, "For what?"

Stacy put her head down and took a deep breath. She obviously had something important to say, but was hesitating. Stacy knew she needed to tell Ryan, because he had gone out on a limb for her like no one else. He deserved the truth, but telling him the truth exposed her to ridicule and she could become an outcast. Her entire relationship with the team would be jeopardized, and what would Ryan think? Ryan could take back everything. Ryan deserved to know the truth about her if he was putting all his faith in her. What would happen to him if he found out later? Then he might have a bigger problem. She wondered what would happen if someone else found out. What would the impact be on Ryan? What if Ryan told someone?

"I'd kill him," she thought. "No I wouldn't. I'd kill myself," she thought to herself.

"Stacy, Earth to Stacy, I'm here, and you're saying nothing," Ryan said.

Stacy had been silent for almost a minute, but it seemed like hours.

"Stacy, what is it? What explanation?" Ryan asked.

Stacy continued her elongated pause, and finally said, "Ryan, I need to tell you something."

"Sure Stacy." Ryan replied.

"No. Please don't say a word; this is very difficult for me."

There was no turning back now. She had reached the point of no return. She figured for an instant she could make something up or just laugh it off, but that wouldn't work. The pressure on her face told a story of a burdening weight and she could see on Ryan's face that he knew it. She looked up and said, "Ryan, I'm going to tell you something. I haven't told anyone. I'm afraid you'll think different of me, but I'm a good person."

Ryan answered, "I—," but was cut off by Stacy.

"Please. I need your word you won't tell a soul. You have to give me your *word*."

Ryan nodded, and motioned as if zipping his lips, she smiled.

He said, "You have my word. What is it, Stacy?"

Stacy continued, "Ryan, I'm really afraid to tell you this. If you tell anyone, I don't know what I would do."

Ryan sympathetically leaned in and said, "Stace?"

Chapter 4

SURVIVAL

The team had performed extremely well over the past eight months. The POS project had been moving very aggressively and it was on schedule in spite of budgetary and staffing issues. Although the pace was grueling, Stacy was able to motivate the group and keep them focused on the end goal. She had absorbed many of the concepts that Ryan had taught her and she was implementing them very effectively.

Stacy and Ryan's job became much tougher when the budgets of all projects were slashed by 10 percent. Even though they were promised sufficient resources and funding, no one had ever accounted for the downturn in the economy and the retail industry's sluggish performance. Cost overruns in other areas of the company were forcing a careful examination of spending across the organization and no department was immune. The POS project had a contingency built into their budget that could absorb some of the 10 percent reduction; however, they were concerned that if any more cuts came, it would spell major trouble for the project.

Unfortunately for Stacy, things had become even more difficult. She had lost two members of her development team. The aggressive pace was a bit too much for one of her employees and, unexpectedly, the employee had quit. The pressure had been so great on him that he started to call in sick at least twice a week and his production had fallen off significantly. Stacy wondered whether the employee was pushed too hard or if he just had a problem. The other employee found another opportunity and left very suddenly. He felt the pressures being exerted on him were not worth the salary he was earning, and therefore jumped at the chance to move. Unfortunately for Stacy, management was showing no signs of authorizing her to replace either of the lost staff.

From the beginning, Stacy had taken control of the entire lifecycle of the project. She had completed a fully loaded resource project plan, which enabled her to allocate the right people for every set of tasks, and she managed their time accordingly. She engineered the completion of the requirements with business users and negotiated agreements to requirements prior to Ryan and Jay's involvement. Ryan was very happy with how Stacy progressed into her new role. During the development of the project plan, he urged Stacy to build contingencies around time and budget in the event of changes, which was lucky for them, since the budget reductions and resignations had forced the execution of these contingencies.

Stacy had spent a lot of time, with Ryan's input, developing the plan and cultivating her management techniques. It was a bit rough in the beginning. She argued with some of the business units regarding the requirements and direction of the project, causing major friction between her and her peers in business units. Ryan, however, was becoming very adroit in negotiating. He knew the key to negotiation was patience and listening; therefore, he was able to ease the tension and guide Stacy toward a better negotiating position by getting involved only when necessary. Stacy gradually changed her approach in dealing with the business units and Ryan was surprised at how good a student she had become. Even Jay noticed her progress and commented on her success during a team meeting.

Ryan had introduced additional project management concepts, which, while not new to the industry, nobody had never used or implemented them successfully at the company. Beyond the standard Gantt Charts, he introduced Pert Charts, Activity on Arrow Diagrams, and helped Stacy develop the resource capacity model. The resource capacity model provided Stacy with a more methodical approach to assigning resources and providing accurate time lines. Using this method, she analyzed the time recorded by each of her employees for various random tasks over the past year. Then, with Ryan's help, she learned to create statistical models to determine which employees were better at certain tasks. From this vantage point, she could assign personnel to the appropriate level of work and have a measurable way to determine more accurate project time lines. This, along with the other tools of project management, gave Ryan's team a window into the bigger picture of what was happening within their group.

The most important lesson Ryan brought to the company was the understanding of constraints within the process of information technology. He helped the team identify bottlenecks in the operation, demonstrated how those bottlenecks contribute to inefficiency and cost, and worked with the team to remove them. Executives in the company had always seen information technology as a black hole of expenses and always quoted the line from industry magazines that 70 percent of IT projects fail. Ryan diligently contradicted the derogatory statements about the IT department by the business units, by producing metrics and quantifiable results demonstrating their success. It was an uphill battle, but it did have an effect on perceptions.

Many of the business units attacked IT, saying its work was inefficient and faulty. More frequently, department heads would complain in senior management meetings about inefficiencies due to their perceived lack of productivity in IT. Jay struggled intensely in these meetings to defend his department against these attacks.

Ryan had seen this pattern develop over the past two years and he worked with Jay to counter the arguments with the data he had collected and the processes he implemented. By implementing the new procedures, processes, and metrics, he quelled many of the arguments but the underlying tension between IT and the business remained. Ryan understood the importance of metrics as an equalizing factor in arguments. Through a quantitative approach, he could formulate the battleground on which he wanted to engage the business units. If he controlled the metrics and the business units failed to counter quantitatively, he would have the upper hand.

The POS project was no exception; its strategic impact to the organization led to increased tension among all the parties involved, making Stacy and Ryan prime targets. In almost every meeting on the project, Stacy and Ryan, but mostly Stacy was the center of attention because she was running the project. The attacks leveled against her centered on late deliverables and incomplete items. Stacy always diligently prepared for these meetings and produced counterarguments to both. In many cases, she demonstrated that items delivered late were due to the business unit's unresponsiveness to questions and reviews. She also quantified that had the business responded in a timely fashion, the project would have been ahead of schedule by almost one month. She had refrained originally from documenting these items in status reports in order to resolve issues amicably, but now she felt she had no choice due to the stinging attacks.

Stacy had become very confident in her ability to manage the project. By implementing project management principles, Stacy had been able to communicate the actual status of the project and keep everyone informed despite the combative nature of the status meetings. In the last six months, she had shown an incredible amount of growth in her new role. Her progress impressed Ryan so much that he wrote a small memo to Jay recommending they explore ways of providing additional growth opportunities beyond their comfort zone to other members of IT. Jay liked the idea, and brought it to his boss, the CIO,

Daniel Hemley, for recommendation and review. Dan, similar to Jay, was the type of manager who loved new ideas. Together they believed that the expense of trying new things could never outweigh the long term benefits of a successful gamble.

On the other side of Ryan's responsibilities, Ryan had given the 'business as usual' team to Tim. This team was responsible for smaller maintenance items, or programming that required less than ten hours of work. This included bug fixes and the new items that the business units would concoct at lunch, and then handwrite the ideas on napkins with salsa. These scribbled notes went to Ryan for implementation, even with the dried up salsa.

Tim's work ethic was perfect for this position. Operationally focused and detail driven, he was perfect for the role. In his role, he could have been considered the mechanic of the group as opposed to the engineer. If there was a problem, they could bring it to him, and his team would turn around and fix it. The team became so good at the processes they developed that one would swear it was a different company. Tim developed very detailed metrics to analyze and promote the performance of his team, which rivaled the work being done by the metrics group. Eventually, these well-defined and consistently reported metrics would be incorporated into the metric group's monthly reporting.

Tim, a hobbyist mathematician, always liked numbers and used them to describe almost everything. He modeled many of his metrics based on the statistical methodology used in baseball called sabermetrics, an unorthodox method of using statistics in baseball to determine baseball strategy. While the formulas in sabermetrics couldn't be directly applied, he understood the thinking behind the metrics. Sabermetrics determines a player's productivity by understanding the importance of certain elements of baseball, such as the importance of an out. By weighing outs more than hits, formulas could be derived using probabilities that stressed players and strategies that avoid outs, rather than homeruns.

Tim tried to translate the concepts into his own group. He created metrics such as "value per response time" to determine the value associated with a developer responding to a service ticket. Tim knew the most important aspect to the company was the value delivered to the business units, which could then be translated into cost or revenue. Using this, he could demonstrate to the developer a prioritization method of response based on the value of the problem and not on the person who yelled the loudest. He also developed metrics based on the salaries of the individuals, allowing him to move more complex and more valuable problems to the best, higher-paid workers.

By using these metrics and indexes to provide quarterly performance evaluations, he was better able to analyze his staff and provide feedback. Some of his staff thought it was too rigid, but most liked it because they knew exactly how they were performing, removing any ambiguity or personality conflicts. Only one person on his team didn't like it, and that was Phil, who consistently scored low on the scale.

Ryan's team seemed to gel and they were performing admirably, in his opinion. They had received responsibility and they were responding. Each member of his team had a particular role, and each knew his or her job. More importantly, they were all looking to expand their roles and take on more responsibility, because they were empowered to do so. At his desk, Ryan picked up a pen and scribbled a list on the inside of a notebook, writing first, "Be honest and true, get qualified people you trust, have them develop a method." He titled the list "Three Keys to Success." He knew these were very important; he had seen it. He couldn't believe how easy it was, but it made sense to him. He believed this team could do anything and, at this pace, the team would be extremely successful, if nothing went horribly wrong.

About a week later, early on a Monday morning, an e-mail went to the entire company announcing Dan's resignation from the firm after only a little over a year on the job. Ryan had read somewhere that the average tenure for a CIO is about eighteen months, so he wasn't completely surprised, but he was upset. He felt he had a degree of loyalty to Dan, not directly, but through Jay. Jay was Ryan's mentor as Dan was Jay's. Ryan read the e-mail further and it said that the Dan was leaving to "pursue personal interests." Ryan didn't like the sound of that. He heard through the grapevine that the Dan was at odds with the CEO over the direction of IT. He wasn't sure exactly what the discussions were about, but the two had made their feelings known in a not so private manner. He had to find out exactly what was going on. He decided to go up and see Jay.

Jay wasn't at his desk when Ryan went to see him. Ryan asked Jay's assistant when he would be back, and Ryan was told that he was out for the day and was scheduled to be out tomorrow as well, that he should try back on Wednesday. Ryan asked for a meeting on

Wednesday morning, which the assistant scheduled for first thing in the morning. As Ryan was walking back downstairs to his cubicle, he wondered why Jay wasn't in today. Jay had always kept him informed of days he would be out of the office, especially if it involved more than a day. An uneasy feeling overcame Ryan like a super cell thundercloud advancing on the horizon.

When Ryan got back to his desk, Stacy and Tim were waiting for him.

Stacy asked, "What the hell is going on?"

"I don't know. I went up to see Jay but he wasn't at his desk and his assistant said he won't be back until Wednesday. I've scheduled a meeting with him on Wednesday."

Tim jumped in, "I don't like the look of this."

"I don't like it either, but there isn't anything we can do about it. We all have jobs to do, so I suggest we get to doing them. We will get everything sorted out as soon as possible."

Tim slowly began to walk away, and Stacy said, "Do you think they're going to let a lot of people go in IT? There's a rumor that they are going to outsource most of IT."

Tim stopped dead in his tracks only a few feet away and began to return while Ryan replied, "Look, I've heard that rumor. Here's what I know, IT costs are too high, profits are down, but the company's expenses as a whole are also up, so it's not just an IT problem. I don't think they are just going to go after IT. If management does anything it would probably be across the board."

Tim and Stacy both looked worried. It was one thing to talk about the organization, but that meant nothing, if they were going to be fired.

Ryan continued, "Second, let's look at our team closely. We have the best metrics, we are producing, we are on budget, or at least close, on the POS. There is no sound reason to do anything to this group."

Tim replied, "Do they need a sound reason?"

"It would be stupid for them to act rashly, especially in light of our production. Do you really think these executives are stupid? I don't."

Tim shrugged, while Stacy said, "I don't either," and then mumbled, "I hope."

Ryan went home that evening asking himself the exact same questions Tim and Stacy had asked earlier. Ryan's dejection caused him to skip his classes, which was very unusual. His mind continued to race over the uncertainty that had befallen them. The difference was that he needed some answers for his team, but right now, no one was answering him. He felt isolated because he did the best he could to keep his team from degenerating. He wondered why Jay didn't reach out to him. Did he know something before Monday? He trusted him and right now, he was disappointed. Jay had always been forthright and communicated everything. Now Ryan was completely in the dark. Ryan thought there could be no way Jay didn't know this was coming. Jay was very close to the CIO and these things don't happen overnight. It puts the organization at too much exposure.

Lisa glanced at Ryan as they were watching TV. Ryan was staring into space, deep in thought. She closed her book, and said, "All right what's going on? You haven't said much, you're staring into space, and you purposely missed class tonight. Spill it."

Ryan said, "Look, I don't exactly know what's going on at work and I really don't want to worry you. It could be nothing, but the CIO unexpectedly resigned today."

She replied, "That's a shame. Why?"

Ryan said, "We were told 'to pursue other interests' but it just doesn't happen that way. He's not even in his office; I mean he's gone, clean desk and all. Funny thing, Jay wasn't at his desk either."

Lisa said, "Do you think more people will go?"

"I don't know. I really just don't know."

"Does Stacy know what happened today?"

"Yes, she is a bit worried. I tried to tell them all not to worry about it because we just have no information, and I don't want rumors spreading. That could cause more problems."

"Well you just do what you're best at."

"What's that?"

"You keep your team motivated. My God, you always try to find the 'silver lining' and those motivational clichés drive me up a wall, but everyone appreciates them, even if they don't tell you, including me."

Ryan felt a bit better after that statement, at least temporarily, but he was really nervous about tomorrow. Thoughts of mass firings and the uncertainty of finding a job in a poor economy raced through his head. But there was nothing he could do; he simply needed to stay focused.

The next morning, Ryan pulled into the parking lot about thirty minutes early, and passed by Jay's parking spot. He was tempted to park there, but changed his mind. Ryan had sometimes played a joke on him by parking in his spot and making him walk the entire length of the parking lot. Instead, Ryan drove to the very back of the lot, parked his car, and exited with his latte. As he turned to walk to the back of the car, he noticed, in the distance, Stacy and Tim talking by the front of the building. He really didn't want to field any more questions, and he was tempted to go around to the other side of the building, but he knew avoiding them wasn't appropriate. If they had a question, he needed to be there for them. He continued walking up to the front of the building; three-quarters of the way there they noticed him and pointed. They anxiously awaited him.

"Did you read your e-mail this morning?" Stacy exclaimed.

"No." answered Ryan, "I left my BlackBerry at the office last night."

Ryan "accidentally" left it at the office. He was afraid there would be some e-mail that would come after six last night, and if it was bad he would be up all night. So he left the BlackBerry in the office, enabling him to have a very good night's sleep. As much sleep as one would expect under these circumstances.

"What did it say?" Ryan asked.

"All IT personnel should come to the first floor training room at 9:30 a.m.," Tim responded.

Ryan looked at his watch. "Thirty minutes? Everyone?"

Stacy looked at him with a glare and slowly said, "*Everyone.*"

Ryan said to Tim and Stacy, "Get your teams together now, let's go to Jay's office. It will be a bit crowded but I want to talk to everyone."

Stacy and Tim hurried in and gathered everyone as quickly as they could. Ryan asked Jay's assistant if he could use the office, and he explained why. His assistant gladly opened the office."

Ryan walked into the office, and noticed something very peculiar. The pictures Jay had on the desk were gone. Status reports and file folders were still on his desk, in the same unorganized fashion as they had always been, but all his personal stuff seemed missing. He failed to notice yesterday if the items were there, and he really didn't want to think of what was actually happening, although he instinctively knew.

As the team moved into the office, with obvious looks of despair and mumbling questions, Ryan said, "Look, everyone, I have no idea what is going on. If I did, I would tell you what I could.

Unfortunately, I'm in the dark as much as everyone else. With that said, are there any questions you have that you think I can answer?"

Ryan looked around; they knew he couldn't answer much. Ryan went on to say, "I can't promise everything will be all right. I just don't know. What I can tell you is that we need to stay as positive as possible. I mentioned to Stacy and Tim we have the best numbers of any group in IT. Try your best to hold you heads up, and when we walk into the meeting, we walk in together."

For a brief moment, there was a bit of a relaxed feeling. They knew he was right. They had all the facts to demonstrate they were the A team. Ryan was trying to create an impression of solidarity and strength, if not for anyone else but his team.

At 9:30 a.m. everyone had gathered in the first floor training room. The room was used for large gatherings and training sessions. It was a stadium-style seating arrangement that could seat about a hundred people. Since there were almost two hundred people in the department, there were many people standing on both sides of the room and along the back. A few people had made themselves comfortable by sitting on steps in the aisles.

Even though people were talking, the decibel level was pretty low. You could see people trying to whisper to each other as if they didn't want to be noticed by someone. Ryan's team was located near the back right of the room. They were able to get a few seats, but most of the team stood along the wall. Ryan looked down at his watch, which said 9:40 a.m., and wondered why they couldn't start on time, if this was such an urgent meeting. Just as he finished the thought, he heard the "tap, tap" on the microphone.

A very tall and slender man, about six foot five, in a dark suit and red tie, with salt and pepper hair, was standing at the microphone. The man opened his portfolio, then adjusted the microphone slightly to have it angle upward to meet his large stature and said, "Welcome, everyone." The man's voice was a very low and deep, with authority behind it.

"My name is Gerald Stone, and as some of you may have heard, the board has authorized a new management team. I am the new CIO for the corporation."

Ryan sighed and knew this had been in the works for a while. Ryan knew there was no way the company could hire a CIO during the course of a few days. Ryan didn't like surprises like this; then again no one does, but Ryan always believed in trying to get as much intelligence as possible to avoid surprises. The CIO was at the center podium flanked by three individuals, all wearing dark blue or black suits and white shirts. The four were so coordinated on stage it almost looked like a dramatic Broadway play. The benign opening lines of the new CIO's comments began with an introduction of the three people behind him. Ryan sensed there would be more than just a few polite opening words; he could feel a crescendo of tension.

"As you may realize by now, things cannot continue to be run the way they have been run. Anyone who doesn't fall in line with the new structure and anyone who cannot follow my instructions will be escorted out. There will be a zero tolerance policy. The department has been operating very poorly for the past year, and we will no longer tolerate inefficiency. We will closely examine every aspect of the department, make decisions that we will execute very quickly, and soon announce a new organizational structure. Therefore, be courteous and respectful to your new management as we devise the new direction for the department. I will expect full cooperation from everyone. Thank you." With that last line, Mr. Stone and his three associates walked out.

There was a stunned silence in the room. You could hear a pin drop, and it was a few minutes before people realized they could leave. The silence in the room was deafening. Ryan thought a theme song to an old Western shoot-out should have been playing in the background. Ryan tapped everyone on the shoulder and said, "Let's go back to our desks." As they travelled back up, Stacy walked next to him.

"What the hell was that?" Stacy said.

Ryan answered, "I don't know. I'm not looking forward to this."

As they reached their desks, they couldn't help but chat about what was happening. Ryan motioned to them to head back to their desks and said, "We will talk away from the office. Try to focus on some of the tasks we need to complete today."

Just as he said that, his phone rang. He looked at the number, and it was Jay's assistant. The voice on the other end of the phone said, "Ryan, can you please come up here, please?"

Ryan replied, "Sure."

Jay's assistant said in a very low whisper, "Your new boss."

Ryan acknowledged, "Thanks," then hung up the phone.

Ryan continued to wonder what happened to Jay. He felt as if he were a prisoner walking on his final march to the electric chair wondering what happened to his cellmate. Ryan thought that if they were going to terminate him, it would have happened already. He made a conscious decision to walk with purpose and to walk with confidence. He wasn't going to be intimidated. He turned the corner, approached the door, and knocked politely but with authority. He didn't hear anything, but he peeked in and saw no one. He thought to himself, "Great, now what?"

Suddenly a hand touched him on the shoulder, and a voice said, "You must be Ryan. Eric Musconi, pleasure to meet you. Please, come in."

Ryan paused for a moment and then followed him in. Ryan looked around the office and thought it was in poor taste for Eric to pile all of Jay's remaining items in a corner. Ryan continued in and sat down. Eric was in his white shirt and blue tie. He was almost an exact copy of Mr. Stone earlier. His voice wasn't as powerful, and he had a more nasal sound to his voice.

Eric said to him, "Ryan, I know this is a shock to you, but the good news is you weren't working for Mr. Alethia too long, so I suspect that you and your team should have an easy time accommodating the change in management. I want to discuss my management style with you."

Ryan was amazed at how direct and blunt Eric was.

"I came from the financial sector, and I have a tremendous amount of experience in building systems. I'm sure I can show you a thing or two. Systems in the financial world are much different than those in retail. They are much more rigorous, and require much higher performance levels, something you're probably not accustomed to."

Ryan knew there were problems here but he didn't think the problems were of the magnitude that Eric was implying. Eric also came across as a bit arrogant in his insinuation that Ryan wasn't accustomed to high performance levels.

Eric continued, "In any event, we will have time to chat later. I need a few things from you though. I need you to give me an organization chart, and I would like you to schedule a meeting with your team and myself for later this afternoon. Can you get that done for me?"

Ryan replied, "Of course."

"Great. Sorry we can't talk now, but I have to be somewhere in five minutes and I needed to meet you briefly and have you retrieve the information on your team. Thanks again, Ryan."

Ryan left Jay's office, now Eric's office, a bit dejected. He couldn't help but feel sympathy for Jay at this point. Ryan's anger increased, however, as he wondered why Jay hadn't called him. He felt he deserved an e-mail at the very least. Jay had mentored Ryan for the past year, and Ryan had learned much about leadership. Now, at this critical juncture, he felt abandoned. Ryan juggled his thoughts and emotions but couldn't reconcile the obvious feeling of complete betrayal. He thought about calling him on his cell phone, however, he wasn't sure if Jay would answer the call. He could have called Jay, but felt that Jay should be calling him. Ryan wanted to drop the whole thing. Ryan couldn't forget it, and it was proving difficult to move on.

At Ryan's desk, Tim approached and inquired as to the situation. Just as Ryan started, he could hear more footsteps approaching. The gate was a very quick and light pattern set of steps. He knew it was Stacy hurrying over to his desk. Ryan decided not to tell them everything that happened in the meeting. However, he did tell them to have their teams ready for a mandatory meeting with the new boss this afternoon.

Ryan then said to them, "Meet me by the elevator in ten minutes. We will get a cup of coffee and head outside for a discussion."

After Stacy and Tim had left, Ryan opened up his e-mail and looked to schedule the meeting. He went into his calendar program to look at people's schedules, specifically Eric's. Eric's day was already full and it was his first day. He picked up the phone to call him, but his assistant picked up the phone.

Ryan asked, "Hey, can you tell me what availability Jay might have this afternoon?"

The assistant noticed Ryan's error and gracefully moved past it, replying, "*Eric's* calendar is pretty booked, but let me ask."

Ryan thanked him for picking up on the error and waited patiently. He waited for a good two minutes on the phone, and began to think to himself, it never took this long to figure out a schedule. Ryan shook his head a bit and knew he had to stop doing that, and just accept what was happening.

"I just called Eric on his cell phone; he can meet at 3:00 p.m. with your team," the assistant said.

Ryan replied, "Thank you. I'll book it in Grumpy."

The seven conference rooms on the floor gave rise to a naming scheme that everyone loved. Ryan thought it was ironically appropriate to schedule in Grumpy or Dopey. Ryan went into the calendar application and invited everyone to the one-hour meeting. As he completed the invitation, it he thought to himself how wasteful this day would become as everyone waited in anticipation for the meeting.

Ryan looked at his watch and noticed that it was about the ten-minute mark, so he hurriedly went over to the elevator. He noticed Tim there and he saw Stacy coming around the corner. He strolled over to the elevator button and pressed it.

Tim inched over to Ryan and said in a very low voice, "So?"

Ryan replied, "Not here. Just wait a few minutes. Let's go to the cafeteria, get a cup of coffee, and move outside."

Stacy hated this cloak-and-dagger act. The frustration on her face could kill someone, but she knew it was the right thing to do. Ryan had told her that from time to time it was better to move a discussion outside of the office where the chance of someone hearing you was remote, a lesson he learned from Jay.

The three bought coffee and began to walk outside the building; they made their way over to a nice grassy area where the company had set up some lunch benches. The original owner of the company, now retired, was very much a naturalist, and had made the area for employees to eat, discuss work, or just have a nice area to contemplate or reflect. The owner believed that work was secondary to everything else, and that there is a purpose to life. He had done many things to try to make his employees' time at the office pleasurable, but over the past two years had abandoned the area almost completely since the owner retired. Tim, Stacy, and Ryan had increasingly used it as an area to have impromptu meetings or discussions away from the other team members. The three had used the area even more, since the issue with Stacy and Phil dissipated.

It was a great spring day, about sixty-five degrees, a little warm for the last week of March. Ryan mentioned to the team, "What an awesome day it is out here. Smells like opening day once again."

Stacy replied, "Yeah, now enough chit chat, what happened?"

Ryan tried to delay the inevitable discussion; however, sensing the urgency, leaned his head down and said, "Honestly, I don't know what the hell is going on. I just met with the new boss, Eric. He is a bit energetic to say the least, but there's something I don't like."

"What?" asked Stacy.

"It's just something. I went into the office. Jay's stuff isn't even fully packed yet. There are boxes with his name shoved in the corner, and this guy is already settled in and getting down to business. Maybe that's the way it's supposed to be, I don't know."

Ryan paused for a bit and explained the brief encounter, finishing with the scheduled meeting this afternoon at 3:00 p.m. Stacy and Tim didn't like what they heard, but they were biased to begin with; Ryan could see it in their body language. Tim's focus was straight ahead as if he had seen a ghost. It was the uncertainty that was concerning them and he knew it. No matter how bad this situation was, they needed to figure out how to persevere. Jay was no longer here, but his team was.

Ryan had a mini epiphany. If he didn't stay positive about the situation, his team wouldn't be positive and, therefore, in order to change their perspective he needed to change his own.

He picked up his head, and said, "Look, this may not be bad. It's sad that Jay isn't here, but he is not, and this guy is. We have to get our stuff done. It can't be that bad, the guy comes from the financial world, and maybe there is something we could learn from him."

Ryan hoped they would buy it. He didn't.

Tim replied, "OK, Ryan, I'm still uneasy, but you're right."

Tim looked at his watch, stood up, and picked up his coffee. "Damn, I have to go," he said. "I've got to get to an operations meeting. I'll talk to you later."

Tim hurriedly went back inside. After a minute of some silence both he and Stacy picked up their coffee and started to walk back. As they were walking, Stacy discussed the situation and her concerns. She told Ryan of all the rumors she was hearing. She had heard from someone that their team would be split, or certain people like Tim would be moved out, or half the department would be fired outright, and the worst rumor of all, the entire department would be outsourced. She thought about how they could outsource an entire department. It made no sense to her. She knew companies had done it, but there was no way it could be successful here, could it?

She prodded Ryan, "You need to find out what's going on."

"Stace, I'm sure I'll know if they want me to know and if they don't, they wouldn't tell me anyway. Don't let it get to you."

"Well, it does. I hate not knowing."

Ryan replied, "Don't worry about it." But Ryan himself was worried about it.

As Ryan prepared for the meeting, he wondered what Eric would say. He didn't say much to him earlier. He knew one of two things had to happen. Either Eric would go over the projects currently in process, or he would ask them all to leave. Ryan's dichotomy of the situation was dangerous, and the rush of emotions leading to the meeting worried not only him, but also every member of his team. Throughout the day, people had been looking to Ryan for some answers, and although Stacy and Tim were the direct line managers, everyone knew instinctively to go to Ryan. He was their go-to guy. He listened to everyone's troubles and concerns, and right now, they needed a listener.

As the witching hour rolled closer, Ryan began to walk around to his team. He was telling his team not to worry, to be positive, reiterating to everyone that the new management had a track record of success or they wouldn't have been brought in, and that he was confident that the new management team would recognize their success. He summarized his comments with a cliché, "Successful people like to be around successful people." That seemed to work for quite a few members of the team, at least for those who were listening. A few of them had already made up their minds and weren't going to listen anyway.

When Ryan walked up to Stacy's cube, he grabbed a paper clip from the desk, stood up on his toes, and tossed the paper clip over to Tim's cube on the other side of Stacy's wall behind her desk. After the click of the paper clip hitting the desk, a voice bellowed, "Yes, Ryan."

Ryan chuckled and said, "Can you pop over here for a second?"

A minute later Tim was at the cubicle with Ryan and Stacy. Stacy had turned away from her computer toward where Ryan was sitting near her desk. Tim leaned against the cubicle wall with his arms folded waiting for something.

Ryan paused, and then said, "I know we only have thirty minutes to the next meeting. Take the weekly status reports and metrics for the past two months, print them out, and put them in a folder. Bring them with you to the meeting."

"Why?" asked Stacy.

Ryan said, "Just a hunch, but really I want to be prepared. I want you guys to show that if he asks any questions, you have the answers available, not just something that came out of your heads."

Tim agreed, and quickly turned around to go back to his desk without saying a word. Stacy—who had never been one for status reports—pulled a folder out from a wire folder organizer, slapped it on the desk, and said, "OK, now what? I hope three months is enough. If not, I'll go to the drawer."

Stunned, Ryan said, "Wait a minute, you mean to tell me you actually have the reports at the ready? Weren't you the one who said that status reports were a lot of bullshit, and that they weren't good for anything but toilet paper?"

She replied, "Actually, I didn't say *just* that. I have to admit, I didn't like them, but it really helped me organize my plan, and I could see problems very clearly before they happened, and it's only been a short time. I modified the original templates you gave me. In fact, the reports are quite a bit different.

"Why?" Ryan said, "You give me a report every week in the format I gave you."

Stacy replied, "I needed more information, so I took your report, added about five different sections coming from different members of the team, and then when I give you the report, I edit it, to what you are looking for."

Ryan laughed, "Why didn't you just give me the report so you don't have to do any extra work?"

Stacy replied, "I thought about it, but at first, I figured you wouldn't like the changes."

Ryan jumped in, "Why? I would've—"

Stacy put her hand up, as if to say stop, and continued, "Ryan, you know you have to stop jumping in, I didn't finish my sentence."

Ryan apologized.

She continued, "Mister Type A. Anyway, then I realized something. The status reports aren't for you. They are actually for me and for my team. When they write a status report, they understand what they are doing, and what they are communicating. Plus, they need different information than you do, and so, they report information to me, then *I* determine what's important and what's not. And boy, does it work well."

Ryan had a big smile on his face. His decision to make Stacy the manager of the group was proving to be the correct one. He knew a good leader gets people to perform above their level, and this was a classic example. Stacy was performing way above where she had been previously in such a short time. He knew she was ready for the meeting, and he was very confident everyone on his team would do well.

Three o'clock rolled around, and the team was all assembled in a conference room. There was a definite feeling of tension in the air. There were thirteen people in the room, not including Ryan, waiting for Eric to show up. Tim and Stacy were near the front of the table along with Tim where they had left an open seat at the head of the conference room table. They had their folders with status reports and metrics ready. Stacy had opened up her folder and begun reviewing the report. She wanted to nail any question without looking at the report. Tim was a bit more nervous, which Ryan picked up on. Tim kept tapping his fingers at the end of the table and gently swiveled in his chair. The rest of the team looked to Ryan, Stacy, and Tim for guidance. The team knew what was in the folders and they were ready to provide support, if asked. No one was really sure what to expect.

Ryan looked up and noticed the conference room clock said 3:05. He figured Eric was running a bit late but would show up at any time. In order to pass the time, Ryan began asking questions about the POS project. He hadn't realized how much his team had progressed over the past few weeks. The confidence and fortitude with which they spoke about the challenges they were facing was a very proud moment. It was very reassuring to not hear whining in light of recent events such as the budget cutbacks, loss of personnel, and now this complete organizational shakeup. Before long, Ryan glanced at the time and noticed that they had been waiting for eighteen minutes.

Suddenly, the doorknob to the closed conference room door turned. Ryan readied himself for the battle to begin. Stacy looked directly at the door like a tigress waiting to pounce on prey. Tim stopped tapping. The door slowly opened. It was a very heavy conference room door, and suddenly a head peaked in. It was Eric's assistant.

"Ryan?" The assistant saw Ryan toward the end of the table and said, "Mr. Musconi, will not be able to meet right now. He has asked that you reassemble at 4:30 p.m."

With that, the assistant backed away from the open door and gently closed it. The team began to get up and file out of the room. One member of Stacy's team, Janet, walked over to Stacy and said, "Stacy, I can't stay. I have to pick up my daughter from day care."

Stacy replied, "There's no way to get someone else to pick her up?"

Janet replied, "Not on such short notice."

With that, Janet's expression turned to fear. This situation scared her greatly. She couldn't afford to lose her job. She was a single mother who was struggling to juggle a career, school, which she had recently completed, and parenting. Her technology skills were very good, and much of her knowledge came from sheer determination.

Janet could absorb concepts very quickly and she shined under Stacy's tutelage. It took her longer than most to complete her Bachelor's degree, seven years, but that was a testament to her persistent and driven personality.

Stacy, turned to Janet and said, "I'm not sure what to do. Let's go talk to Ryan."

Janet and Stacy walked back to their desks with Ryan. Janet's eyes welled up. The pressure she had been feeling was getting to her. She was deathly afraid of losing her job.

Sensing the pressure, Ryan put his arm on her shoulder and said, "Janet, don't worry about it. It's only the first day of this change. It won't be *that* bad. Just leave at your normal time. No one can expect such changes to people's schedules on such short notice."

Janet seemed reassured, and while still nervous went back to her desk.

Ryan turned to Stacy and said, "I'll deal with Eric on this if he says anything. He can't possibly expect her to stay. Anyway, she was here at the right time."

The team stayed at their desks waiting for the 4:30 mark. They shuffled papers, surfed the Internet, read the news. No one on the team could do any work. They endured the continuous ordeal of waiting. Waiting was the hardest thing for them. Ryan could sense it, and walked over to a few cubicles where he tried to crack a few bad jokes. Ryan needed it himself, he was more nervous than anyone else, but he didn't want anyone to know.

Ryan glanced over to another cubicle across the aisle, and noticed Phil. Phil seemed peculiar. It wasn't a bad peculiar, just odd. Ryan couldn't put his finger on it, but all day Ryan had noticed that Phil was removed from the rest of the team. He had a dumb grin on his face and kept to himself. This was odd for Phil, since he usually just complained or grumbled. Ryan's gut told him something was wrong, but he discounted it, thinking that maybe Phil had turned a corner.

The team reassembled at the appropriate time, and once again, they herded liked cattle into the conference room. Almost everyone had the same seats. Ryan, Stacy, and Tim were ready for battle once again. Tim reviewed his numbers this time, and Stacy was gritting and itching to get to her points. Ryan looked at the two of them and hoped they were ready for this. He was ready with his arsenal of reports and presentation. He wondered what exactly he was ready for. He had no idea what this meeting was about and neither did anyone else.

The clocked continued to tick 4:33, 4:37, 4:40. Eric was still MIA. At 4:45, Ryan got up and walked toward the door. He opened the conference room door to look for Eric's assistant. He looked out and to the right, and saw the assistant's cubicle empty. Ryan walked a few feet down the hall to peer around the corner to see if he could see anyone who might be able to tell him where Eric was.

He walked back to the conference room but now it was 4:49. The people in the room were very uneasy. Ryan knew his team was very uncomfortable right now, and this wasn't going to be good if Eric showed up.

Ryan said, "Let's give it another ten minutes."

The time passed, 4:52, 4:57, 5:00.

Ryan said, "OK, it's 5:00 p.m., not sure what has happened, so let's go. Have a nice evening, everybody."

He then turned to Stacy and Tim and said, "Wait a minute, would you?"

Tim and Stacy hung back. After everyone left, he turned to them and said, "What do you think?"

Stacy and Tim both shrugged, and then Stacy said, "Well this sucks. Obviously, he doesn't respect people's time. I'm glad we didn't keep Janet back."

Ryan replied, "Me too."

After a brief pause, Ryan continued, "OK, let's go. I know we said we agreed earlier to head over to Zesty's but I'm not really in the mood right now."

Stacy and Tim both agreed. They all walked out together, collected their things, and left for the day.

Later that evening, Ryan picked up his BlackBerry around 8:00 p.m., and noticed that he had an e-mail from Eric. The e-mail read:

Ryan,

Sorry about missing the meeting today. I would appreciate you giving me more time in the future, since some of my executive meetings last a bit longer. We will need to discuss.

Also I came looking for you at 6:30 and you were gone. Let's talk in the morning.

Eric

Ryan exclaimed, "What?"

He couldn't believe what he read. Ryan read right through the e-mail.

"More time?" he exclaimed, "We waited thirty minutes for that son of a bitch."

Lisa could easily hear from the other room and came in. "What happened?" she asked.

Ryan explained what happened in the meeting and then showed her the e-mail.

She said, "At 6:30? What is he a workaholic?"

Ryan was so pissed at the first part of the e-mail that he completely ignored the second part. Eric obviously expected him to stay past 6:30 p.m. That wasn't going to work. It could be unbearable if this was the expectation. He knew things would change, but it wasn't reasonable to expect to upend everyone's life.

As hard as he tried, he couldn't remove the anxiety he was feeling. What was Eric going to do next? What would he say to the other members of the team? What were his expectations? Ryan glanced at the time and realized it was already 12:30 a.m. He just needed to get some sleep and deal with it in the morning.

Unable to get a restful sleep, Ryan got out of bed at 5:30 a.m. The situation had bothered him so much, that he barely got an hour's worth of sleep. He tossed and turned all night and just couldn't relax his mind enough. He doggedly picked himself out of bed, and took a brief shower. After he slowly started to become more coherent, his mind once again took over and replayed the previous day's events. In his mind, this situation was completely ridiculous and was threatening to spiral out of control.

Ryan completed his morning ritual with the eight-hundred-pound gorilla on his back. As he pulled into the building parking lot, he noticed quite a few more cars in the parking lot than other times when he arrived early. He wondered if Eric's was one of them. As Ryan made his way into the building and toward his desk, he noticed that the lights in a few offices were on and one of them was Eric's. Ryan hadn't seen an e-mail on his BlackBerry this morning, so he figured that was a good sign. He looked at his watch, which said 6:55 a.m.

"This guy is crazy if he does this every day. He puts in twelve-hour days. Maybe it's just because he's new and, once he gets secure, he will settle in," Ryan said slightly aloud in an attempt to rationalize the entire situation.

About fifteen minutes later, as Ryan was responding to e-mails from the day before, a voice startled him. "Ryan, glad you could make it today. Where is everybody?"

Ryan responded, "Hey, Eric."

Eric laughed as he replied, "Sorry I startled you."

"No problem. What do you mean where is everybody?"

"I mean its 7:10 and no one is here except you." There was an awkward pause when Eric continued, "You know, I came looking for you at 6:30 and you weren't here."

"I didn't know you needed me to stay last night."

"I meant this morning. I looked for you about 6:30 a.m. and you weren't here. Come to think of it, you're right. I looked for you at 6:30 last night too. What a coincidence. Come down to my office, let's chat for twenty minutes."

Ryan responded "Sure."

Ryan had a big problem with this. He figured if Eric was looking for him at 6:30, there was definitely an expectation being set and not being met, and this was only the second day. Ryan wasn't sure how he was going to deal with this. He didn't like this impromptu meeting he was about to have and he suddenly became very nervous. Ryan gathered a few papers and a notebook, locked his computer terminal and headed toward Eric's office. Eric was about a hundred feet ahead of him and Ryan wondered why Eric didn't even wait for him.

As Ryan entered Eric's office, Eric motioned with his hand to Ryan to have a seat as he sipped his coffee. Eric opened up with a few pleasantries, and then paused as he glanced at some papers.

"Ryan, I looked over some status reports last night and I want to get a clear understanding of how your team operates. I have a copy of the organizational structure and I want to go over it with you, and finally, I want to discuss my expectations."

Ryan replied, "Sure."

Eric continued as Ryan began to take notes, "It seems as though your group has done well compared to the rest of the IT groups. These metrics that I am looking at demonstrate that, relative to the other areas in IT, your group has done well."

"Thank you," replied Ryan.

"Don't thank me yet. Here is my problem. I consider your group the best of the worst. Where I came from, your group would probably be fired collectively and would be outsourced to some third world country where I could get better productivity at half the price."

Ryan was stunned and said, "Well—"

Eric interrupted Ryan, "Don't speak, until I ask you a question. I'm not here to listen to excuses. I'm here to tell you what will be done, what I expect, and what you will do—or you won't be here. I'm going to set a new level of metrics that will require a performance increase of approximately 50 percent and I will ask for recommendations from you to cut your staff by three people."

Ryan couldn't say a word, but he was fuming.

Eric continued, "Now, with regard to your structure, I see you have two primary groups that are responsible for your area of development, and they are headed by," he paused to review the document, "Stacy Gilfoil and Tim O'Malley. This structure will not work. If you only have two lines reporting to you, I probably don't need you. However, I think you have value, so I want you to create a more horizontal structure. I will work with you on this structure. We anticipate that a more horizontal structure will help spread out the work and remove unnecessary lines of decision making."

Eric continued to review the structure and circled one box and drew and arrow toward the edge of the paper, and wrote the word "out." He then said to Ryan, "In addition, after discussion with my senior management team, we are going to move Phil out of your area. He will be moved into another area of IT, but have a dotted line reporting structure to me."

Ryan for a brief moment was very happy to be rid of Phil, but that was too easy, something was wrong.

Ryan asked, "Eric, may I ask why he is being moved?"

Eric replied, "Well, he used to work for one of my colleagues at the firm that we came from. My colleague has moved here with us, and is heading up the enterprise resource planning group where inventory control and logistics are being run. Phil knows how to work with him and is a great resource to tap."

Ryan was amazed, but it now made sense. Phil must have been informed about this, and that's why he never said a word and had that stupid grin on his face.

"I hope there is no issue with this, because we have already have spoken with him and it takes effect immediately. He mentioned to us that you really don't have him on any critical projects, so we felt it would be a simple move. He will be reporting at the same level as you."

Ryan couldn't understand how that schmuck got promoted in a day, up two levels and now he was his peer.

Eric continued, "Finally, Ryan, I think you have a lot of untapped potential. However, you need some guidance and you need good examples to follow. You yourself need to be a good model for everyone on your team. I expect you to know every detail that your team is doing. You should be updated almost daily so that if I ask you a question you have the answer. I don't want to hear that you have to find things out, I could do that. You don't have a very large group. I do. Therefore, I have to ask questions and you just need to know the answers.

"Am I making myself clear, Ryan?" he asked.

Ryan, still stunned, simply nodded.

"In addition, there's an old adage that says if you want to succeed you should be in before your boss and leave after your boss. Now I don't expect that every day, I know things come up, but this isn't a nine-to-five job. I expect you to put in the hours required to get the job done and that generally means ten- to twelve-hour days consistently. If you're doing less, I probably haven't given you enough work and that probably won't happen. I expect that from all my employees, and collectively we *will* become the best group in the company. I accomplished this at the bank and I *will* accomplish it here. That's why we get paid big dollars, any objections?"

Ryan knew it was futile, because if he objected, he probably would be fired. He would just have to see what he could do. He shook his head and said, "No objections, anything else?"

Eric replied, "Nope. I look forward to working with you."

Ryan replied, "As do I," but he didn't mean it.

Ryan left the office dejected. He wasn't sure what to do next, or how he should act. He kept thinking to himself how Eric, in one day, was dismantling the team he had established. He wondered what he should say to the team, since they had turned their department into something they wanted.

He wondered if anyone would quit. Actually, he was certain some would quit and seek employment elsewhere, but he wondered who would go first and how. Would it be on their terms on Eric's terms? Ryan was genuinely nervous about his own position; he expected the others were as well.

As Ryan went back to his desk, he noticed the time was approaching 7:40 a.m. He had a very quick meeting with Eric, relatively speaking. He heard someone in a cubicle tapping away at the keys, and as he approached the cubicle he knew who it was. It was Phil. Phil hadn't shown up a single minute early in the last year, yet today he was over an hour and fifteen minutes early, at least.

He peeked into Phil's cubicle, and said, "Morning, Phil. You're here early."

Phil stoically responded, "Morning, Ryan. Yes, I had to come in early. Jim, the new executive in charge of the inventory system came to me yesterday and told me I was reporting to him. He mentioned that I would have a critical role. I'm not sure how they picked me, but I'm glad someone recognized my talent."

Ryan replied, "Phil, I spoke to Eric, he told me you used to work for them. So it doesn't take a genius to figure out what happened."

Phil replied, "Oh, he told you. We'll then I will also assume he told you how critical I was to them at the bank."

Ryan shrugged as if not to let on what he knew and didn't know. Phil continued, "Ryan, I didn't like working for you, and now those days are over." Phil began to lower his voice and whisper, "I know where all the skeletons are. I would stay very clear from me, because I'm not a person to lie. If asked, I will tell my superiors what I know."

Ryan wasn't fazed because he knew there was nothing wrong, but he did worry that Phil would fabricate issues.

Phil went on his mini diatribe, "In fact, you might want to tell some of your people they should start looking to get out, because they won't be here long. I'm going to make sure of that."

Ryan had enough and said, "Phil, you're a bit too big for your britches. I don't care what you have to say to anyone. I will say, be careful who you step on to go up, because they will be there on your way down too."

Phil just laughed and turned away. Ryan had never seen Phil like this. He never mistreated Phil and always tried to treat him fairly, but for some reason, Phil and he never clicked. Phil obviously had an agenda at this point.

Ryan walked back to his desk and continued his work. He reviewed some reports and examined some code for about an hour before Stacy walked in.

"Good morning, Ryan, any news?" Stacy asked.

Ryan replied, "Tons, we have a big problem, I think. Let's wait for Tim and have a discussion." Ryan turned to his computer as Stacy walked away nervously; she hadn't heard that much trepidation in Ryan's voice before. Ryan sent a meeting invite to Tim and Stacy to block off thirty minutes at 9:15 and marked it urgent.

At 9:15, Tim and Stacy walked over to Ryan's desk and Tim said, "Coffee?"

He replied, "Most definitely."

Tim and Stacy gracefully strolled out of the building; however, Ryan had been looking over his shoulder to see if anyone was watching. Ryan had looked down the hall as if he were looking for prison guards at a POW camp.

As they exited the building, he moved Tim and Stacy from their normal bench to an area with some extra trees and at a sharp angle to the face of the building where Eric's office was. Ryan had reason to be a bit paranoid after this morning's meeting. While there was a threat of rain for later in the day, the thick overcast clouds resembled the dreary feeling each of them had.

Ryan began to explain what happened in the morning meeting. He explained in great detail how the events of last night and this morning were all tied together and that he wasn't sure how this was going to work out. Stacy was particularly concerned about the change in organization. Ryan explained how Phil was moved out and his history with new players. Stacy was relieved that she wouldn't have to work with him anymore.

She didn't think twice about Phil until Tim asked, "Do you think he will try to sabotage us?"

Ryan replied, "I never would have believed it, but yes. I knew he was a jerk, but I didn't see him as a complete opportunist like this. Stay as far away from him as possible."

Tim replied, "Should we start looking?"

Ryan replied, "Look, I can't tell you what to do, but let's wait and see what happens. Maybe it's just a scare tactic."

Stacy said, "I hope you're right."

The next few weeks went by. Ryan was definitely not himself. He arrived early, but not too early. He was in by 8:00 a.m. nowadays, and made sure that Eric saw him. Ryan's work habits also changed dramatically. Instead of being the go-getter and resolving issues head-on, he became gun shy in making decisions and it really showed. He wouldn't make a decision without Eric first approving it. This began to slow the projects down, but Eric preferred being consulted first.

Even though Eric spoke negatively about micromanagement, Ryan knew that's exactly what was happening. It was a way for Eric to feel more important. Ryan became increasingly frustrated that he just couldn't do his job. Ryan also noticed that Eric would get a high from being consulted. It was a way of getting the spotlight turned in his direction to demonstrate his importance to the organization and to himself.

Ryan also noticed a difference in Phil. Phil was strutting around the office, taking his cue from the new management, telling everyone what was wrong. He never offered any assistance or solutions to problems, but he was quick with the jab at everyone. His attitude toward Stacy became increasingly antagonistic, and the two were butting heads even more than usual. Stacy, fully knowing the situation, backed down more times than she should have, Ryan thought, but he understood the circumstances, and didn't have much to offer.

About a month after the changeover, a management meeting was called with Eric, his colleagues, and their respective teams. This was a mandated meeting by the new CIO for all the application development groups. During the meeting, the group heads reviewed the organization once again. At this meeting, the executive team collectively began issuing edicts to quell some of the disruption that had been occurring over the past few weeks. Ryan knew the disruption was directly related to the ambiguity of the organizational structure established. Employees within the IT group didn't really know their roles, and previous established leaders within the department were stripped of their responsibilities in decision making.

Ryan had remembered some of the papers he read about micromanagement. It was easy to recognize the warning signs for micromanagers. Micromanagement occurs through an inappropriate level of control and decision making from superiors. One of the results of micromanaging is an increasing level of disengagement from daily activities due to the lack of trust and responsibility. Ryan knew he was definitely at this stage. He couldn't give a damn about the current situation. Unfortunately, he had a team to worry about, and he was going to have to figure out a way to weather this storm or risk his disengagement infecting other members of his team.

He tried to keep his team motivated by accenting the positives and attempting to challenge them outside of the office. In one case, he gave Tim a great exercise to develop a set of metrics that would enable him to predict the cost of outages based on the time of day and day of the week. This exercise had no bearing at all on the projects at hand, and no one really cared about numbers at that level of detail.

After a few more weeks had passed, with the organization now two full months into the restructuring, another meeting was called. This time, however, a select group of individuals was invited, including all of

Eric's reports and Phil. It was odd that Phil was in this meeting since he didn't report to Eric. At the meeting, Eric noted that Phil's boss couldn't attend, and that Phil would act as surrogate.

Eric opened the meeting with his customary review of the agenda and established his rigid expectations. Once Eric had finished listening to himself talk, Phil chimed in, "Ryan, the inventory control team has noticed that your team is unable to supply us with orders from the Web site in a timely fashion. In fact we have found numerous errors in the data we do receive and basically find it completely unusable."

Ryan was blindsided. This was a setup, and Phil was the mastermind. Phil had actually been the original coder months ago, and once again, Ryan had to take him off the project to actually get it moving and back on track. Furthermore, since Phil now reported into a different team, the requirements were changing on a daily basis, and the Web team couldn't decipher what was being requested, even though countless meetings were requested and conducted. The teams could never get on the same page.

Phil continued, "Eric, I deeply regret to inform you, that we have tried every way we know of to reconcile this, but we are not getting cooperation from the Web group, especially Stacy."

Ryan said, "Excuse me? You haven't given us a complete set of clear requirements in over a month, and everything you do give us, contradicts the previous documents you provide."

Eric yelled, "Enough! Ryan, you will not speak until I address you. I happen to know that Eric's boss reviews the requirements and he would not produce incomplete requirements. Now sit there and be quiet until I get all the facts from Phil."

Phil continued to produce example after example of integration problems. Ryan wasn't allowed to say a word, but the expression on his face could kill a bear in its tracks. His ears turned red and his eyes completely fixated on Phil. He was being sabotaged, and brutally sabotaged, by the guy who couldn't get his work done. What made it worse was that Eric was buying all of his crap. The few times Ryan tried to interject, Ryan was hushed like a child by Eric. Finally, when Phil was done, Ryan had geared up for a major rebuttal.

Eric then chimed in and said, "Look, I don't have time for this nonsense and incompetence." Ryan thought for a moment he was about to be vindicated and that Eric was going to see Phil for who he truly was.

Eric continued, "I have to go upstairs for a meeting in five minutes. Ryan, see to it that you address all of these issues by next week. You have seven business days, and if you can't do it, I'll find someone who can."

Ryan sat in his chair with his jaw open, as if a cat had scrambled out of the office with his tongue. Phil, who was walking out with Eric, turned to Ryan and with a grin on his face and gave Ryan a quick, sarcastic salute. Ryan could hear Phil continue on, "Eric, I also need to talk to you about Stacy."

Ryan was shell shocked as he went back to his desk. Things couldn't get any worse. He was being sabotaged and it was nothing more than a matter of time, before he would get fired. Phil was going to make sure that happened, and there was almost nothing he could do. As he continued to stare at his desk looking at the document Phil had put together, he needed to figure out a way to get the situation from a loss position to a position of stalemate. He knew he couldn't win, but he didn't want to lose. He continued to tell himself that things would get better since they couldn't get any worse.

Just then a knock came on Ryan's cubicle, it was Tim.

"Yes, Tim, PLEASE tell me you have good news," Ryan said.

"Ryan, I need to talk to you about Stacy," Tim said

Ryan asked, "What?"

"She left hysterically crying and we can't find her."

"What happened?" he asked

"We were having lunch in the cafeteria, and then Phil came over," Tim replied.

"What did he do?"

"He was just being stupid, He told her there was a rumor going around that she was a lesbian, and that explained why she never had an affair. He's up to his old tricks but this time it was blatant, cruel, and unprofessional conduct. "

"Are you kidding me?" Ryan replied.

"This asshole's a piece of work. I know she's upset because quite a few people were talking about it," Tim responded.

Ryan picked up his cell phone and called Stacy. She didn't answer. He picked up his stuff and went to look for her outside near the benches where the team congregated. No luck. He called Lisa and asked her if she had heard from Stacy, and he explained why. She told him that if she did hear from Stacy that she would call him. Finally, he called Zesty's and the manager, a good friend of theirs, said yes, she was at a table in the back sobbing. Ryan called Tim and told him that if anyone asks, to say he had a family emergency.

Ryan made it over to Zesty's he looked around to see if he could find her, and the manager pointed over to the far right table. He slowly made his way over, and sat down.

Even though he already knew, he asked, "Stacy, what's the matter?"

She replied, "I'm sure you know by now, don't patronize me."

"OK, I won't. Stacy, I want you to know. I didn't tell anyone. Your secret was safe with me."

She replied, "I know. You and Lisa were really the only two friends I told outside of my circle. It's too late now though. I tried keeping it a secret and it was wrong, but I didn't want anyone to say anything. I made a mistake. I know Phil saw us together. I knew it too. I just knew it."

"Stacy," Ryan said, "It's not the end of the world. Look, don't let it bother you. There is nothing to be ashamed of at all. You are who you are and your friends care about you no matter what, and we will stand behind you. That's what the team does."

Stacy nodded. She had tried to keep it a secret, but she knew she probably shouldn't have tried. She was quiet for about ten minutes and then turned to Ryan and said, "You know, Ryan, the good in this is two things. First, I can be who I really am, and you really allowed me to do that. I appreciate it."

Ryan replied, "You're welcome."

She continued, "More importantly, you never betrayed my trust. For that, I am grateful. I know I can really count on you."

Ryan once again thanked her and said, "Stacy, even if we weren't friends, I would still not repeat anything said to me in confidence. How can you have a good solid team, if people don't trust you, and if you don't trust them? It just doesn't work, and if that means keeping a secret, or it means just listening, then that's what I do. I learned how important that bond of trust is between coworkers, especially in the hierarchy, and I try my damndest to make sure it never gets violated."

Stacy was comfortable knowing that her colleague would back her up. It was important to her, and she wanted him to know how she felt. While she had told Ryan of her lifestyle, she never really discussed it. Now, she continued to discuss her life in greater detail, and explained to Ryan that moving her into a management role gave her more confidence. It helped her come out of the shell, and enabled her to expand out of her comfort zone. It was her breakout period.

She discussed her future in ways Ryan hadn't heard before, what she would do and what her ambitions were. She was very driven and angry at the same time, and she was determined to use that anger for a greater purpose, herself.

Ryan was more comfortable that Stacy would be OK. She continued on, talking about her life, her job, her dreams, and in the process she got a few jabs in at Phil's expense. Ryan saw the expression on her face. It was going to take a lot more than just his words but Ryan hoped that Stacy knew he would stand by her 100 percent.

Ryan remembered that integrity was a critical component of being a leader, but he fully began to realize that leadership was more than just going into battle. He had to listen, and be a good communicator. It was more than just the job. It meant being there, when they wanted, not when he wanted. It meant a different level of sacrifice.

Ryan had never read anything like this in his classes or in any other book. His schooling hadn't prepared him for this situation, but it did prepare him to be ready for anything. He knew his instincts were right, because it felt right. He was doing the right things, and therefore he resolved to continue.

Chapter 5

HUMILITY

Over the course of the next eight months, Eric made Ryan's life a living hell by employing methods designed to frustrate and marginalize Ryan at almost every turn. Ryan would be a mandatory participant at 7:00 a.m. meetings called by Eric for which he had no input or contribution and would merely be a passive observer. He would also be required to produce and reproduce status documents, presentations, and spreadsheets that would never be used except to be filed in Eric's drawer or tossed aside because the content would be outdated by the time it was completed. Instructions given to him would never be precise and were often ambiguous with illegible notes scribbled in the margin, requiring him to constantly redo submitted work. It was an endless circle of uncertainty meant to demoralize and force him to submit to Eric's style of management, a style resembling a medieval serfdom.

Over the past few years, he had worked very hard to achieve success, but now he was marginal in Eric's organization and his responsibilities diminished greatly. Having developed a successful, independent and metrics oriented team, he wanted to do more than become a scribe at meetings, and take direction from Eric. It felt as though he had travelled through time and landed back at his first job with Jeff. Like Jeff, Eric was egotistical and controlling, but unlike Jeff, Eric was technically and more politically astute with the credentials to back it up. He was a graduate of the Kellogg School of Business at Northwestern, and he made sure everyone knew it. Ryan was never as impressed with any of it as Eric would have wanted, and while it was a top rated education, Ryan clearly understood the importance of implementing the knowledge as opposed to merely obtaining it.

He avoided Eric as much as possible and limited the extra time he spent in the meetings. Ryan was even able to miss a full twenty days of work during the same time period, by attending conferences and off-site meetings, scheduling vacation, and scattering in a few strategically positioned sick days. Eric's engagement in other projects with Phil caused a lack of focus and attention to Ryan's behavior. The brief amount of serenity for Ryan couldn't last forever, but it provided him with some rest and sanity he sorely needed.

Eric's busy schedule also provided Ryan's team with a brief reprieve from his petty antics and prevented him from reorganizing the area. Eric constantly reminded everyone of his intent to reorganize, but never followed through due to other priorities. This enabled Ryan, Stacy, and Tim to continue their work, so long as they flew under the radar and didn't bring attention to themselves or their projects. Care was taken by the three to minimize conversations in the office to avoid being overheard by Eric or Phil. Eric would on occasion act, as a demonstration of his authority, to countermand any direction provided by Ryan, which led to more confusion for the team.

Stacy and Tim, being removed from the direct line of fire, had an easier time than Ryan since he was Eric's real target and acted as a buffer for them. They didn't have to attend the same meetings or constantly be in Eric's office being unjustly criticized for his writing or defending the team's position on its work. It was apparent to them that the stress on Ryan's face was slowly eating away at him. She commented to Tim that Ryan's face has aged about ten years since Eric took over. Ryan was a man of thirty-three now, but he began to look closer to forty-three. They knew he worked hard to prevent the buildup of stress, by meditating and exercising, but there was no doubt he was losing that battle.

Work on the POS project continued even though Stacy and her team were now severely handicapped by Eric's budget cuts and staff reductions, which would ultimately doom the project. The project had also lost senior IT management support, and the CIO had threatened to shut it down at least twice over the past two months. However, the chief marketing officer was adamant about implementing the new POS, which had cost his department over $1 million in the past eight months. The CMO knew that without the CIO's support, the project would fail, but if it failed, he would ensure the CIO paid a heavy price politically. Stacy cherished the thought of a senior management political blowup, and hoped the CMO would ultimately win the battle. She poured her heart and soul into the project and defended it passionately.

Tim's group continued its work almost unimpeded, delivering smaller items, and fixing bugs by using the methodology and metrics he had developed. Many of the executives had been implicitly trained by Tim to ensure that the value to the changes were quantifiable. Tim's methods were so effective in changing the mind-set of the business community throughout the organization, that he had gained notoriety and respect among the senior leaders of the company. They understood the methodology and metrics, and while some didn't care for them, they all respected the process and knew it was futile to challenge it.

Although both of them were performing as well as could be expected, they knew it was only a matter of time before Eric would intercede and change their operating structure. Eric, always looking for the spotlight, needed to be the center of any success within his group, and since Stacy's project was all but officially killed, the next most logical area of interference would be Tim's group. Ryan worked very hard to keep Eric away from Tim to let him continue to perform, but he wasn't sure how long that would last.

Having his group systematically eroded, Ryan was desperate to leave the company and find a new role elsewhere, but until he found the right opportunity, he had to endure the hardship facing him. He tried convincing himself that it was a learning experience, just like the ones before, only this one proved to be much harder physically and emotionally. All that was left for Ryan were feelings of frustration and anger, and it was increasingly difficult for him to conceal. Ryan was successful, however, in establishing a new and implied role for himself, by becoming a self-appointed buffer for Stacy and Tim. He believed that if he could continue to be the target of Phil and Eric's attacks, they would avoid Stacy and Ryan, allowing them to do their jobs and insulating them from the pressures he faced on a regular basis. Stacy and Tim could easily see how Ryan was stepping in between them and Eric—although he never told them explicitly—and while they discussed it with each other, they never mentioned to Ryan that they knew or how much they appreciated it.

Stacy's troubles with Phil, however, hadn't subsided, but her approach was different. She had been taking a more passive-aggressive stance with Phil as he continued to make jabs at her lifestyle. She merely brushed him off and ignored Phil at every turn. The more she ignored him, the more agitated he became. Many of her colleagues were concerned that Phil's rising animosity would get worse, but no one was sure how far he would go.

Still, Ryan did try his best to keep Stacy out of Phil's firing line by ensuring minimal contact between the two; however, Phil focused his attention on discrediting the POS and Stacy by continually providing misinformation to Eric. He spent much of his time documenting the deficiencies and issues of the POS in an effort to deflect the cost overruns and blunders of the inventory system he controlled. Ryan couldn't comprehend why management couldn't or wouldn't see through the obvious façade, and he was puzzled as to why they never sought the truth about the projects.

Everyone on Ryan's team knew that the comments made by Phil were very damaging, and both Tim and Stacy spent an enormous amount of time retorting Phil's statements, which Eric had accepted incontrovertibly. Unfortunately, due to the rumors continuing to circulate of another impending organizational change, every member of Ryan's team was in self-defense mode. They all worried that in less than a month; they would be out of a job and therefore couldn't allow spurious comments to be unanswered. If a change was going to occur it would occur at the end of the year, which was less than thirty days away, and thus everyone's stress level was elevated due to the holiday season.

One early December morning, five days before Christmas, Ryan joined Stacy and Tim in the cafeteria for a coffee. They had been in the cafeteria five minutes before Ryan joined them.

"How is everyone doing this morning?" Ryan asked. Unfortunately, he didn't get the usual canned response.

"Not well," said Tim.

"What's the matter?" Ryan asked.

Tim paused as though he was shaping an answer. His eyes stared down at the table, and Ryan noticed that Stacy was looking intently at Tim as though they both had something to hide from him.

"I've got...," Tim paused again and then said, "The pressure is really getting to me. I can't keep producing variations of status reports and counterresponses to every one of Phil's lies. This is unbearable."

Ryan replied, "Guys, I know this is tough, but hang in there." The new fiscal year is approaching and other companies should be hiring. You might find other opportunities elsewhere. Forget this place. Things will work out, just hang in there."

Something was different though. Not only did Tim not reengage the conversation, but the look on Stacy's face was very somber. She looked pale, very pale. Ryan looked directly at Stacy and asked, "Are you OK?"

"Fine," she replied and after a very distinct and deliberate pause continued, "we are just under a lot of pressure right now."

It was obvious from their responses and their body language that they were hiding something. He knew they were under a lot of pressure, but there was a cloud hanging over this conversation, and the tone in their voices was indicative of another problem. His team never kept anything from him, and now he knew something was deliberately being hidden. Hoping they had a good reason to remain silent, he decided not to press the issue.

As Ryan got up from the table, his BlackBerry buzzed and so did Stacy's. They both received an e-mail simultaneously for a meeting in ten minutes on the POS. As Ryan was about to curse Eric out, his phone rang. The display on his phone said, "Eric Musconi."

"What the hell does he want?" Ryan said aloud.

Stacy looked patiently at Ryan, knowing, based on Ryan's responses and the e-mail a few minutes before, that Eric was on the phone. Stacy stood very still next to Ryan, trying to determine the content of the conversation, based on Ryan's responses on the phone. There were no details in Eric's e-mail about the meeting, just that they were both to attend, so she was desperate for some insight and her impatience wouldn't allow her to wait until Ryan was off the phone.

"Ryan, I'm very disappointed in the progress of the POS system. I want to let you know that the CIO has informed me of his decision to officially cancel the project," Eric said over the phone.

Ryan exclaimed, "Eric, but the system is close to being finished!"

"It's not a debate. This meeting is to get a final disposition report to the CIO, who will then present it to the board. Get your ass up here, and bring Stacy."

Eric then hung up the phone abruptly without giving Ryan a chance to respond. Eric had executed another of his classic attacks, giving Ryan no time to offer any response. Ryan did notice the unmistakable voice of Phil in the background, which aggravated him even more than Eric's tirade about the POS system. He knew Phil would also attend the meeting, spurring the demise of the system and deflecting the deficiencies in his group.

Stacy said, "What did he say?"

"He's cancelling the project."

"What? How can he do that?" she said.

"He's giving a final disposition report to the CIO for presentation to the board, where they will announce the termination of the project."

"What happens to us?" she asked.

"I don't know, he didn't say. We need to get up to the meeting. Let's go and see."

"I'll stop by my desk and get the latest status reports, I'll give them something to chew on," Stacy said.

"Don't bother, just bring a notebook. It's already been decided."

Any remaining hope Stacy might have had, disappeared. She was prepared to defend her turf like a lioness defending her cubs. However, after hearing the exasperation in Ryan's voice, she had become despondent and fear began to overtake her. She wondered if she would be fired or if members of her team would be fired. All she had left was to walk in and attempt to save her job and herself; she wasn't going to back down even though it seemed hopeless.

As they walked into the conference room, several members of Eric and Phil's team had already been seated. The room was silent and no eye contact was made as they moved to the far side of the room and sat down. Phil and Eric entered the room about thirty seconds later, and sat next to each other near the head of the table opposite Stacy and Ryan. As Phil sat down, he stared directly at Stacy as if he was expecting a shoot-out. In response, refusing to back down, Stacy never took her eyes off him. The other participants in the room were all looking intently as if they knew a scuffle was about to occur. It was no secret in the organization, that Phil and Stacy were at odds. Phil had made sure everyone knew his opinion of Stacy and he took creative license in explaining how he dealt with Stacy.

Eric opened the meeting immediately and bluntly with the purpose of providing a final disposition report recommending the termination of the project. Eric described budget overruns and issues related to the project, mostly directed at inefficiencies of Ryan and Stacy, and thus Phil decided it was a perfect time to make his opinions known.

"I wholeheartedly agree with Eric's assessment of the project and I would recommend that upon its termination we transfer all remaining resources, budget, and personnel to the inventory control system project, under my direction, to ensure we complete the most critical project in the organization. We are a bit short staffed and could use the help."

Eric nodded his head and was about to speak when Ryan said, "If you want to cancel the project, go ahead, but I keep my resources. It's my team and I will use them appropriately."

Eric wouldn't have had any issue eliminating the entire staff, even though he could potentially lose some resources. In Eric's mind, he could easily make the case for transferring problem resources to another area, and refitting his department with the resources he sorely wanted. However, he wouldn't be dictated to by anyone about his department.

Eric responded, "That's not for you to decide. I will make that decision, but I will keep it under consideration. I have to decide what's in the best interests of the company and the team."

Stacy had had enough, "There is nothing wrong with the POS project. It was a well-funded, appropriately staffed project from the beginning—until you decided to sabotage the project. In spite of that, it would have been completed if we had been given accurate and consistent requirements from Phil."

This started a barrage of comments between Phil and Stacy. The tension in the room escalated to a very high level; curiously, Eric didn't intervene and allowed the conversation to escalate. Ryan thought this behavior was very strange for a control-minded manager like Eric. He tried to get Stacy's attention to have her calm down, but she never looked in his direction. Her eyes were completely fixated on Phil as they continued their argument.

Phil pounded his fist on the table and said emphatically, "I'm tired of your criticisms, Stacy. We gave you everything we needed and you couldn't deliver. We have a very tight time line and a critical project and you are deliberately sabotaging us."

"You're the one sabotaging us, and you know it. Everyone in this room knows it. You all have a hidden agenda." Stacy had completely lost her composure at this point.

Ryan tried to stop her, but before he could, Eric stood up. "I've had enough of this. Everyone be quiet. Ryan, come outside with me. I don't want to hear a word from this room."

Ryan stood up and walked around the table to exit the room. As he looked back he could see Stacy looking in his direction with an expression of remorse; he nodded his head in response as a sign of solidarity.

Outside of the conference room, Eric was furious and directed his anger at Ryan. "You better get Stacy under control or I will fire her on the spot."

"What about Phil? If Stacy is culpable, then so is he."

"I'm not talking about Phil, I'm talking about Stacy. She works for you."

"There is a definite disparity here. You are letting him get away with that conduct, and it is impossible for anyone to work in that environment."

"Then maybe I should fire her, because I'm not having Phil fired. You're going to support Phil one way or the other, even if I have to fire Stacy to do it."

Ryan was a bit perplexed, this conversation now flipped from Stacy to him. "You mean *I* need to support Phil, or you will fire Stacy."

"I have no problems firing you, but it's easier for me if I have your support. You will support Phil or I will have Stacy fired, and if you still don't support him, I'll fire you."

Eric then walked back into the conference room with Ryan few seconds behind. Ryan walked slowly and deliberately around the conference table back to his chair, pulled the chair away from the table, and sat down staring in a downward direction directly at the table. Stacy was looking at Ryan from the moment he walked into the room but he never looked in her direction as he was replaying the conversation in his head. Stacy was nervous because Ryan looked shell shocked and oblivious to his surroundings. A deafening silence had overtaken the room as everyone awaited Eric's direction. Ryan looked in Eric's direction and noticed Eric whispering to Phil who, after a few seconds, had a suspicious grin on his face.

Ryan leaned over to Stacy and in a soft voice said, "Let it go. We will talk outside. Just let it go. Trust me."

Stacy whispered back, "Let what go?"

"Just don't argue, keep silent. I know it's frustrating, but I need you to keep quiet."

Stacy nodded but was obviously disappointed. She sensed something happened outside the conference room, and for Ryan to be so adamant, the conversation must have referred to some dire consequences for her.

Eric, across the table from Ryan, clasped his hands with interlocking fingers, and directed his comments directly at Ryan and Stacy. In a deliberate tone he said, "Based on the status and its poor design, the POS system will be recommended for termination, and I will subsequently decide what to with the resources based on what is in the best interests of the department. I will make that recommendation to the CIO."

With those final comments, the participants began to file out of the room without further discussion. While everyone proceeded out of the conference room swiftly, Stacy and Ryan remained seated, waiting for everyone to leave before they would get up. Ryan turned to Stacy and was about to speak when he noticed out of the corner of his eye that Phil was the only other person who hadn't left his seat. Ryan paused for a moment and made eye contact with Phil, who at that moment decided to get up from his chair. However, unexpectedly, Phil didn't proceed toward the door. Instead, he had made his way across to their side of the table with the dumb grin on his face once again as if claiming victory. He edged closer to Stacy and leaned his head down between Stacy and Ryan

"Now who has the last laugh, dyke. Your boyfriend can't save you now."

Stacy was appalled as was Ryan. She wanted to grab him by the throat and deck him. Phil had been very callous in the past but this comment crossed the line. Ryan stood up to put some distance between Stacy and Phil.

"Get out." Ryan said in stern and deliberate voice.

Stacy bit her tongue, but was furious as Phil edged away from them toward the door. Stacy never looked away from him; she wasn't backing down and she wasn't about to be intimidated. Phil continued to exit the conference room, turned and glared at Ryan and pointed to him as a warning, but Ryan wouldn't be intimidated either.

Stacy and Ryan walked out of the conference room together and proceeded to the elevator bank. Not saying a word to each other, they both knew exactly where they were going, outside the building. Stacy's anger was manifesting itself physiologically as her ears were bright red and Ryan could feel a lump in his throat with his mouth becoming very dry due to the intense set of emotions that had engulfed him. They both did everything in their power to stay quiet until they were outside the building.

Just as they opened the door to leave the building Stacy yelled, "That son of a bitch. I would have decked him. I would've." Stacy knew better, but if they were at a bar, it would have been an ugly scene. Now what the hell do I do? Phil is so far up Eric's ass, I'm screwed. He's really out to get me."

"You're going to HR.," Ryan said.

Stacy replied, "What?"

"When we are done here you are going to HR. Tell them exactly what happened, and what was said. Don't leave out anything. I will then go to HR to confirm the story, but first I will go to Eric."

"What's HR going to do? These departments are all fluff, and all they are is a mouthpiece for management."

"Some of them are, but you have no case if you don't get it documented. This is harassment, and if it's not handled, it's a major lawsuit."

"What are you going to tell Eric?" she asked.

"I'm going to tell him I'm reporting Phil to HR. I'm not going to tell him you are, just me."

"Aren't you afraid he is going to fire you?"

"Of course, but that could happen anyway. Stacy, Eric told me if I didn't get you in line he would fire you, and if I didn't support Phil he would fire me. He is out to get us, but mostly he's going after me. He wants me to capitulate to him. This is a power play on his part, an ego trip. I will do my job, and if that's not enough and he wants to fire me, so be it."

"Why don't I just quit, that will make it easier on you. I don't want to deal with this anyway."

"Then he wins, and it doesn't solve the problem. What about the message you send to the rest of your team? I'm not giving up yet, and neither should you. Go to HR and get it documented. Let me know how it goes."

Ryan and Stacy went back into the building. Stacy continued to walk past the elevator bank and made a right turn down the corridor into the HR department. Ryan waited at the elevator bank to head up to Eric's office and formulated his thoughts, ultimately deciding on short, and direct.

Upon exiting the elevator, he turned right and began to increase his gate toward Eric's office. His movements became stronger and more deliberate as the rage and determination began to build like the pressure of a volcano within him. Arriving at Eric's office, he was fully prepared for a confrontation; however, the moment was anticlimactic since Eric wasn't in his office. Eric's assistant told Ryan he wasn't sure where Eric was, but he would call Ryan when he returned.

Walking back to his desk, he wondered how long he would have to wait for Eric. He knew Eric would probably go ballistic when he spoke to him, but he was ready to confront him on this and other issues. He had finally reached his tipping point and had made a conscious decision to act against the mistreatment and the obvious unprofessionalism. He was relieved that Stacy was formally discussing the situation with HR. This gave Ryan the sense that it would be harder for them to fire Stacy since termination would have the appearance of being retaliatory; however, that would all depend on how HR handled the situation.

Time seemed to progress very slowly as he looked at his watch and noticed that thirty minutes had passed with no word from Eric's assistant. As he picked up the phone to call him, an e-mail notification from Stacy popped up on his screen. The e-mail said she was still in HR, and she was about to meet the SVP of HR, and the chief legal counsel. The e-mail implied she was having productive discussions with the department. He kept his fingers crossed that Stacy would stay calm while discussing the incident since her deliberate and blunt communication style served her well in some cases but not in all and it had come back to haunt her in the past.

He wanted to be ready for his inevitable discussion with Eric, which probably was the most difficult discussion in his career and he was hoping not to revert to Stacy's communication style when he spoke to Eric. He turned his chair to face his computer terminal and Googled "harassment." After coming up with twelve thousand hits, the first hit was from the U.S. EEOC. He found that harassment was conduct that was unwarranted, severe, and pervasive. Using that definition, this situation represented harassment and Phil was most certainly guilty of it. How Eric would react, however, would be interesting, since he knew that if Eric protected Phil, he would be culpable as well.

As he jotted down some more notes from the Web sites, he received a call from Eric.

"Hello, Eric," Ryan answered

"What did you want, Ryan? I was told you were looking for me."

"Yes, I need to see you."

"I don't have time for you now, and *you* have work to do. You don't have time either."

"I need to see you immediately, it cannot wait." This was the most emphatic Ryan had been with Eric since he had started working for him. Ryan's voice could be intimidating at times, and Eric surprisingly backed down and invited him up, albeit reluctantly.

He nervously walked up to Eric's office even though he had the upper hand since Eric had no idea why he was coming up. Continuing, he concentrated on calming himself down, and removing the nervousness, by becoming more confident about what he was about to do. He feared being fired on the spot, but he knew if that happened, the company could potentially be liable. Unfortunately, that wouldn't do him any good in the short term since lawsuits take years before they are eventually resolved. Regardless of the consequences he had resolved to follow this path and do what he felt was right.

At Eric's office, he walked in without waiting for Eric to wave him in. This was very out of character for Ryan, who was always very polite and knocked before entering anyone's office. It was surprising for Eric as well because he always demanded that everyone be acknowledged before entering. Eric didn't have a chance to say anything to him, because he took control of the situation and the conversation immediately. Upon walking in, he proceeded to close the door firmly. Then he turned and stood behind the chair in front of Eric's desk.

"Listen carefully, sir," Ryan started. Eric was completely stunned by this abnormal behavior. Ryan addressed him as sir, as though he was in the military. He decided to be overtly professional to ensure nothing could be used against him.

Ryan continued, "I'm leveling a formal complaint against Phil for harassment and unprofessional conduct against Stacy. My decision to formally document and level this complaint came as result of the meeting we left earlier where Phil had made a severely derogatory remark to Stacy, which is cause for the charge of harassment. I will provide you with a copy of my written complaint when it is completed and after I speak with HR."

"I'm glad you came to me first. We can easily stop this. I will be more than happy to speak to Phil and straighten him out. Thank you for bringing it to my attention, there is no need to report it to HR," Eric replied, although in a soft voice, as if trying to appease.

"With all due respect, sir, I can't do that. This is a pattern of behavior that I have not acted upon previously and it would be unethical and unconscionable for me not to formally act at this time."

"You're overreacting, and I won't tolerate this. It's your word versus his. You have nothing," Eric replied more angrily.

"You're wrong; remember he said it to Stacy. I overheard him."

"Off the record then, I will make your life miserable here. You make one misstep and I'll have your ass thrown out so quickly you won't know what hit you. You either get in line, or you will be out."

Just as he finished that sentence, his phone rang.

Ryan was watching Eric intently to see the expression on his face. He instinctively knew that was a call about the situation. Eric listened but didn't say a word. It was a brief conversation, that he concluded by saying, "I'll be right there, sir."

"That was Mr. Stone," Eric said in a low voice. "I am to meet him in HR immediately along with Phil."

After a brief pause, Eric got up out of his seat, grabbed the blue pinstripe jacket off the back of his chair, and put in on. As he pulled on his shirt cuffs to straighten them out, he said while looking down at his arms, "Get out, now."

He didn't push his luck, he answered, "Yes, sir," and left the office with Eric a few steps behind. He turned to the right, while Eric turned to the left. As he continued down a few steps, he turned his head to get a look at Eric, who was walking at a fairly brisk pace, and noticeably agitated.

When he went back to his desk, there was a light on his phone, indicating a phone message had been left. He dialed into his voice mail and entered the password, which spelled leader. As he listened to the envelope of the voice mail, he was puzzled at the extension from which the message came, extension 8212. Then the message played.

"Ryan, my name is Sandra Whyte from human resources. I need to speak with you urgently regarding a member of your team." Please contact me as soon as you get this message at extension 8212. If I am not there, please have me paged. Once again Sandra Whyte, human resources, extension 8212, matter is urgent."

He had expected a call from human resources, and upon hearing the message, a grin began to appear on his face. He knew this would be an embarrassing situation for Eric and Phil, but they deserved it. On one hand, he savored the thought of Phil and Eric squirming in HR and feeling a bit of heat for their arrogance and antagonistic attitudes. On the other hand, he hoped things wouldn't get worse and that the situation would be adequately resolved by HR and not swept under the rug. He threw his head back and looked up at the ceiling in a bit of exasperation because he really wished the situation never occurred at all.

Anticipating the conversation he was about to have with HR, Ryan grabbed a notebook and set it on the desk in front of him. He opened up to a clean page ready for note taking. Once set, he took a deep breath, picked up the phone and began to dial. On the other end of the phone, he heard the rings and wondered if she would be at her desk. On the third ring, the phone clicked and he heard, "Hello, Ms. Whyte speaking."

"Hello Ms. Whyte, you left a message for me earlier. This is Ryan from IT."

Ms Whyte was a very pleasant person, and he had on one occasion visited due to a personnel-related problem. She probably wouldn't remember him but he remembered how personable she was and how much concern she showed for the employees of the company. She had a very good reputation of being a great listener, which made her perfect for a role in HR.

She explained that the reason for her call was to gather more information regarding the investigation currently underway while being careful not to use the employee's name over the phone. After a few brief questions about his involvement and his perception of the incident, she asked him to come down to HR for an interview regarding the situation. He informed her that he could be down in five minutes if she was available. She appreciated his quick response, and told him she would be at her desk waiting, but that they would move to a conference room and that one other person from HR might join her. He acknowledged and consented to having other HR personnel in the conversation.

As he headed down to HR, he glanced around, looking for any sign of Eric, Phil, or even the CIO. He became increasingly concerned that one of them would spot him on his way to HR and was afraid of retaliation, a trait that was obviously inherent in them. Although scared, he kept a cool head and tried to stay confident since he knew what he was doing was just. Their behavior could not be allowed to continue and while it was easy for anyone to keep quiet, he could not and would not. As a party to the incident, he felt obligated to communicate it and would work within system. More importantly, it was for Stacy, his most trusted lieutenant, and under no circumstances could he abandon her.

Upon reaching HR, he walked along a corridor with six glass-walled conference rooms, all of which had their vertical shades turned to prevent people from looking in. As he continued down the corridor, he could hear the Phil's distinct higher pitched voice getting louder. He turned his head as he approached the last conference room on the right and caught a glimpse through a crack in a pair of vertical blinds. He could briefly see the anger on Phil's face, and as he continued to walk he could definitely hear the anger in his voice. He wasn't sure if

Eric or anyone else form IT was in the same room, but it didn't matter, he moved quickly to ensure that he wasn't seen.

He noticed Ms. Whyte as he turned left away from the conference rooms. She was standing by her cubicle speaking to her colleague. Ryan approached her and said, "Hello, Ms. Whyte, a pleasure to see you again."

Ms. Whyte was a slender African-American woman who had a wonderful smile and very power laugh. Her smile and mannerisms could calm any irate employee or provide a much needed lift to a stressed worker. She was a family woman who had many pictures of her very 3 athletic boys on her desk. She clearly understood the pressures faced by working parents in the corporate world and she brought a very sympathetic ear to all of her conversations with employees.

"Hello, Ryan, I knew your name sounded familiar but I couldn't place the face. I'm sorry we are meeting again under such circumstances. Let's move to an empty office," she said.

They walked about twenty-five feet to an empty office on the right. The office, which had been empty for two months, belonged to a vice president that had recently retired from the company. It was a spacious office with bare walls but very nice plush carpeting. The desk was made of solid mahogany and the chairs were pure Italian leather. He could only imagine what other decorations might have been in the office when it was occupied.

The office was situated away from the conferences rooms, which eased Ryan's fears of being seen or heard by roaming eyes and ears. He followed her into the office where she asked him to have a seat as she made her way around the desk. Once there she picked up the phone and made a brief call letting the person on the other end of the phone know where she was. It was a short and seemingly cryptic phone conversation, which didn't help allay Ryan's concerns. It was uncertain to him if someone was joining them or if she was notifying someone where she was in case she was needed.

After hanging up the phone, Ms. Whyte, noticing Ryan was a bit tense, said, "Relax, Ryan, you know why you're here. We spoke to Stacy and she told us you were in the room when the incident occurred. She has the highest regard for you and your professionalism. She's been speaking with us for over an hour."

"Wow, she's been talking to you guys all that time?" Ryan asked

"Yes, she has. This is a very serious situation, and it's not an isolated incident either, but it is the most egregious and obvious."

Ryan was astonished that this had happened before so he asked, "With the same person?"

"Actually, I can't discuss specifics but let's just say it's a pattern by a few individuals in the same area."

Now Ryan was amazed. He wanted to ask why nothing had been done about it before, but thought it wasn't really appropriate since she said she couldn't discuss specifics. It was interesting to think that HR might have been notified of the behavior from anyone else in the department and, if so, why nothing been done to correct the situation.

"Ryan, by the look on your face, I know you have a ton of questions, but I really am not at liberty to discuss anything. I would like for you to tell me what happened in the meeting this morning and please just stick to the facts and provide as much detail as possible."

He began to recount the meeting and the events from earlier, but sidetracked to provide a longer history of the issues between Phil and Stacy. He looked to her for acknowledgement that the historical perspective he was giving was acceptable for the purposes of the conversation. Ms. Whyte acknowledged by simply nodding. She welcomed the information, and would tell him if anything was superfluous.

He continued to talk for about thirty minutes going through in very good detail all the incidents that occurred in the past from the rumors of the affair to the rumors of her homosexuality. He indicated that never before had Phil shown such callousness as he did in the meeting earlier in the day. She appreciated the feedback, since it helped to demonstrate Ryan's objectivity. His objectivity began to wane after the discussion about the meeting. He was so incensed by the comment and complete disregard Phil had shown to his fellow worker that it made him physically sick to his stomach as he became more enraged. Sensing the buildup of anger, Ms. Whyte, who studied psychology and human behavior patterns, gradually turned the conversation away to a benign topic to calm Ryan down.

Pausing for a minute, he took a few deep breaths and took a sip of water to calm his nerves down. He hadn't reached that level of anger in all his life, and the feeling was despised. Losing control of his emotions was never a trait for Ryan. He was afraid that losing complete control of his emotions would make him appear biased in regard to the incident. He looked at Ms. Whyte and said, "Please forgive my outburst. I'm obviously showing too much anger right now and I should be calmer."

"Actually, it's nice to see someone in your position care that much for the well-being of your employees. We encourage our managers to be mindful of the feelings of their employees, but unfortunately, we never reward that behavior, in fact some might say we frown upon it by concealing it," Ms. Whyte said.

"I trust my people and I want them to trust me. I want them to know I will do the right thing when the time comes," he said.

"Are you sure it's just for them? Maybe you want to know that you will do the right thing when the time comes," she said with a smile on her face.

She was right on target. He did want to know that he would do the right thing at the right time. It was something that had haunted him for years, since the day Subbu was fired. He never completely forgave himself, but he did learn from the experience, and today was a day that he could step up and do the right thing.

"Some people would have come in here and told me the story and ultimately downplayed it. You, however, gave me the full story, including the historical perspective and your emotions. It was genuine and sincere."

"I'm sure other people would do the same in my shoes," Ryan said.

"I've been in HR for fifteen years and while I've had similar situations, everyone was so fearful of losing their jobs that they sugarcoated the stories. Right now, I have full corroboration of Stacy's story, and once we get the other side of the story we will be able to act accordingly," she concluded.

"Do I need to speak to anyone else?" Ryan asked.

"Not at this time, but I may ask you back shortly. Why don't you go get some lunch and if we need you we will let you know."

He thanked her for her time and they shook hands. As he walked out of the office, he had a major sense of relief but he wondered about how any repercussions might affect him and Stacy. He knew that Eric and Phil would react to the situation but he was not naïve enough to believe they would change their ways. They might temporarily change their behaviors but there was more of a chance of a leopard changing its spots than Phil and Eric changing permanently. What puzzled Ryan more than anything else was Eric. Phil was a malcontent and ego-driven person, but Eric, he thought, would have been more polished. He couldn't understand how Eric had become so successful with his style of management, which seemingly rewarded and condoned

Phil's poor behavior. He strongly believed that as a senior executive who came from the financial world, Eric would have been more professional and more sincere. At some level, he hoped he would learn something from Eric, because he always wanted to believe that Eric would teach him some important lessons in management or technology, but he was wrong, and now he wanted nothing from him.

As he walked back through the corridor where he entered HR earlier, all the conference rooms were empty. Looking at his watch, he noticed that the time was 12:15 p.m., which meant everyone was probably out to lunch. He wondered if there would be more meetings in the afternoon or if he would be called in to speak to someone else. He expected to receive a call from Eric at any time asking him to come to his office. There he expected to get lambasted by Eric and even potentially fired. He was worried he would get no protection from HR, especially since Sandra never mentioned it.

As he approached the elevators, his phone rang. Ryan grabbed the BlackBerry off his belt and turned it to show the display. Stacy was calling him from her cell phone; he knew she was out of the building. He quickly pushed the down button at the elevator bank and then answered the phone.

"Hey, Stace, how'd it go?" Ryan asked

"It went as well as could be expected. Not something I really want happening, to tell you the truth. Let's talk at lunch, you coming down?"

"I'll be right down."

As if on cue, he hung up the phone and the elevator door opened. He stepped in and pressed the number one. The doors closed and he proceeded downward, while his thoughts continued to drift toward the inevitable meeting with Eric. The more he thought about it, the more he became uneasy and agitated. In his mind, he could see the anger on Eric's face, vividly; he could feel the tension of the meeting and the yelling that would accompany it. Ryan's heart began to race in fear, and he worried about having no protection from HR. While Ryan knew that HR would not tolerate certain behaviors of unprofessionalism, there were other ways to get a point across, and fear was one of them, especially in light of looming cuts to the organization.

As Ryan walked out of the elevator on the first floor, his phone rang again. He turned the BlackBerry, since he never put it back on his belt, viewed the display, but didn't recognize the number. He hesitated for a moment, not sure if he should let it go to voice mail, but on the third ring, he relented.

"Hello?"

"Hello, Ryan, this is Andrea from Mr. Stone's office," the female voice on the other end of the phone replied. Andrea was Mr. Stone's assistant, a polished executive assistant with a slight British accent. She had come to the company with Mr. Stone, and had worked with him for over fifteen years in that capacity. She was always quick with a smile and had a very soft voice, which everyone affectionately referred to as the British stiff upper lip.

Shocked, he paused for a moment since he wasn't expecting a call from the CIO's office. The call was in obvious reference to the situation, since Gerald Stone's assistant had never called before. He was already out of the elevator when he glanced toward the revolving door and he saw Stacy outside the building. He decided to wait and finish the conversation before he continued walking.

"Yes, Andrea, how can I help you?"

"Ryan, the CIO would like to meet with you at two. It is imperative that you clear your schedule," she informed him.

"Not an issue, I will make sure I am there. May I ask what it is in reference to? Should I bring anything?"

"Sorry, I don't know. I was just asked to set up the meeting," she replied.

"OK, thank you, I'll be there."

He hung up the phone and clipped his BlackBerry on his belt; he glanced through the front windows of the building where he noticed Stacy outside the building on the phone. Proceeding through the doors, he approached Stacy. As he neared, she hung up the phone and turned to Ryan.

"Guess who that was," Stacy said.

Ryan shrugged his shoulders and hastily Stacy responded, "Mr. Stone's office. I am to meet him at 2:00 p.m."

"You too, I just received a call from his office to meet him at 2:00 as well."

"That's seems odd. I know what he wants to talk about, it just seems strange that both of us would be in his office together, don't you think?" she said.

"It is strange that both of us would be together for a meeting of that nature." Ryan paused for a moment and then asked, "How did your meetings go?"

Stacy went into detail throughout their lunch. She explained how HR was appalled at the behavior and had mentioned that this didn't appear to be an isolated case. Nothing was substantiated or proven and therefore no action had ever been taken. There had been rumors of sexual harassment and unprofessional behavior but no one had ever had the courage to approach HR and formally complain, which tied their hands. Sandra assured Stacy that there could be no repercussions against her and that the individuals involved would be dealt with should the accusations be verified appropriately, but Sandra wasn't allowed to provide any more details at until the investigation was completed.

Upon returning to the office, Ryan sat down at his desk to review some e-mails; however, before he did, he lifted himself from his chair and slowly walked outside his cubicle and around the corner, where he had a view of Phil's desk. He slowly peered around the corner but didn't see any movement at Phil's desk; however, he didn't have the best angle, so he continued to move closer. As he neared the cubicle, he noticed the desk was clean and the monitor screen was off. Phil wasn't at his desk, and it seemed as though he hadn't been at his desk all day.

He then walked over to Tim's cubicle, which was two more cubicles away and across the aisle from Phil's. He startled Tim, who was typing an e-mail on his keyboard, but quickly changed the screen once he noticed Ryan was standing there.

"Have you seen Phil at all today?" he asked.

"Earlier. I know he was here this morning but, come to think of it, I haven't seen him since very early this morning," he replied.

He wanted to know if Phil had come back from HR, and it appeared that he hadn't. He thanked Tim and began to walk away slowly, as he listened intently to Tim resuming his typing. He thought Tim was hiding something, since earlier in the day when he was with Stacy in the cafeteria and changed the subject he and Stacy were discussing. This was particularly odd behavior for Tim, who was a very open individual who never had any secrets and shared his entire life with Ryan and Stacy, especially over the past year. Ryan had come to respect Tim's integrity and dedication to the team and had considered him not only a valuable member of the team, but a close friend as well.

He looked at his watch and noticed that the time was approaching the 2:00 p.m. mark. He proceeded back to his desk to pick up a notebook and pen. Before he left for the meeting he decided to check his e-mail, unfortunately for Ryan, he always had an urge to check his e-mail many times, which sometimes bordered on the compulsive side. Upon opening his e-mail he noticed a meeting request that included all of Eric's reports, entitled "New Fiscal Year Efficiencies," scheduled for tomorrow at 4:00 p.m. Ryan shook his head and wondered what this meeting would be about. Another of Eric's meetings meant to glorify the "Caesar" and satisfy his ego. Noticing that he might be a few minutes late, he ignored the e-mail and hurriedly made his way to Mr. Stone's office taking the stairs to get there faster.

Approaching Mr. Stone's office, he heard Stacy's voice from the office, sounding unexpectedly relaxed and jovial. He glanced over to Mr. Stone's assistant who smiled, nodded, and raised her hand in the direction of the office, acknowledging to Ryan her permission to proceed directly into the office. Once in the entryway, he made eye contact with Mr. Stone, but before he could utter a word, the low and bellowing voice of Mr. Stone preempted him.

"Hello, Ryan, thank you for coming," Mr. Stone said.

"Yes, sir," Ryan responded.

"Please have a seat." Mr. Stone motioned to Ryan to take the empty seat in front of his desk to the right of where Stacy was sitting.

"Stacy, Ryan, thank you for coming. I want to apologize personally to the two of you for the conduct of one of your colleagues earlier this morning. We have had a few meetings with senior IT leadership and human resources and I can assure you that the problem will be adequately dealt with in accordance with the policies of the company."

Mr. Stone continued to talk directly to Stacy for approximately five minutes. He gave his philosophy on cultural diversity and tolerance, and emphatically apologized to Stacy for the hurtful and callous words Phil used, although he never mentioned him by name. He then turned to Ryan.

"Ryan, I have asked you here for two reasons, first, because you were an unintended victim of the remarks made and, second, because I want to give you my assurance that you and Stacy, as a member of your team and mine, have my full support and backing."

Ryan was impressed and overwhelmed by the words and tonality of Mr. Stone. He showed a great amount of humility and appreciation for his two employees, completely catching Ryan off guard. He had expected a polite but stern and distant lecture. He never expected to hear the CIO of the company talk to them about their feelings and discuss the situation at a personal level. He was showing them an appreciated amount of genuineness and sincerity. It was refreshing to have a senior manager provide this level of understanding, which he never expected.

The meeting lasted forty-five minutes and ended with a pleasant handshake, a promise to follow through on preventing intolerance in the department and personal commitment to Stacy and Ryan to have his door open should they need to speak to him. Both he and Stacy left the office in a much better emotional state than when they walked in. As they left Mr. Stone's office they continued to discuss how impressed they were with Mr. Stone and their utter disbelief at how their meeting progressed. They continued their conversation in the elevator area with their obvious pleasure being echoed as their voices grew gradually louder by the acoustic nature of the dome-like elevator bank.

They waited for about twenty seconds before the elevator indicator sounded off with its light high-pitched bell. They gradually moved to the elevator, whose directional light pointed down, and waited for the door to open. As the door opened, both Ryan and Stacy took a quick step back and immediately froze at the sight of Eric and Phil standing at the door of the open elevator. Eric and Phil were paralyzed at the sight of Stacy and Ryan, and they all looked at each other in the manner of an old Western standoff. Eric gathered himself, looked away from the two of them, and walked deliberately between them with Phil right behind. No one said anything to each other and no gestures of any kind were made. The two sides were content to disengage each other as quickly as they were engaged.

Upon entering the elevator, Stacy pressed the button for their floor and waited for the door to close, then turned to Ryan and said, "They're going to see Stone."

"Yep," he replied.

"That should be interesting. Do you think he was really sincere and that he will actually take action?"

"Some sort of action has to happen, what it is, I don't know. Either way it's a major problem for them, including Stone."

The day ended without any further incidents, meetings, or discussions with anyone. Ryan's team was abuzz about the incident and they were clamoring for more details; however, when asked, Ryan thought better of answering directly. He politely told his team that he was unable to discuss any issues about other employees, allowing HR to handle the situation and keep the discussions limited to the appropriate parties, which was the proper way to handle the issue. Personally, he liked to keep everyone on his team as informed as possible, but the circumstances around this incident were on a need-to-know basis only for the protection of everyone involved.

The next morning was relatively quiet, progressing slowly and with very little activity across the floor. He had been at work for over two hours and there was no sign of Phil or Eric, which was very unusual. He looked forward to completing the day and starting his vacation, and the only thing between him and his vacation was the 4:00 p.m. efficiency meeting that Eric had scheduled yesterday. He hoped the day would continue to be uneventful and that the meeting was just another one of Eric's attempts to hear himself speak and provide insight into his strategic vision for the department. His vacation would provide him with a much-needed break from the intense pressure he was feeling. He began to daydream about the things he would do over the break, away from the office. He closed his eyes for a brief moment to take a deep breath of relaxation as he thought of relaxing on his couch without the worry of seeing Eric for nine days.

Stacy gently tapped him on the shoulder, interrupting his daydream, and said, "Ready for your vacation?"

"Absolutely, I need a break, how about you?"

"I'm taking a day or two." Her expression softened as she looked around and continued, "More important though, I wanted to let you know that I spoke to both Eric and Phil today."

"You did? What did they say?" he asked.

"Well, I was called to Eric's office about an hour ago, and I was apprehensive about going. I was going to speak to you first, but you weren't at your desk."

"I've been here all morning, you must have looked for me while I was in the men's room, sorry," he said.

"That's OK. The meeting was brief. Sandra from HR was there. I felt very awkward being in the same room and I never made eye contact with Phil. Eric made Phil apologize, and Eric apologized in the same manner Mr. Stone had. Then Sandra had a brief discussion with me, letting me know that Phil was to attend sensitivity training classes sponsored by HR, a permanent mark would be on his file, which would affect his next year's review, and that any more outbursts against her would result in his termination."

"Wow, she said that?" he asked.

"She said some other HR stuff during the meeting, but as we exited the room, she said that HR was making a statement about the behavior being exhibited in IT and that it wouldn't be tolerated. She also told me off the record that he was going to be moving to another manager to eliminate the need for him to communicate with me directly, and that you and his manager must attend any meetings where he and I are required. She said she would talk to you later about that."

"Interesting, so how did Phil look?"

"Well, I really didn't make eye contact with him, but it was definitely a forced apology from both of them; but I must say," she then lowered her voice and with a big grin, she said, "it was nice to see them both eat a slice of humble pie."

Ryan couldn't help but smile at the pill Eric and Phil had to swallow, but he knew this type of situation should never have occurred, and he knew the real problem wasn't resolved. He doubted whether it ever would be resolved. Phil's behavior was a problem that could be remedied either by a sincere change in behavior or by termination. However, the undercurrent created by his management and Eric condoning or at the very least ignoring the behavior, was more difficult to rectify. This very visible group of executives had received a mandate and a tremendous amount of power within the organization, which fostered a belief of invulnerability. The consequences of this incident may have temporarily shaken that perception, but it was doubtful that it had been broken. There was too much at stake for this group, and as long as they could control the information, they would have the upper hand in controlling the situation.

The afternoon wasn't any more exciting than the morning. Ryan was still daydreaming about his vacation, and had no intention of preparing for the 4:00 p.m. meeting with Eric. Expecting Eric to provide a lecture on the upcoming years strategic efforts, he figured it was futile to prepare any reports that could assist in the direction of the company since Eric would immediately dismiss anything he produced. There was no longer any doubt that layoffs were imminent; however, he believed the damage to his team would now be minimal due to the events of the past few days. He knew that every member of his organization was performing at a high level and received very high reviews, and the obvious targets of Eric and Phil's attacks were now off limits.

As Ryan entered the conference room for the 4:00 p.m. meeting, he noticed he was the first one in attendance even though he was only a few minutes early. It seemed strange that Eric's cronies hadn't appeared yet, many of whom abided by Eric's manifesto of being either at work or at meetings before him. Ryan took his seat, and began to doodle in his notebook as he waited for someone to show.

Five minutes passed, when Eric appeared. He closed the door gently and avoided eye contact with Ryan until he sat down. Ryan asked, "Is anyone else coming?"

"No, I've met with everyone already. This meeting is just with you and me."

Ryan suddenly became nervous, assuming he was about to be terminated so he took a few deep breaths to try to calm himself down. His mind began to race with how Eric was going to terminate him and what he would need to prepare for HR, but he began to believe with certainty that the ax was about to fall on him. Accepting his fate and noticeably nervous, he exhaled deeply as he responded to Eric's statement, "What exactly is the agenda?"

"The agenda is very simple. As you know we have to make major cuts in the organization, and as such we have had to make very tough decisions."

"I understand," replied Ryan as if to acknowledge he was being fired.

"Now, off the record, and I'll deny ever saying this. You are on thin ice. Your little stunt saved Stacy, and we apologized because Phil shouldn't have said what he did. Nonetheless, I have organizational decisions I need to make."

Ryan nodded and thought this was taking a bit longer than necessary, but looking at the expression on Eric's face he noticed it turned from one of avoidance to a stare of vengeance. The confusion increased with every passing moment as he wondered, if he was about to be fired why wasn't this being done in the presence of HR personnel.

Eric continued, "Ryan, as I said, you are on thin ice. Since I can't fire Stacy for her poor performance, I should fire you. However, I'm not going to do that. I don't want to risk any more problems with HR."

Ryan didn't say a word; he just stared at Eric intently, not knowing what to expect. Eric looked at his watch and almost immediately, Ryan glanced up at the clock on the wall and noticed the time was now 4:16; he wondered if there was any significance to the time. Eric then picked up his BlackBerry and dialed as he signaled to Ryan to wait a minute by holding up one finger. He wondered why Eric would make a phone call in the middle of a meeting, and what could he possibly be discussing. Eric turned away from him and hunched over as he whispered into the phone. He felt a bead of sweat slowly traverse down the side of his face as he felt the blood pressure running to his head from the uncertainty of the situation. The increased tension, he believed, was designed to intimidate him, and it was working. Ryan couldn't calm himself down at this point. His breath was shallow and he began tapping his foot on the floor.

"Ryan, I just needed to call human resources to verify something," Eric said.

He was now perplexed. If he just said he wasn't going to fire him why would Eric call HR? Would he be moved? What was he doing?

"Tim has just been terminated as part of our planned layoffs for fiscal efficiency," Eric said

Ryan felt his heart skip a beat and he was now speechless once again. How could Eric fire Tim, who had worked diligently to produce some of the best results in the company? Tim was a valued member of the team, a great worker, and one of the nicest people anyone could ever meet. Of all people, Tim didn't deserve to be fired under any circumstances.

Eric stared directly into Ryan's eyes with almost an evil gaze as he said, "I terminated him, because I couldn't terminate Stacy or you. Remember, you still work for me and all I need is one screw-up on your part and I will get rid of you for cause or you could resign on your own at any point if you choose, but one way or the other you will lose."

Eric stood up and as he walked toward the conference room door with Ryan still in utter silence, he turned to Ryan and concluded, "I'll deny this part of the conversation if you go to HR, but if you do, you may become their target for trying to manipulate the situation for personal gain. Good luck and enjoy your vacation."

Eric left the conference room with almost the same grin Phil had on his face, two days before. He thought to himself, the company would handle with utmost visibility the incident between Phil and Stacy but was either oblivious to the real problem or unwilling deal with management appropriately. The road ahead for him would be very arduous and painful. There was no conceivable way for Ryan to be successful as long as Eric was seeking any opportunity to deride or chastise him.

Ryan left for the day feeling dejected but simultaneously somewhat relieved. He still had his job for the moment and at least for the present he would be out of the office on his vacation. The pressure and tension at the office was taking a toll on his health, which was noticeable by his increasing weight and the colonization of his scalp by silver hairs. All he wanted was some relaxation time, without any of the worries of the office; unfortunately, the heavy burden of Tim being fired trumped relaxing. All he wanted to do now was to go home and sulk for a while.

Later that evening around 10:00 p.m. as he was sitting in his living room staring blankly at the TV, the phone began to ring. He thought about answering it, but thought it best to let it go to the answering machine. Lisa, obviously annoyed, hurriedly ran across the house to pick up the phone in the kitchen. Ryan didn't discuss the situation with Lisa when he came home because he just wanted to be left alone for a while. The holidays were only a few days away and he didn't want to think about it anymore. He would have been content to curl up in a shell and hide for the next few weeks, but it was obvious that wouldn't happen. He thought about calling Tim many times since he left the office but he would wait a day or two. Ryan was scared to speak to Tim, because he wasn't sure if Tim would blame him and he didn't want to relive the events of the past few days at this moment.

"Oh my God," Ryan heard Lisa's voice from the kitchen.

He leaned to the side of his chair so that his left ear had a better angle to listen. As he listened, he could tell by Lisa's tone and language that she was talking to Stacy. Stacy must have spoken to Tim and he figured she was telling Lisa, which now meant Lisa would chastise him for not telling her. She never liked hearing office stories from Stacy first, because it gave the appearance that they didn't talk at home. In this case, it wasn't a conversation he wanted to have or was ready to have; he hoped that speaking to Stacy would help him garner the courage to call Tim tomorrow.

"Ryan, you need to get the phone," Lisa yelled from the kitchen.

"Coming," he replied.

Ryan made his way out of his chair and walked down the corridor to the kitchen. He looked at Lisa's face, and noticed the complete glare and expression was not one of anger but one of concern. It was a bit puzzling as he lifted himself on the barstool in the kitchen and rested his elbow on the raised kitchen counter. The lights were off in the kitchen except for the two spotlights above the raised countertop. Lisa handed him the phone without saying a word but her lips moved as they mimed the word "Stacy."

"Hey, Stacy, what's up?" Ryan asked.

"Well, I didn't see you leave today and I needed to speak to you. What happened at the meeting?"

Ryan wasn't ready to tell her, but as they started to talk he became less anxious and was more amenable to discussing the meeting. He explained how Eric called him to the 4:00 p.m. meeting where he thought he was attending a general meeting with all of Eric's reports. He laboriously gave her details starting from the moment he walked in the conference room where he was the only one there.

"Get to the point, what happened?" she emphatically said.

He paused for a moment trying to decide where to restart the story. He gathered himself for a minute and finally said, "Eric sat down, started to lecture me, and then told me he had fired Tim for the proposed layoffs."

There was a silence on the phone, and he faintly heard a whisper on Stacy's end. Ryan heard no anger on the other side, and he became concerned because this wasn't the response he anticipated. He had expected to hear some cursing and maybe even the violent clearing of a desk, however, the silence was deafening and Ryan listened intently to the other side of the phone. He could hear a faint whisper increasing in volume saying, "Oh my God, Oh my God. No."

"Stacy, I know this is upsetting. I'm very upset as well. I'm going to call him in the morning."

The sobbing increased but she wasn't responding to anything Ryan was saying, it was as if she was having a separate conversation. He lifted his head turned his to the left and noticed a dark shadow in the hallway leaning up against the wall. The silhouette was definitely Lisa's. She was in the hallway listening to the conversation. Ryan called down the hallway, "Lisa?"

The silhouette then appeared from the shadow and into the indirect light from the spotlights above the counter. Her facial features slowly became more apparent as she entered farther into the light. Ryan noticed her eyes had welled up with tears but she wasn't saying anything. He asked, "Lisa, what's wrong?"

Stacy hearing the question over the phone said, "Ryan, earlier today when I was speaking to Phil, remember when you asked how we were doing and Tim said, 'not well'?"

"Yes, but he said he was tired and frustrated and the stress was getting to him."

Stacy began to sob, which Ryan could easily hear over the phone, and during a ten-second silence, Ryan's heart began to palpate with increasing speed and force. She exhaled over the phone and said, "Tim told me he had been diagnosed with throat cancer."

He couldn't believe the disaster that had unfolded. Tim, who had become a star on the team and who developed into a great manager, had a great career ahead of him, and now this horrible disease would sideline him. To add insult to injury he was fired for no other reason than vengeance, which wasn't even directed at him.

Lisa grabbed the phone from Ryan, still with tears in her eyes, as he remained motionless in his seat as if he had frozen into a block of ice. Lisa put the phone to her ear and said, "Stacy, why don't you come over, I think we all could use some coffee and company."

Lisa, who had tears streaming down her face, then hung up the phone after Stacy had agreed to come over, and put her arm around Ryan. Lisa was crying because she knew Tim had a young family—he'd been married for only four years and had two toddlers—and now he would be going through the most difficult time in his life. His family would not only struggle with the life-threatening condition, but the loss of income as well and the uncertainty that would accompany it.

The pressure had finally become too great for Ryan. He closed his eyes, dropped his head into his hands, and began to cry.

Chapter 6

DESPAIR AND HOPE

The Christmas holiday passed for Ryan, which had become the worst holiday in his entire life. His thoughts on Tim and the events of the past week consumed him, preventing him from enjoying the most festive time of the year. How anyone could enjoy a holiday without some remorse for a close friend and colleague, mired in one of the worst compound situations anyone could face, was unimaginable. Worst of all, his fear of condemnation by Tim completely paralyzed him and prevented him from conjuring up the courage to call him. He considered calling Tim a few times, but each time his mind raced ahead, believing that in some way he was responsible for Tim being fired, and he couldn't bear the thought of Tim placing the blame squarely on him.

On the one hand, he stood up for Stacy; if he hadn't, would Tim still be around? Had he just given Eric what he wanted, would anything have changed, and would it have saved Tim's job? He wondered if he had known about Tim's cancer earlier, would he have acted the same way? The fact that he was even giving credence to the notion that he would have changed his behavior made the situation even worse. He struggled to move on as the stress and pressure of these thoughts burdened him like the weight of the world.

Even if he had summoned the courage to call Tim, he couldn't think of anything to say. He couldn't tell Tim exactly what Eric told him, and how could he be believed anyway? If ever confronted, Eric would simply deny the conversation ever occurred, placing Ryan in a more difficult situation with Tim. Ryan knew there was little chance Tim would reach out to Eric, but this was the confusing thought pattern racing in Ryan's head. While he believed his friendship with Tim was strong, he wasn't as confident that Tim would understand, especially in light of his added condition.

The situation reminded him of the incident years ago with Subbu, which he increasingly realized affected him more deeply than he first believed. He doubted whether this time he had done enough to protect his team. He second-guessed himself over every minute detail and questioned every aspect of his motives over the past few weeks, wondering whether he overemphasized protecting Stacy at the expense of others on the team, and asking himself whether the needs of one person outweighed the needs of another. There were numerous ways to handle any situation, but were all options explored, or was there anything missed? Ultimately, he believed he did the right thing, but doubted his actions and wondered whether the right outcome will always succeed the right course of action.

The stress pushed him into a mini state of depression, for the two days after Christmas. He put on a good show for his family, but seized every chance he found to excuse himself from the gatherings. Lisa understood how much pain he was in, and allowed him to disengage for a few days, but she wouldn't let him do it for too long. She tried talking to him briefly, but he politely refused to discuss the matter. She watched him closely to make sure he wouldn't act rashly, but she saw no indication of a major problem yet.

By the third day, he began to open up a bit, and discussed various conversations he could have with Tim. She acted out a few lines at his request, to try to ready him for a mini barrage of personal attacks. Lisa mentioned there was really no way to know how Tim was going to react, and it was better to just listen rather than worry about a conversation. The most important thing, she told Ryan, was to focus on his health and not his job. He didn't believe it was that simple, since he was the one with the job, and Tim was not, but he knew she was correct and he had to summon up the courage to call him. He needed to find a way to charge up the hill and hope for the best.

He decided to call Tim from his car, giving him an opportunity to drive around and think about what he could say. Calling from his car also gave him many good excuses to get off the phone, he thought, should the conversation turn bad. He grabbed his winter coat, phone, and keys. Then he turned to Lisa and told her he would call Tim from the car and that he would be back shortly. Lisa wished him luck and told him not to worry but most of all just listen to Tim.

Looking out his front door, he noticed the gentle snow that had started to fall. The temperature was just under freezing and the quiet and the gentle nature of the falling snow had a calming effect. The air was very easy to breathe as he took a few deep breaths to calm himself down before reaching the car. As he entered his car, he grabbed the steering wheel with both hands and gripped it tightly, once again breathing deeply and noticing the vapor as his breath condensed in the air in front of him. His heart started to beat more intensely as he imagined the conversation. His thoughts were so intense that he was oblivious to the freezing cold wood grain portion of the steering wheel on his gloveless hands.

As he pulled out of his driveway, he decided to head for the expressway, which would give him a comfortable drive without many interruptions such as lights and stop signs. As he neared the expressway, which was only a mile from his home, he picked up his earpiece and plugged it in his ear. Then, using voice activation, he dictated the number to dial. It seemed like ten seconds before a connection was made; with each passing second, his chest slowly compressed as the intense pressure continued to build. He heard a click on the other end as though someone picked up the phone. He was about to say hello when he heard the distinctive three-note tone from the phone company of a number not in service. He picked up his phone and glanced at the display. Ryan noticed that he inverted the last two digits of the phone number.

Terminating the call, he attempted to dial again, this time being more deliberate than the last time at reciting the phone number into the headset. He waited for the connection, and after two quick seconds, the phone began to ring, drying out his throat while his hands began to sweat as he waited anxiously for someone to answer. After two rings, Tim's answering machine answered the phone on the other end. He immediately thought of hanging up, but decided to leave a message for Tim and asked that he call him back.

Overcoming his fear of calling Tim had proved fruitless since he merely had a conversation with the answering machine. On one hand, he felt relieved that he didn't have the conversation, but this was merely avoidance and he knew that it was imperative to talk to him both as a colleague and a friend, but there was no doubt as to how hard this was for him. If the situation was just cancer he could have easily picked up the phone, but knowing that Eric had fired Tim in retaliation for what Ryan did was almost unbearable to discuss.

He realized almost immediately that he hadn't spoken with Stacy in a few days. Wondering whether she had spoken to Tim, he decided to call her and find out. He dialed the number for her cell phone, figuring she wouldn't want to discuss any personal matters on her office line. Stacy, unfortunately, was in the office during the short week between Christmas and New Year's. She always liked working those days because everyone was usually out of the office and it was like a ghost town.

"Hello," Stacy answered her cell phone.

"Hey Stace how's the office?" he asked.

"Everything is very quiet, unusually quiet. I haven't seen Eric or Phil at all this week. Eric's door has been closed and Phil didn't seem to be at his desk," she said in a soft voice so as not be overheard.

"I'm not surprised. I figured they would be out this week. To tell you the truth, I'm not looking forward to coming in next week," he said.

"I completely understand. At some point things will blow up."

"Stacy, I wanted to know if you spoke to Tim."

"I didn't, but I did speak to his wife very briefly. I actually called him four times over the past three days before Gina actually picked up the phone last night."

Gina, Tim's wife, rarely spoke to his office colleagues. She was shy and lacked self-confidence dealing with people, which was uncharacteristic from her boisterous Italian family. Gina never answered the phone and usually let phone calls go right to the answering machine. It was rare that Stacy even spoke to Gina, which was a clear indication that something was very abnormal. Stacy had spoken to Gina only twice before and both were in person, once at Gina and Tim's wedding reception and the other when Stacy was invited to their house for their first son's christening.

"You spoke to Gina? What did she say?" he asked.

"Well, I thought he wasn't returning my call, and it turns out I was right. She mentioned that he isn't returning any phone calls, and he is very depressed. He doesn't understand what happened at the office and is very concerned for their well-being, and that it will be hard to get treatment while looking for a new job."

"Oh, I just called him and left a message. I wonder if he will call me back."

"I doubt it. In fact, don't count on it. I promised Gina I would call her back tonight, and I told her to call me if she needed anything."

Ryan and Stacy continued their conversation, and decided that they, including Lisa, should discuss ways they could help Tim. They were all eager to help in some way, but it would be difficult not knowing what help was needed. Stacy and Ryan nominated Lisa to be the point of contact because she was always the best at talking to people. He told Stacy that she should tell Lisa, because Lisa would probably kill him when she found out.

When he arrived home, his resolve to find other employment turned to clear action. He put aside his depression over the workplace and Tim's situation and decided to spend some time revising his resume and looking at the job boards. January would be a good time to find employment since positions often open up at the beginning of an employer's fiscal year. He made his way to his home office and in the process mentioned to Lisa that Stacy would be coming over for coffee in the next day or two to discuss Tim's situation. She asked him why, but he continued into the office as if he hadn't heard her.

He sat down at his computer and decided to retrieve his e-mail from his home account. He hadn't reviewed his e-mails in about five days, so he was sure there would be at least three hundred e-mails, with 95 percent being spam. As he scrolled down the list, he noticed one e-mail entitled, "Catching Up." Looking across the screen to the right he noticed the sender and was stunned. The sender, he thought, had some nerve to send an e-mail at this time and refer to it as "catching up." He believed the e-mail was simply a request of something rather than a friendly reengagement. After almost a year of no contact, Jay wanted to talk to him and catch up.

He was infuriated and angry at the person he trusted so much and considered his mentor, even if for such a very short time. Jay never said good-bye to him, no handshake, no call, and no e-mail. He just left and never even attempted to communicate. Ryan reached out numerous times with calls to Jay's cell phone and e-mails but never received a response or acknowledgement. It was a very poor way to handle the situation and Ryan felt Jay didn't deserve a response back to his e-mail.

Ryan's loyalty though wouldn't afford him the luxury of being spiteful by not responding. While he suffered from the pain of abandonment, he was simultaneously excited at renewing the contact he so desperately needed a year ago. He knew that having his mentor at this time could help him deal with the two situations at hand, and could possibly provide sorely needed guidance. Even if he couldn't, it would be nice—in an almost therapeutic sense—to talk to someone not closely involved. Ryan's biggest concern was reestablishing his close ties with him only to have the relationship disappear shortly thereafter. Another betrayal of trust might be difficult to overcome and ultimately kill the mentor relationship, but he decided to give J the benefit of the doubt and he opened the e-mail.

The e-mail had a friendly salutation and requested that Ryan call him as soon as he could to discuss an opportunity. It was a short two-line e-mail, with no details about the opportunity and more importantly no apologetic tone as he would have expected about the long gap of contact. It was a very detached e-mail for a person whom he admired and respected, and thought the feeling was mutual. He had expected Jay to at least provide some insight as to where he was and what he was doing or even inquire as to Ryan's current situation. Ryan was very disappointed, and debated whether he should respond since it didn't appear that Jay was very interested in a dialogue.

Once again, his loyalty ultimately proved victorious over his bitterness. Figuring there was more to be gained in reestablishing communication, he responded in kind with a short four line e-mail of his own that indicated his desire to discuss the opportunity and his pleasure to speak with Jay again. He offered to meet him for lunch the next day and provided his home number. He didn't think it was worth writing a long, drawn-out e-mail about how he felt, or even offer any indication of his displeasure at the way Jay handled his departure.

Later in the evening, as he was watching TV with Lisa, he mentioned the e-mail to her. She asked him how he felt about meeting up with Jay. He explained how much disappointment he felt, not at his departure, but at the complete detachment from a person whom he highly respected and one of the most important figures in his career. Facing him, if he accepted the invitation to lunch, would be a difficult task for him, and he told Lisa that he wasn't sure how he would handle it or even whether he would bring up how he felt about it. Lisa told him if the situation came up, he should ask J, because he deserved an answer and ultimately a good mentor relationship should be able to overcome some turbulence.

Lisa was a good listener and she knew exactly what Ryan was thinking before he even said a word. She knew how hurt he was because she remembered the anger he expressed during the discussions they had months after J's departure. They continued their discussion for another twenty minutes when they both heard his cell phone ring in the kitchen. Ryan jumped from his seat, leaving Lisa alone to suffer through the monotonous reruns on TV.

When Ryan returned five minutes later, he made his way back to his chair and looked at Lisa as if to continue their conversation, when she interjected, "That was Jay, wasn't it?"

"Why would you say that?" he asked.

"How many times do I need to tell you? Intuition."

"It could have been work or Stacy," he said with a smirk on his face.

"Who was it then?" she asked.

After a pause he replied in a soft voice, "It was Jay."

She laughed and asked whether he accepted the lunch meeting. Ryan told her that they would be meeting for lunch the next day, and that the short conversation was very friendly and relaxed. Jay had asked about the current situation at work, and how the members of the team were doing. Most of the tension Ryan felt about the meeting seemed to dissipate and his anxiousness turned more toward excitement at seeing his old friend. Lisa was certain the discussion would go well since the tone in his voice was more upbeat and confident and he seemed less focused on the detachment and more focused on a reunion.

Ryan woke up the next morning and was more optimistic than he had been for quite a while. He opened up his laptop computer at the kitchen counter and drank his coffee while reading the news on the Internet. He even decided to retrieve e-mails from work, which he hadn't done since the day he left the office. A few e-mails were from Eric, obviously demonstrating his authority by his demands and his constant need to send copies of the e-mail to twenty plus people. Ryan laughed at the tone of the e-mails and completely disregarded them. In a sense, he had become immune to Eric, there was nothing left for Eric to take from him, and Ryan no longer cared. The worst possible scenario would be his termination, and Ryan thought that wasn't such a bad thing at this point in time.

The next day, Ryan drove to the restaurant, arriving to lunch twenty minutes early. His obvious excitement led him to leave his house much earlier than necessary. Waiting in the parking lot, he decided to call Stacy to let her know he was meeting Jay. Upon hearing the news, she was very happy to hear that he inquired about them. Similar to Ryan, she was fond of him and was disappointed that he never remained in contact. Stacy told Ryan next time they go to lunch to be sure to invite her. Ryan decided not to mention the opportunity that Jay wanted to discuss, especially since he had no idea what it was.

Ryan then turned the conversation to discuss Tim.

"Did you speak to Gina last night?" he asked.

"Briefly, Gina mentioned that Tim is harboring a lot of resentment and that some of it was misplaced. When I asked her what that meant, she mentioned that he believes you protected me and abandoned him, and therefore we are both to blame."

"Wow, I'm shocked that he would think I would abandon him or that I was given the choice between the two of you. If I'd had any insight as to what was coming I would have told both of you."

"I know, but Gina said he gets this way sometimes, and will take it out on the world for a few weeks. She promised me she would talk to him and invite us over, and that it would just take some time for him to get over it."

"I hope so, I really want to talk to him, and explain everything," he said.

"Me too," Stacy replied.

Ryan closed the conversation and entered the restaurant. It was an old favorite of theirs when they worked together. The place served the best ribs on the planet and Jay was a rib fanatic. He would always joke about the ribs, calling them "gravity ribs" because the meat was so tender it would fall off the bone by the force of gravity.

As Ryan looked around to see if Jay was already seated, he noticed him in the back corner of the restaurant. Ryan began to chuckle at the sight of Jay, who noticed him as well, and raised his hand to flag him down. He was wearing the signature plastic bib given by the place with the name Ribz printed on it. He was like a kid who couldn't wait to get to his favorite eatery, anticipating a complete mess with barbeque sauce painted across the lower half of his face and coating every finger.

He walked over with a big smile and opened up bellowing "Hello."

"Hey, Ryan, it's great to see you," he said as he stood up and shook Ryan's hand.

"Great to see you too, I'm glad we could get together again," he replied.

They exchanged pleasantries and ordered beers as they sat down, each making small talk of how their families were and of their genuine delight at this hastily coordinated reunion. Ryan was surprised to find out that Jay was now out of the IT industry altogether and that he had formed a real estate company. He was buying and selling residential and commercial properties throughout the county and enjoying the role of an entrepreneur. He explained to Ryan that he left the field because of his disdain for the politics and the uncertainty that accompanied the executive-level positions. He said that, while it was nice for a while, when his boss retired, and they asked him to leave too, it seemed like a good opportunity to try something new.

Ryan was impressed, since an endeavor like that is very risky. He knew Jay was not risk averse, being an ex-marine, but it was still an impressive undertaking for anyone to leave the comfort of his or her field and attempt a radical new direction.

J regretted that he wouldn't be able to work with Tim and Stacy and especially Ryan in the future. He said that Stacy and Tim represented the foundation on which that department was built, but that Ryan was the architect of their success. He mentioned that of all the people who had ever worked for him, Ryan had the most potential, stretching far beyond the technology skills he possessed. He had never had a subordinate so interested in making his team work efficiently for their own benefit. Most of the people who had worked for him were more interested in satisfying their own ego and their insatiable appetite for technology.

Ryan still hadn't asked the question he wanted to pose, and instead, discussed Tim's situation, which would be a perfect lead-in to the situation at work. Jay was horrified to find out that Tim had throat cancer, and asked if there was anything he could do. Ryan also told him that Tim was fired about two weeks earlier.

"Why was he fired?" J asked.

"Well, that's a long story. Let's order first."

They examined the menu, although they weren't sure why. It wasn't as if they were going to order anything different. It would be the usual full rack of ribs, and the customary vegetable to say they ate healthy. When the two beers they ordered finally came, Jay proposed a toast to a speedy recovery for Tim, to which they raised their glasses and took a refreshing swig.

After they had ordered, Ryan explained what happened with Phil and Stacy starting from the time when Phil made reference to her homosexuality. Ryan didn't think it was proper to tell him the truth about her lifestyle so he just kept the conversation continuing as though it were rumors spread by Phil. If Stacy wanted him to know about her lifestyle, she could tell him. He then detailed the conversations that he had with Eric about his order to get Stacy under control and his implicit demand that he capitulate. Ryan may have taken some creative license, by inserting more colorful language than necessary, but the content was accurate. He recounted with the incident that led to the disciplinary action of Phil and Eric; the meetings with HR, Stacy, and the CIO; and the final conversation with Eric that culminated with Tim's termination.

Jay was appalled, but not surprised, by how the company allowed that behavior to continue and not take real action by terminating the group.

"That's exactly why I can't be in the industry. I don't want to deal with those situations anymore," he said. "I've seen too many situations that made people miserable and destroyed careers, and while I tried my best to rectify what I could, it was never fully under my control, and therefore, I resolved to work for myself so that I was responsible to, and for, no one."

It disappointed Ryan that he would no longer have the opportunity to work for him. He felt he had so much to learn and Jay was a person who had the experience, morals, and values to teach him how to be an excellent leader. Now, Ryan's hope for additional mentoring vanished, and he would be on his own. Ryan became increasingly confused as to how such a brilliant and honorable man could be forced from an entire industry. As Jay continued to speak, Ryan began to doubt Jay's leadership capabilities, which produced a cascading effect in his mind of how Jay originally disengaged and how the permanence of his abandonment was being manifested.

Ryan interrupted and said, "I have to ask you a question. You know I have a lot of respect for you and I appreciate your mentoring and everything you did for me when we worked together. But after you left, I was really disappointed and a bit angry that you never contacted me. I left you messages and sent e-mails asking what happened to you. Why didn't you ever respond?"

"Well, I received your messages and I appreciated them. However, I really wanted to distance myself from that place. I intended to contact you once I'd had time to think. For the first week or two, I gave some thought to my career and my future in the industry and I needed some time to myself."

"I understand, but it would have been nice to just send me an e-mail, saying you were fine. All of us, Tim, Stacy, and I, were really confused as to why you never called."

"That's very nice to hear that you guys were thinking of me," he replied, "but I also wanted to prevent you guys from any backlash because of your connection with me. I knew the crew replacing us and I had been informed of their intentions. They are a very vindictive bunch, as you well know by now."

"I still don't understand why you couldn't have sent us an e-mail just to stay in touch. All I'm saying is it would have been nice. I learned so much from you in a short period of time, and you taught me that leadership was more than just getting people to do their work," Ryan said.

"Thank you, Ryan, I appreciate the faith you placed in me, but I think the one thing you needed was to be on your own at that point, and not be tempted to use me as a crutch. I've kept in touch with other people at the company and I've been keeping tabs on you to make sure you were all right. Everyone says you're doing a stellar job."

"Who?" Ryan asked.

"You know James Ward?"

"You stayed in touch with the chief marketing officer?"

"Yes, he calls me from time to time and we have had lunch on occasion. He said you're doing a great job in spite of the morons running IT. He has a great deal of respect for you."

Ryan's disenchantment with this conversation was growing and he thought it best to slowly change the subject. It seemed as though the more he pressed, the more questions it raised. He couldn't understand why Jay would have more constant contact with the CMO than with his former team and he began to doubt most of what he was being told. He wasn't sure what he could trust anymore.

Jay then said, "I almost forgot the reason I wanted to speak to you. I've had some conversations with the CIO of SportsCentral USA, initiated by a mutual acquaintance, over the past few weeks who offered me an opportunity at SportsCentral USA for the head of development."

"Are you going to take it?" Ryan asked.

"No. I told them I could recommend an individual with impeccable qualifications who could build a team and help create a strategy for them. Are you interested?"

"Absolutely! Thank you," Ryan said.

Elated at the prospect of having an opportunity that would give him the chance he desperately wanted to employ the techniques he had learned and manage a group, he hoped, with the support of management. Ryan began to ask questions about the CIO's personality and potentially what he was looking to accomplish.

Jay detailed his conversations with the CIO and explained how the vice president of application development he had recently removed for failing to create an appropriate strategy to make the retailer a significant player in the online space. The CIO, according to Jay, had a vision for his company, but needed key personnel who could take his vision and make it a reality. He didn't want people who were high maintenance, but rather, entrepreneurial leaders who could challenge him and never be afraid to tell him when he was wrong. The plan, he articulated, was a very ambitious one that directly targeted Paltz, which explained why they originally reached out to Jay.

"It sounds like a great opportunity. I know I can do this," Ryan said.

"I know. That's why I recommended you. They want to hire very quickly, so be prepared to move. You will get an interview, because I already explained your current position and what you did for me—the resume is just a formality. Get me your resume and I will forward it to them."

The rest of the lunch was more upbeat than when they had initially sat down. Ryan was energized and excited, making the horrors of his current job almost seem miles away. As they were leaving the restaurant, they shook hands as Ryan said, "Thank you very much for thinking of me for the position, and please stay in touch. Maybe we can do lunch in a few weeks and I can invite Stacy and Tim."

"That would be great. I'm looking forward to it." he replied, and then departed. The only thing left for Ryan was to send his resume and wait to hear back from J and SportsCentral USA.

Two weeks went by, and Ryan hadn't heard anything from Jay or anyone from SportsCentral USA. He grew increasingly disillusioned, as he had sent three e-mails to him, with no response, in an attempt to arrange another lunch as they had agreed. He began to doubt whether the opportunity was authentic or if Jay had some ulterior motive, but that didn't make sense. He could think of no other possible motives Jay might have had.

Unfortunately, his patience was wearing out. While the anticipation of an interview continued to build, his current job was depressing him. The situation at the office remained unchanged and the all the participants seemed to progress as if nothing had never occurred. Eric and the management team now implicitly viewed Stacy and Ryan as pariahs, and they both knew it was a matter of time before something would transpire leading to their ultimate dismissal. There had been no other apparent actions taken by HR, and it seemed as though the matter had simply faded into the background.

Luckily, his patience was finally rewarded when he received the phone call for an interview. He was surprised to learn that the interview was being arranged directly by the CIO's office and not through HR. The woman who called carried a very soft voice with a Midwestern accent. She inquired as to his availability for the next morning, and since Ryan was eager to move forward, he agreed to arrive early the next morning. She thanked him for his amenable response and provided him with directions and instructions, which included proper attire and the CIO's expectations of the interview.

He became nervous that this was indicative of a very stiff company, and as such, would most likely not hire him due to his age, nor was he certain they could employ a modern technology strategy. Jay mentioned in their lunch about his age possibly being an issue; however, Ryan was determined not to let age become a factor. While some executives viewed youth as a liability due to lack of experience, he resolved to make it his greatest asset.

Later in the evening, sitting at his computer, he reviewed his resume, examining every detail, and deliberating over how he would answer potentially tough questions, especially those centered on his age. He Googled historical figures whose age could have played a role, in an attempt to find examples of the impact of young leaders throughout history, although he wasn't sure how well this approach would be received.

In the middle of proofreading his resume, the phone rang as if on cue to merely interrupt Ryan's work. Ryan picked up the phone and answered in an agitated manner. On the other end of the phone, Stacy, who had called to vent, gave Ryan a sarcastic earful about being polite to people who call his house. Ryan laughed and apologized, explaining that he was intently working on his resume for an interview the next day. Stacy was surprised by the interview, mostly because she had no knowledge of it and expected to be consulted. She knew there was no reason to be consulted on Ryan's life; however, she felt empowered to be his sounding board and wanted to make sure he was doing the right thing. Stacy was beginning to act like the big sister Ryan never had, and while he openly challenged it, he never diligently suppressed it.

He explained to Stacy with whom he was having the interview and how it transpired. Stacy demonstrated irritation at not knowing some of the details earlier. She thought Ryan should have told her about the prospect earlier, especially since it came about during the lunch conversation with Jay weeks ago. Ryan explained he didn't want to be too optimistic, and that he felt more comfortable just allowing things to happen, if they were to happen at all.

She was genuinely excited for him and she wished him luck and ordered him to call her immediately after the interview. She made it very clear, in the particular way Stacy could, that if he didn't call, she and Lisa would have a discussion about his behavior. Ryan laughed and promised he would call in the afternoon. Just before he was about to hang up, Stacy said, "One more thing."

Ryan acknowledged her and waited for her to continue. After a pause Stacy continued, "If you get the position, will you take me with you? I can't take this place anymore. I'm drowning."

"Stace, I don't want to look too far ahead but if I can, of course I would bring you. I just need to make sure there is a position available. Hopefully, I will have the authority to do that, but since I don't know if I will, and since I don't have the job yet, let's just cross that bridge when we come to it," Ryan replied.

"I just need to get out."

"Well, you should start sending out your resume."

"I already have, but I haven't received any responses."

"They will come, be patient. Let's see what happens tomorrow."

"OK, good luck. Is Lisa there?"

"Yes, I'll go get her," Ryan replied as he yelled to Lisa to pick up the phone.

The next morning, Ryan was ready for the interview. He arrived at the company headquarters twenty minutes early and progressed very quickly through the security desks and reception areas. It was eight o'clock in the morning and the floor was empty, except for a few, what appeared to be, executives. The receptionist greeted him warmly and asked him if he would like any coffee, to which he respectfully declined. He waited in the reception area for ten minutes before a voice he recognized asked for him. It was the woman he spoke to before to arrange the interview, the CIO's assistant.

"Ryan, good morning, please follow me."

"Thank you, ma'am," he replied, and then proceeded to follow her through the two glass doors leading to the executive offices. As he walked down the corridor, he noticed the offices were closed and dark, and couldn't help but notice that many of the executives weren't at the office yet, a stark contrast to the situation with his current employer. He continued to walk with the woman, who noticed the nervous look on his face and said, "Don't be nervous, you come highly recommended, and Mr. Wheeler is looking forward to meeting with you. Mr. Wheeler is a great person to work for and he is looking for honest, hard-working people to be a part of his team."

"Thank you again," he replied.

They continued to the corner office where she opened the door to Mr. Wheeler's office and proceeded to introduced Ryan. Ryan quickly glanced at the name plate adjacent to the door. He thought it odd that it only said A. Wheeler. Normally the nameplate would have the individual's full name.

"Welcome, Ryan, I'm so glad you could come on such short notice," Mr. Wheeler said as he stood up and reached across his desk to shake Ryan's hand. "Please have a seat. Can I get you anything—coffee, water?" he asked.

"No thank you, sir," he replied as he sat in the leather chair in front of Mr. Wheeler's desk.

The assistant closed the door behind Ryan, and he began to shuffle in his seat to become more comfortable. He glanced around the room and noticed quite a few pictures of what appeared to be his family, including soccer action shots of what he assumed were his daughters.

"Do you have children, Ryan?" Mr. Wheeler asked, noticing that Ryan was looking at the pictures of his children.

"Yes sir, one boy, a very active preteen. He plays almost every sport he can, but he loves baseball and soccer," Ryan replied.

"Wonderful. I have three children. Two twin daughters in college," he said as he turned their pictures toward Ryan. "Star soccer athletes, they are. I was very lucky; they received full scholarships to Duke and UCLA."

"Impressive," Ryan replied.

"Thank you. I also have one boy who is a senior in high school. Doesn't play sports but is set on political science and hopefully will be accepted shortly to Georgetown."

"That's an excellent school, he must be very bright."

"He isn't naturally academic but he works very hard, and I am very proud of his determination. Sometimes he is too stubborn; he gets that from his mother."

Ryan laughed with Mr. Wheeler and he was feeling more comfortable by his openness and unintimidating demeanor. Mr.

Wheeler provided Ryan with a brief history of himself not from an egotistic perspective but providing a perspective of the struggles he had faced as a young man. He mentioned how he grew up in Northern Virginia with a father who was a career diplomat and served the State Department just after World War II. He attributed most of his aggressiveness to the fact that he was the youngest of five boys who were all very competitive. He had a small tour in the navy but decided to pursue civilian interests after his first tour was completed. He stood six foot six and was very slender with a calm, relaxed face and a baritone voice, limited hair, and dark rimmed glasses. Ryan thought he could sit and have a beer with this man, but more importantly, he began to feel he could learn a tremendous amount from this man from his experiences. Mr. Wheeler's openness about his family and his life obviously made him a person one could have a conversation with, but there was something else about him that Ryan couldn't quite put his finger on.

After a few more minutes, Ryan began an explanation of his career and his various experiences. He provided some detail regarding his educational experiences, his interests, and his goals. Finally, Ryan concluded with the colleagues he had met and his great respect for Jay. He was hoping to avoid the conversation on why he was leaving, although, if asked, he was prepared with a very canned answer.

"Ryan, tell me what is the most important trait a person can have for this position?" Mr. Wheeler asked.

"Well, honestly, sir, it's not technology. While it's important to have a good technology base, what I have learned is that a person who is managing a group, such as the one you are hiring me for," Ryan said, fully aware he was attempting to subconsciously suggest whom Mr. Wheeler should hire, "is a person who can effectively manage through communication and resource alignment."

Mr. Wheeler's interest was noticeably piqued by the look he gave Ryan. He wasn't expecting a managerial answer. Ryan knew, almost everyone who applies for management positions in IT, focuses on technology expertise; however, there were many cases he studied in graduate school, where the leaders knew technology, but they weren't the experts, and they focused on becoming experts in management.

Ryan added, "The real trick is getting experts who can work together. Some technologists are very ego driven and keep solutions to themselves. I try to promote the opposite. Get bright people together and let them do their jobs and encourage them to impart their knowledge."

Mr. Wheeler was again noticeably impressed, and he put the resume down and began discussing management techniques with Ryan. They bantered back and forth about how to handle certain situations, and while they didn't exactly agree, they shared one belief that became readily apparent. Inaction and indecision were the worst traits for a manager.

"In all my years in this industry, I have never come across an individual like you. Many people have walked in here talking about technology and where the industry is going, but no one has ever just discussed management, and definitely not in the way you just did," he said.

They went on to discuss the company and the position for which they were vetting Ryan; however, it became clear to Ryan that he blew this interview away. They discussed the problems in the organization, and the way the team was currently structured. The conversation turned from inquisitive to consultative, which Ryan knew was a great sign.

The discussion went on for almost an hour and half before Mr. Wheeler said to Ryan, "When Jay mentioned you to me, I was very skeptical, especially because of your age. I know why he recommended you, and I can tell you that I don't see your age as a problem. I want to interview a few more people, but I must say you are at the top of my list."

"Thank you, sir."

Ryan left the interview feeling like he won the lottery. The position was perfect for him, and it gave him the opportunity to set a direction and execute on that vision. This was a great opportunity for his career, becoming a vice president of development, and there was no doubt he was excited about the opportunity. Ryan would just have to wait for the official word.

Waiting would be the most arduous task for him, but he never believed waiting would turn into uncertainty. Expecting to hear back from Mr. Wheeler within a week, he was distressed when six weeks went by with no direct communication from him. He left a message after the third week, and after the fourth week, he finally spoke to Mr. Wheeler's assistant, who mentioned that he was out of the country and wouldn't be back for another week. Still, he thought, by now he should have heard something at least via e-mail.

He became disconcerted at the prospect of not being selected for the position. Everything, he thought, lined up perfectly for him, and he was under the impression that the position needed to be filled quickly. There was no indication to him that this process should have taken this long, and now he began to feel as though he was the problem, and that he shouldn't have expected anything.

It was now early March, and the situation at the office wasn't getting any better. Ryan was tired of fielding questions from Stacy about whether or not he had heard back from the company. While he kept a positive outlook, Stacy knew it was getting to him and so she ceased her inquiries, sensing the subject was a bit sensitive. Each day would be just another day of swimming in molasses where there was no excitement and no direction, and senior management was simply massaging their egos. The saving grace for Ryan was his determination to finish his MBA, which provided him with the focus he needed to get through the days.

Ryan was nearly complete with his MBA with only his current class remaining, which was an independent study with a professor of management whose specialty was strategy. He was tasked with researching various strategies such as Porter's generic strategies of an organization whereby companies can either be cost leaders or differentiators but not both simultaneously. He also researched the blue ocean strategy by Kim that focused on creating value in areas where competitors were not likely to follow such as Southwest Airlines and Cirque de Soleil.

In researching these theories, he was fascinated by the similarities and differences contained within them. Once again, he was faced with the reality that there was no magic bullet in creating and implementing strategy. With so many different strategic concepts, what was certain was the fact that there was absolutely no certainty. This realization triggered another image for Ryan. Sun Tzu, he remembered, in his classic *Art of War*, provided guidelines by which a general or commander could increase their odds of victory in any conflict. He remembered the importance of a commander's ability to utilize his troops effectively, which meant employing the skills with perfect timing. This meant that a commander must avail himself or herself with information about where the battles would be, what the terrain would be like, and what the environmental situation was. Armed with that information, Ryan focused his attention on the various levels of organizational conflict: intradepartmental, interdepartmental, and multi-organizational.

Managing all of the conflict would be very difficult for a manager at any level, but what Ryan understood from his research was simply the fact that the recognition of the existence of all of these conflicts was a principle of successful management. Armed with that information, he postulated managers should attempt to understand and resolve conflict within their departments or direct reports. Managers also need to be wary of competing interests by other departments that could implicitly or explicitly sabotage their departments. Managers should be astute enough to recognize normal competitive behavior among organizations and their impact on projects, deliverables, and other assets. Finally, managers should be aware that competition extends to indirect competitors such as other industries vying for both limited resources from customers or limited availability of assets, e.g., human capital, whereby other companies seek to poach quality resources from other organizations.

Ryan presented all of the information to his professor to proofread the concept prior to finalizing his paper. The professor, impressed by the research, allowed him to proceed with the paper and made some suggestions to enhance the content. The professor also allowed him to progress down a track of researching a particular, more dynamic method of implementing any given strategy derived. The work, based on presentations given by Col. John A Boyd, USAF, demonstrated how to organize and direct a team to execute a given strategy by following and reinforcing the key principles of trust, intuition, mission, and agreement. What struck Ryan was the simplicity of the principles, how connected they were to the way great companies, such as Amgen and Walgreens, operate, as shown by the research conducted by Jim Collins for his book *Good to Great.*

Ryan was interested in this type of information. It was practical knowledge that he could utilize and if employed properly would make everyone, including himself, successful. He craved the information that would help him become an elite manager, the type of leader sought after by companies to help turn around problems. This type of situation raised his adrenaline levels and enabled him to look beyond the problems of his current situation.

By now though, his focus on his final class was the only thing keeping him sane. Two months passed from the original interview, and there was no word from Mr. Wheeler's office, until late one Thursday evening, when he received a phone call directly from Mr. Wheeler. He phoned Ryan's cell phone specifically after hours to have a slightly longer conversation. Driving home from work, Ryan answered the phone, trembling slightly, as he knew what the call was about and he hoped the conversation would be positive. He quickly deduced, however, that it would be odd if the CIO were calling him just to reject him. While that was a possibility, he thought that would be too sadistic, especially for the man Ryan met eight weeks prior.

"Ryan, I wanted to let you know that at first I had serious reservations about your ability to handle this position, primarily due to your age," Mr. Wheeler said.

"I understand, sir, but as I mentioned, I look at my youth as an asset, it fuels the fire in me to be aggressive and persistent. I guarantee I won't be complacent," he responded.

"I am fully aware of that. I checked your references and I am very impressed. I made one final call to Jay and we spoke about you at length. Your philosophy toward management and your ability to execute, make you an asset to any organization. If you are willing to learn to temper some of your aggressiveness, I would be more than willing to work with you."

"As long as I can be myself, I would love the opportunity to work with you and learn from you."

"I would expect nothing less. Ryan, I will be sending you an offer letter this evening in an e-mail. I would appreciate a quick response, we have much to do," he concluded.

"Thank you sir, I'm really looking forward to working with you."

Ryan hung up the phone and joyfully yelled. He couldn't believe that he was about to receive the opportunity he had long sought. He couldn't wait to get home to tell Lisa so he called her and, before she had a chance to say hello, he began to rattle off the entire conversation, barely coming up for air. Lisa could hear the excitement in his voice and was ecstatic for him, believing in her heart he truly deserved this chance.

The next morning, Ryan prepared his resignation letter and planned how he would handle his exit. Receiving the e-mail the night before was the final punctuation mark, and his entire body language changed literally overnight. He hadn't called Stacy yet; he reserved that for an in person discussion.

At the office, he waited for Stacy to arrive to tell her the good news. He decided to wait until after he spoke to Stacy to submit his resignation letter to Eric. He wanted to ensure that Stacy had a heads-up just in case Eric went on one of his tirades, and since it was a Friday the weekend would provide a buffer.

When Stacy came in to the office, he immediately motioned to her to come with him for a cup of coffee. Arriving at the elevator, Stacy turned to Ryan and said, "What's going on? You are way too chipper this morning."

Ryan didn't say a word but signaled to her that he was waiting for the elevator to arrive. When the elevator arrived, the door opened and they proceeded into the empty elevator. As soon as the door closed, Ryan opened his mouth to speak, but barely uttered a sound when Stacy jumped in and said, "You got the job, didn't you!"

"How the hell did you know that?" Ryan asked in complete disbelief that his surprise was now thwarted.

She looked at him and said, "How many times do I have to tell you?"

"I know the intuition thing again," Ryan begrudgingly replied.

"Actually, I'm kidding. Lisa called me last night," she replied.

"Hell, I should just post my entire life on MySpace."

"Congratulations, Ryan. That's really great," she replied.

They talked about the new position, and Ryan explained what he would be doing and what Mr. Wheeler explained to him. Stacy was genuinely happy for him and concurred with Lisa's opinion that he deserved a shot. Then her body language began to tell a different story, which Ryan picked up.

"What's the matter, Stacy?"

"I can't help but think what would've been here, had we been given the chance. I also think of Tim all the time and our entire team."

"I do too, but it will come around. I know Tim isn't yet ready to speak to us or at least me, but I have faith that he will. He's just going through a tough time."

"Please take me with you," Stacy said, changing the subject but stating what she really felt.

"Stace, as soon as I get a chance, I promise I will bring you over," he replied.

"Anything, I just need to get out of this hellhole, and I can't seem to get any interviews."

"Stace, you're one of my key people. The first chance I get for a position that fits you, I will bring you in," he replied.

With that final comment, they began to walk back to their desks. Stacy was looking for some reassurance that Ryan wanted her to work for him. It was an opportunity for her to gauge how much Ryan valued her insomuch as it was to get a job in another firm.

Arriving back at his desk, Ryan noticed that Eric was roaming the halls. Instead of sitting down, he grabbed the two envelopes on his desk containing his resignation and walked toward Eric. When he finally caught up with him, he asked Eric for a quick moment of his time. Eric reluctantly agreed and proceeded to his office.

Eric entered his office and asked Ryan why he wanted to speak with him.

Ryan decided to just open up with the resignation and handed one envelope to Eric and said, "Eric, I just wanted to let you know that I am resigning from the company effective two weeks from Monday." This was a bit of déjà vu for Ryan, and he expected the worst; however, that didn't happen.

"Well, sorry to see you go, but you don't need to wait until Monday. Why don't you just bring me your laptop and you can leave today," he said in a polite voice.

"OK, let me go back, I'll pack up my things and leave," he replied.

Ryan left the office, packed up a small box of his personal items and logged off his computer. He brought the computer back to Eric's office, with Stacy watching intently almost the entire time. As he handed the laptop to Eric, Eric wished him luck. Ryan wasn't quite finished yet; he had to make a stop at HR to officially close his tenure.

He went to HR and looked for Ms. Whyte, who luckily was at her desk. He explained the situation to her, and provided her with a copy of the resignation letter. She was appalled that Eric arbitrarily told him to leave without consulting HR first. She conducted a brief exit interview and explained to him what his benefits were and that he would be paid for the two weeks. She would ensure that his file was updated properly and she would personally ensure, as best she could, that his file wasn't tarnished.

Finally, she asked Ryan if he had any questions that she would be able to answer about benefits or the exit interview. She handled the entire process very professionally and if he had thoughts of any questions, Ms. Whyte had probably answered already. She wished him luck on his new endeavor, but just before she concluded the conversation, she placed her pen on the table and paused.

"Ryan, I want to thank you for speaking up on behalf of your employee. It took a great deal of courage to do that, in light of the atmosphere here."

"Actually, I've been in a position once before, where I didn't speak up and it became much harder for me to deal with later," Ryan replied.

"While generally, we, in HR want to do the right thing, and many times we do, but it really takes executive-level support to follow through on these initiatives, which we just don't have here. Not all companies are the same, and we really try to do the best we can to protect our employees."

It was odd how the conversation seemed to turn more apologetic on her part. He never expected an apology because he understood the dynamics, and he always thought she did a fantastic job.

Ryan said, "I knew you were there for Stacy and me over the past several months, but the realization was, that unless there was another egregious act, there wasn't much more you could do. You and your team were exemplary in dealing with the situation, and I want you to know that I appreciated it."

She thanked him for his honesty and understanding. There was obviously more to the situation than was readily apparent, but it didn't matter, he was off to a new company to start fresh. They shook hands and he walked out of the conference room, but as he exited HR, he was surprised to see Eric walking toward the double glass doors. Ryan galloped the last two steps and pulled the door open, smiled, and motioned with his hand inward to allow Eric to come in first. Eric's face turned red as he had not expected Ryan to be in HR, and he was probably especially perturbed at Ryan's flippant grin.

For the first time since he met Eric, Ryan was in control. He was in control of the entire situation and he knew Eric hated it. As much as Eric wanted him to go, it was all about control for Eric. He was never able to get Ryan to succumb, and now there was no chance; in fact, now they would be direct competitors, although Eric didn't know that yet.

Ryan reflected on the situation and realized two key things. He contemplated the amount of control one actually has, and believed that the more one tries to control a situation, the more control one actually loses. It seemed contradictory; however, something seemed right about it. Eric always tried to control everyone, and although he was able to exert some authority and have some people succumb, he could never really control them. Leadership doesn't require followers to succumb, it requires followers to do what is necessary, and in some cases without being told. In those cases the leader controls the situation, without really controlling it.

Finally, Ryan thought of a question Ms. Whyte asked him during his exit interview. She asked him whether he learned anything, which surprised him. He answered her by telling her that he learned a lot from Jay and others in the company, but not much from Eric. However, he couldn't help but think as he was driving home, that he learned some of the most valuable lessons from Eric. He summed up all of what he learned from Eric in one simple statement. He learned what ***not*** to do.

Chapter 7

CHALLENGE

Three months after Ryan had finally landed in the new opportunity, he thought about the events in his professional and personal life that had transpired over the past year. He weathered the storm of a furious and unpredictable superior, worked through personnel issues as well as he could, attempted to keep his team motivated under the specter of vengeance, and succumbed to the reality of the frailty of life itself. It was, most definitely, a life-changing period for him. He knew through all of the adversity, there were lessons he was required to learn and he would need to employ those lessons in order to make things better for him and his new team.

He recognized the signs of discontent among his new team but allowed them time to adapt to his style of management. It was expected that there would be some resistance to an outsider taking the helm of the department and even reasonable for them to be skeptical about Ryan, especially in light of his age. However, everyone, including Ryan, had received ample time to adjust, and now it was time to turn the department around.

Ryan's management team had five direct reports with a total of sixty-one people in his department. His direct reports were a seasoned group who had been with the company an average of fourteen years. The previous head of the department, Mr. Tony Daegle, had been with the company twenty-four years before he retired. There was a lot of speculation around his retirement based on his confrontations with Mr. Wheeler, who had at the time of Mr. Daegle's departure, been the CIO for only a year and half. Ryan, having the unwelcome experience of observing these types of situations before, understood how some retirements are engineered. The team was sympathetic and a bit disappointed at Tony's departure, and Ryan's introduction compounded more distress and anxiety in the organization. Mr. Wheeler never consulted anyone about Ryan's hiring, nor did he seek any input into his hiring from anyone on the team. Ryan knew, based on a conversation he and Mr. Wheeler had prior to his hiring, that his actions were designed to prohibit any negativity toward any prospective candidate. Mr. Wheeler understood that changing this department would require a radical and possibly risky move to remedy the inertia created over the years.

Ryan wasn't sure whether the team would accept him; however, he didn't need their acceptance, he needed them to produce, and it really didn't matter whether they liked him or not. He questioned, however, whether he could trust them or if they would ever trust him. Eventually, he believed, he could come to trust some members of the team, but he needed to be wary of subtle sabotage, or worse, outright sabotage. If he could garner their trust, then he would be successful, thereby developing this perceived weak and ineffective team into a strong, positive, and valued group.

Of the five direct reports, Bill Lavicik, the director for Web development, was the most outspoken and most confrontational. He had developed a very strong relationship with Mr. Deagle over the years, and resented, very openly, Ryan's presence in the position. Out of respect for his feelings, Mr. Wheeler allowed Bill to express himself without retribution, however, he made it very clear that he was to be professional, courteous and, in no uncertain terms, perform his duties at the level expected of his position. Bill had no issue with the directive and he knew how to do his job well; he did, however, take full advantage of the privilege afforded him. Mr. Wheeler knew his allowance of Bill's attitude could invite disaster; however, he needed to deal with Bill in a very sensitive manner.

Bill believed he was the only candidate for the VP position since he had twenty-one years with the company. Furthermore, he became incensed that the selection went to an individual fifteen years his junior. His attitude of entitlement was exactly the reason why Mr. Wheeler refused to consider him for the position. Technically, Bill was adept at his job but had no working knowledge of the newer technologies that could meet Mr. Wheeler's strategic vision. Mr. Wheeler also suspected that the purported success of Mr. Deagle and Bill was the result of an effective spin campaign, and that many of the systems were fraught with deficiencies, which would ultimately be exposed.

Rebecca Sey, in charge of project management, and James Southard, responsible for mainframe applications, also now reported into Ryan and had twelve years and twenty years, respectively, with the company. Both had some reservations about Ryan, but did not demonstrate, at least outwardly, any disdain for his selection. Each of them had issues with Mr. Wheeler's direction, but they were loyal and knew how to execute their jobs very well. Rebecca had struggled within the company for a promotion to her position, and felt constrained by the glass ceiling in place at the company. Ryan's hiring simply proved that point, even though she never really believed Mr. Wheeler would promote her to that position. James, on the other hand, was very complacent in his position and had contemplated retirement on many occasions over the past two years. The increased politics and belligerent attitudes in the office had become more of a nuisance and, at fifty-five years of age, he relished the thought of an early retirement.

The final two managers reporting into Ryan had each been with the company just under ten years, but with smaller responsibilities and much lighter resumes. Robert Fitzpatrick, who preferred to be called Bob and was five years Ryan's senior, handled new technologies, but was limited by Bill in terms of responsibilities. Mr. Deagle had always maintained a dotted line relationship between Bob and Bill, in effect, giving the perception that Bob reported to Bill. While Bob's responsibilities overlapped Bill's responsibilities directly in very few areas, he never had the authority to completely control what his team delivered. Bill always took credit and, in many cases, usurped Bob's authority, and assimilated his accomplishments where it was advantageous for him to do so. Unfortunately, the previous management condoned this behavior and, while Mr. Wheeler attempted to curb it, the pressures of other priorities were too great for him to deal with smaller personnel issues. He hired Ryan with the expectation that he would effectively deal with these types of organizational issues.

Finally, there was Michael Wilkes, who was two years Ryan's junior, and was put into a new position last year. He was responsible for corporate reporting, which produced information for various departments across the organization. His department had a small group of five developers who basically worked on mundane tasks designed to support the fringe elements of the organization. Their group had no real authority and worked on items the organization considered of little value. Both Bob and Michael were very pleased with the changes Mr. Wheeler implemented and they believed there would be increased personal opportunities to learn and grow within the organization.

The problems for Ryan were not just limited to the obvious dysfunctional structure of his team, although it would be daunting in the immediate future. The group had some unique personalities and opinions that he would need to work with; however, bringing the department to a significantly higher level of performance would be a challenge.

Ryan's challenges became very clear during a private status meeting with Mr. Wheeler less than two months after his arrival. Mr. Wheeler provided Ryan with his vision for the department and issued his mandate. Mr. Wheeler focused on three major improvements for the department, which included streamlining operational activity in the department, replacing the antiquated point of sale and inventory system, and creating an online shopping site rivaling the top online retailers in the country. Secretly, Ryan chuckled at this plan because, by itself, it was a sound set of initiatives, but the expected twelve-month time frame for its completion was unrealistic. It also felt like a bit of déjà-vu for Ryan.

During Ryan's one-on-one meeting with Mr. Wheeler, where he received the mandate, he told Mr. Wheeler he would come back with a plan for the implementation, but made no promises as to the date due to the aggressive time line. He clarified, briefly, why he thought the date might present an issue; however, he would research options very quickly and provide a recommended approach. Ryan quickly countered his boss's discontent with the need to absorb the direction, examine the personnel, establish the process, and ensure proper implementation sensitive to the time line, while deliberate enough to deliver a quality product. Mr. Wheeler passively agreed and reserved judgment until Ryan completed his assessment.

Ryan contemplated the effort required by the team, especially given the circumstances surrounding the mandate and the team's continued apprehension with him. Understanding they needed a common goal, he focused all of his attention on ensuring their understanding of what Mr. Wheeler was asking. During his next weekly status meeting, he solicited feedback from his team trying to ascertain their thoughts about the projects. His attempts at extracting opinions continued to fail, due to their experiences of condemnation and suppression, which prompted him to ask one final question to his team.

"Does anyone here think this set of initiatives is feasible?" he asked.

Bill immediately stood up and in a daunting and deliberate voice as if to demonstrate his authority within the group and suppress any opposition to his position, said, "Ryan you're a nice kid, but you need to understand when Mr. Wheeler says it needs to be done in twelve months, there is no debate. Let me run these projects and I will deliver what Mr. Wheeler wants."

Bill was a very large man, standing six foot, four inches and weighing almost three hundred and twenty pounds, who used his size as best as he could to intimidate any dissenters in his vicinity. He would often make sure people's opinions were swayed prior to any meeting to ensure any objectors could be handled effectively. Since many executives had implicitly allowed his behavior, he became emboldened over the years.

Ryan, stunned by Bill's brazen ridicule, had two choices; deal with the comment either immediately or privately. Unfortunately, he had no time to debate the issue and he responded almost instinctively, "Bill, first, don't refer to me as 'kid'. I'm sure you understand how unprofessional that sounds, and second, it's not accurate, although I'm flattered you think I'm younger than I actually look."

The response generated laughter from the group and created an atmosphere in the room Ryan had yet to experience in SportsCentral. Their body language signaled approval and he believed from their expressions that the comedic and subtle but stern reprimand was long overdue. Bill wasn't too pleased with Ryan and he took issue, although silently, with the tacit approval from the people in the room.

Ryan, attempting to play down the confrontation, continued, "Let's get down to business, I'll ask again and this time I would like someone else to answer. Does anyone think this is feasible?"

The conversation gradually increased as the team became more comfortable. The interaction among Rebecca, Michael, and Robert, and ultimately James was very constructive, and while Bill did participate in the conversation, he was much more reserved than his original opening salvo. Throughout the meeting, they interacted in a reserved but positive debate trying to determine the exact requirements as well as the feasibility of Mr. Wheeler's requests. The team agreed in principle that they could complete some of the projects in the period proposed, however, they could not complete the work in the requested time frame.

The meeting turned south at that point, when Bill mentioned that their opinions didn't matter and if the CIO requested something to be completed in a particular time frame, it was their job to accomplish the task. Ryan immediately disagreed. The projects themselves weren't important and neither were the time lines, what was important was to understand the business rationale for doing the projects, including the why and when.

"That's not for us to decide, we are just tasked with getting the job done," Bill stated.

Ryan responded, "We need to change the way we approach these things. We are assigned tasks and projects because the business needs it for a purpose. In the same way as you cannot fill two pools with a single hose, let's understand the purpose and maybe we can fill the right pool first."

"I've never seen any of our managers go for that. How do you know Mr. Wheeler will go for it?" Rebecca asked.

"I don't, but I need to try. Everything can be negotiated; we need to state the facts, understand what's important, and focus our efforts there."

There were a few hesitant smiles from the group, who were more than a bit apprehensive and cautious not to be too excited about the prospect of Ryan's approach succeeding. Ryan could tell that no manager had ever solicited opinions or comments from the group before, and there comes a time in an organization when the cries, which fall on deaf ears, are simply silenced by futility, which clearly explained the collective hesitancy to speak up. He hoped to change things from both perspectives since it was imperative to ensure truthful and abundant communication.

He was still very uncertain about the trust he may have garnered or the trust he could place in the individuals, especially Bill; however, he stood up from his seat and concluded the meeting with one final statement.

"I know many of you have reservations about my ability to handle this position. I will not try to convince you with words about my capabilities, but I will demonstrate my ability through actions. I assure you, I will do everything I can to effect change in the organization, and I promise I won't disappoint you."

By itself, the comments were benign, but for a few of the team members, it showed a great deal of change. Not once did he mention what *they* had to do, instead, he focused on what he would do for them. His words demonstrated the difference he was trying to bring to the organization. Across the room, almost everyone sat attentively as Ryan spoke and they all refrained from doodling or letting their attention wander, as Ryan's words captivated them. For some it may have been a sign of hope for a better team, while for others it may have been simply an instinctive response of watching a disaster unfolding. Either way it appeared as though everyone in the room was ready to give Ryan the benefit of the doubt that he could succeed where others wouldn't try.

Over the next few days, Ryan compiled all his notes and gathered some metrics from his team. In less than forty-eight hours, he formulated a presentation that he would give to Mr. Wheeler that outlined a plan for action based on the mandate. He knew it wasn't what Mr. Wheeler was expecting, but he needed to do it and fulfill the commitment he made to his team. The lengthy presentation was thirty-five pages and, although he knew he should condense it, he felt there was no way to make the case in fewer pages. It was imperative to provide the summary strategy in the first two pages and the metrics supporting the recommendation in the last fifteen. The middle pages served as a chronology of tactics to implement to arrive at a successful conclusion.

Ryan intently reviewed the presentation he put together in the past two days; however, there was no more time for edits, as Mr. Wheeler had called him into his office to review the strategy. He resolved to go in and be firm in his stance, while ensuring he was amenable on any issue of critical importance. Ryan wanted this time. This was the time he needed. This was the time for Ryan to prove what leadership was—doing the right thing at the right time for the right reason.

Mr. Wheeler had been expecting Ryan when he walked into his office. But Ryan didn't expect the two other senior executives in the room, the SVP of marketing, Maureen Woo, and the SVP of logistics, Jim Blake. Maureen had been with the company four years and had extensive experience in retail marketing. She led one of the most successful online campaigns ever, netting the company a revenue increase of 25 percent last year. She was a very strong-willed person who knew what she wanted and she knew how to make things happen. Jim was a more methodical person, very operations oriented. He managed to cut logistics and delivery expenses by 5 percent last year. He had been with the company ten years and was an expert in managing transportation systems. Together, their departments constituted about 80 percent of the entire IT workload, which was exactly why they were in the room.

Mr. Wheeler apologized to Ryan for having the other executives in the room, but he felt it would be more expeditious to have the key stakeholders in the room. Caught off guard, Ryan nevertheless knew he prepared for Mr. Wheeler and, therefore, he could deal with anything. Nothing in his report was political and only he was responsible if the report had any shortcomings. In short, he felt prepared for this situation.

He briefly introduced himself to the executives for, while he had met them before, they didn't really know him. He spent only a few minutes on his prior experience, and instead focused time on his thoughts around delivery of projects. In an almost professorial fashion, he related the main characteristics of successful delivery with a family of three sisters. He called the younger sisters quality and timing, while he called the big sister purpose.

Maureen laughed and said, "So you mean they fight each other all the time."

Maureen and James laughed since each of them had had siblings. James had five brothers and sisters and Maureen happened to be the big sister with two younger sisters, and they both clearly understood the analogy. Ryan never intended for his line to be a joke, but it was a great icebreaker. Unfortunately, she spent the next five minutes discussing sibling rivalries and it took some coaxing from Mr. Wheeler to get Maureen back in tow.

Ryan said, "It's a great analogy, the sisters are always fighting but, while no sister is really more important, it's the big sister, purpose that serves as the guide. If our work is guided by purpose and we focus on quality and timing, everyone will be successful."

The room seemed to buy in to his comments, at least for now, and he thought that at this point he had laid a foundation, albeit serendipitous. He would now need to deliver the report that demonstrated why all the projects couldn't be done in the time expected and provide the reasoning behind it. His nerves were a bit frayed at the thought of giving bad news to three of the most senior executives in the company.

He opened his presentation to the title slide, which displayed on the very large forty-two-inch flat screen plasma TV in Mr. Wheeler's office. The three executives were sitting at a round table about fifteen feet directly in front of the wall where the screen was positioned, and Ryan was standing in front of the table to present his findings and recommendations. With a confident voice, he opened up by saying he was not going to meet their expectations, choosing to be perfectly clear immediately. The stunned looks on their faces told a story that probably could have been a Stephen King novel, but Ryan continued, "I cannot in good conscience tell you something that you want to hear, if I do not believe it is something that can be achieved or should be attempted. I beg your indulgence for patience as I demonstrate what I believe to be a formidable strategy that enables us to maintain our staffing level, minimize consulting costs, deliver the projects in a timely fashion, and minimize the risk to the organization."

He seemed to grab their attention well and he didn't offer an opportunity for questions at the opening. Quickly, he progressed into the list of projects that Mr. Wheeler had asked of him and it was here that his slides introduced the concept of purpose. Why did we need to replace point of sale systems? What was the reasoning behind a new inventory system? What was the organization's goal to create a premium-level online shopping system? More importantly, he asked why the work should be done simultaneously.

When he asked whether they all thought the work should be completed in parallel, their replies resounded unanimously affirmative due to the highly competitive nature of the marketplace. His response questioned their reasoning and silenced the room.

"If we do them all at the same time, how do we know all three will work together properly? Shouldn't they work in concert with each other?"

"Of course," Maureen replied.

"Then we should ensure key systems work first because if one system fails the others will fail as a result, and if that happens we would not be able to compete effectively," Ryan replied.

Ryan thought they should have realized what he saying before he brought it up, but from the looks on their faces he wasn't sure. The three projects came from three different departments: retail, online, and logistics; it was easy for their intricate relationships to be an oversight since the time lines were very aggressive. Each department focused on their own productivity metrics without fully understanding the downstream consequences across the organization. There had been no coordination among the departments, which could prove fatal as other companies had realized.

He went on to explain that he examined the symptoms of the problem with the company's falling market share, poor customer satisfaction, inability for customers to get the right product, shrinking margins, and declining productivity of warehouse workers and in-house store workers. Based on a report written six months ago by Mr. Blake,

70 percent of the problems involved the inefficiency of the logistics system.

"You actually read my report?" Mr. Blake asked.

"Ryan asked me last month for the business plans and other related reports given to senior management in the past year," Mr. Wheeler responded.

"Yes, sir, I wanted to understand how the business works and what direction it wants to take. In order to do my job better, I need to understand how everything works, maybe not at a detailed level, but at the appropriate level that will enable me to understand how and why the business runs."

"I'm impressed," Mr. Blake said.

Ryan smiled, knowing he was on a roll, but he needed to finish the presentation and close the sale. Unfortunately, he was still only on the first page. Ryan continued with the report that Mr. Blake wrote, and demonstrated that if they implemented a new inventory system that enabled easier integration using standard technologies, they could guarantee time lines of orders to both online and retail store customers; manage inventory levels, which would impact margins positively; potentially increase customer satisfaction; and, among other things, help streamline the IT department. The caveat, he said, was that they needed to agree to postpone the point of sale system and the online system until they were in the final phase of testing of the inventory system—a period of about nine months—in order to divert key resources and position the best technologists and subject matter experts within the organization.

"But I need the online system soon or we will continue to lose market share. I've been told it will take approximately one year to build a new online system, not to mention the two years to build the point of sales system!" Maureen exclaimed.

"I understand; however, if we have a solid inventory system that can integrate with other systems well, the savings in time and money could be as much as 30 percent, maybe even more. I could explain all the technical reasons why if you like, but I am sure you would find that discussion as boring as I do," Ryan replied.

"You're saying that the online system could then be completed in a seven- to nine-month time frame and reduce its cost by almost half a million dollars?" she asked.

"That's the general idea. Understanding how all the business processes interrelate and then working to rectify the major hurdles first will enable us to develop technologies much sooner and meet the needs of the organization."

Mr. Wheeler, sensing a bit of apprehension, discussed the need for the senior executives to coordinate their needs as part of a broader strategy. He acknowledged that when pressure is being exerted, it is easy for anyone to lose sight of the larger picture and that while each project appears different and services different parts of the company, each of the projects is inexorably linked and, therefore, should be considered as such.

The team in the room began to discuss the importance of each of their projects, what should come first, arguing their points with each other, and discussing the benefits to the company. Ryan was perplexed at the intense discussion because the answer to him was so obvious; however, he enjoyed listening to the conversation and the debate. He wondered whether this type of discussion had occurred before.

Mr. Wheeler stopped the conversation and said to Ryan, "Thank you for the presentation, Ryan. I know you're not finished, but I believe the discussion we are having is at a pivotal point. I would like to have you present your findings again later, maybe today or tomorrow, if you don't mind."

"I don't mind at all. I'll make myself available," Ryan replied.

As he exited the office he overheard Mr. Wheeler on the phone with Julia, his assistant, asking her to please arrange a meeting with the six top executives of the company. Apparently, Ryan's message seemed to get through and he was elated. He convinced his management to reconsider—at the very least—their overall strategy for the projects and the recommendation being a team effort was the icing on the cake. Hoping the other executives would at least be open to his options, he realized he probably had done something no one at his level had done before in the company. He said no.

When Ryan arrived back at his office, Rebecca noticed him enter his office and left her cubicle to inquire about what happened. She noticed by her watch that Ryan arrived thirty minutes earlier than expected, which meant either they canceled the meeting or it went horribly. She had been skeptical that his strategy would work and, in fact, had mentioned to others in the group that he was too green to realize it.

Knocking on his door frame, she said, "You got pummeled, didn't you?"

"No, actually it went very well," he replied.

"But you're back so early, what happened?"

"Well, Maureen and Jim were apprehensive at first, but Mr. Wheeler received the message loud and clear, and slowly he made them understand what I was proposing. In fact, he excused me from the meeting and had Julia call a meeting with the other executives to discuss options."

"Well," she said in a skeptical tone, "don't get your hopes up. This company doesn't respond to change very well."

"If I don't try, then what use am I? If we don't raise the bar collectively we will never grow, and I have to risk my job if I intend to do it well."

Rebecca was silent, because she still believed that it was a futile effort. Here was this young manager who came from the outside and is willing to risk being rebuked because he believes he can make a difference. She had never seen a manager in any company take a stand in the same manner as Ryan. She knew he potentially risked his job and standing within the company just by even the thought of differing with the most senior executives in the company. It appeared though, at least for the moment that Ryan had succeeded.

Later that afternoon, Ryan received a call from Mr. Wheeler's office asking him to stop by prior to leaving for the day. Ryan quickly made his way to the office unsure of the topic of conversation. He was hoping to receive approval for his plan, although he didn't think a decision would have been made that quickly. When Ryan reached Mr. Wheeler's office, he firmly knocked on the door frame, and received an acknowledgment from Mr. Wheeler, who was on the phone, to proceed in.

Once he was off the phone, he began to tell Ryan how well the meeting went this morning, and the subsequent meetings afterward. Although he hadn't consulted every major stakeholder of the projects, the numbers reported in his presentation gave him ample evidence to gain the support of Maureen and Jim. He explained how impressed he was with Ryan to have the intestinal fortitude to stand up for what he believed in such a professional manner and he now understood why Jay originally recommended Ryan without hesitation.

Mr. Wheeler changed the subject rather rapidly to inform him of a potential problem within his organization. Prior to the meeting this morning, Bill had come to his office to alert him of what he believed was a "potential issue of enormous consequences for the company." He disagreed vehemently on how Ryan was handling the department and

Project Focus, as they had now labeled the strategic vision. Bill began a five-minute diatribe of his history in the company and his ability to deliver everything asked of him. He then mentioned to Mr. Wheeler that, if needed, he would take over the group of projects to ensure they would get completed. Bill used the information collected in the team meeting and not only was he attempting to sabotage Ryan but the entire team for his own self-gratifying purposes.

Mr. Wheeler said to Ryan, "I told Bill that it was your job," as he pointed to Ryan, "to handle this project, but that I appreciated Bill's time."

He sought to downplay Bill's obvious confrontational and subversive attitude by dismissing Bill's comments. He was a very patient man, but his patience was running very thin with Bill and he wouldn't allow Bill to continue his activities and attitudes for very long. After a brief sigh, realizing that this problem was becoming more of a nuisance, Mr. Wheeler continued, "Ryan, I didn't want to deal with Bill because I thought it appropriate to let you handle this as you see fit," Mr. Wheeler said.

"Thank you. I think he had his pride hurt a bit in the meeting. I am not apologetic for anything, but I'll keep an eye on him and make sure nothing adverse happens."

"You should also know," Mr. Wheeler said, then paused for a moment and continued, "never mind, it's not really important. Thanks for coming by."

"No problem, please keep me informed if he has any more concerns."

Ryan walked out of the office when he heard Mr. Wheeler yell for Ryan. Ryan went back into the office where Mr. Wheeler said, "Remember that position you wanted to hire for to handle the POS system? I'm approving the position. I know you have someone in mind, Sheila?"

"Stacy."

"Right, well, I'll approve the position, but go through the normal HR process and bring her in for an interview. HR will have to approve the candidate, and I would like to meet her as well."

"Of course, thank you."

Ryan had been trying for months to get a position for Stacy, who was languishing at her job. The company had removed of all her staff, and she was in charge of code reviews for some of the other developers. Unfortunately, developers ignored recommendations she made because their superiors knew there was no consequence to ignoring Stacy; in fact, the behavior was a condoned practice. It was obvious they were trying to push Stacy out and she was working diligently to get out, although unsuccessfully.

He hurried to desk, to make the phone call and tell her the good news, but he would temper his enthusiasm in case things didn't go as planned. The prospect of bringing Stacy on board excited him because he would be able to get Stacy out of a very bad situation, but more importantly, he needed someone he could trust, and now he was very wary of his team, although he hoped for change. He knew Stacy could cultivate a few relationships, especially one with Rebecca. It seemed that Rebecca felt out of place in an old boys club with Bill and Jim and, maybe collectively, Stacy and she could counter them, especially Bill.

On the phone, when he told Stacy the good news, he could hear the exasperation of relief over the phone. She also tempered her enthusiasm, only because she was at her desk when she received the phone call. Ryan explained the procedure and explained that someone would call her for an interview in the next week. He hesitated to give her more information until they had an opportunity to talk in person, but he wanted to prepare her for the interview and make sure she understood the situation she was about to enter. Then, for a brief moment, there was a deafening silence over the phone, which was out of place, when Ryan heard Stacy's voice say quietly, "Thank you. I thought you forgot about me."

"Never, I was pushing for this opportunity, but I met up with some resistance, it just took longer than I expected."

They finished their brief conversation and hung up the phone. He couldn't wait for Stacy to come in for the interview because he knew she was perfect for the role and would be a great asset for the company. He immediately called the HR department to finalize all of the paperwork and ensure all the final approvals were completed, and subsequently submitted her resume to HR. The HR representative told him they had already received the approval from Mr. Wheeler, and they would contact Stacy in the next day or two.

Over the course of the next few days, events moved very rapidly, more rapidly than anyone expected. Stacy was called in for an interview, for which Ryan prepared her in great detail. He wanted to ensure she was fully ready for an interrogation; however, it was almost unnecessary. She met with Mr. Wheeler after her interview with HR, and the two of them talked soccer almost exclusively. Apparently, Stacy, who never spoke much about her college years, was the captain of her soccer team at University of Massachusetts. Mr. Wheeler and Stacy talked about college athletics and that his daughters were attending universities on full athletic scholarships. She used the time wisely to talk about her experience as captain and the ways she leverages the experience in her management style.

Ryan, upon hearing the revelation of Stacy's past, said to her, "You're full of surprises, aren't you?"

"Yep, I never really talked about my past out of fear, but over the past year it's become easier. I'm more confident, and really, I have you to thank."

Ryan appreciated the comments, but he knew Stacy just needed an opportunity and he really didn't have much to do with her increased confidence. She had that blunt streak; it was just a matter of channeling that forceful energy in a more positive direction.

Stacy had received high marks from all her interviewers, and HR made the offer only three days after her final interview. The report from HR indicated that she was an extremely talented individual who possessed a lot of energy and enthusiasm and would be a great asset to the organization. One comment Ryan couldn't help but notice was a reference to a leadership quality that the organization would greatly benefit from in the years to come. He knew that comment must have come from Mr. Wheeler.

While Stacy prepared to begin her new job, he was busy giving presentations and sitting in meetings about his proposals. During a marathon session of meetings, with many senior and midlevel managers on a Friday afternoon, Mr. Wheeler announced a rearrangement of the set of initiatives of Project Focus. To Ryan's surprise, it was his plan almost exactly as he had laid it out. The name was obviously a not-so-subtle reference to one of Ryan's slides around purpose and focus, and it received some laughter from the audience when Mr. Wheeler presented it. It was announced that Project Focus was a three-year-plan, which moved away from the traditional one-year initiatives, and which now had received the support of the CEO and chairman. It was an ambitious plan, which started with a mission to methodically turn around the company technologically. The plan described how they would cut the IT costs by 10 percent over the next three years, and detailed the method by which they would establish themselves as the premier technological company dedicated to the customer, a position they felt would give them a unique competitive advantage in the marketplace. It rearranged the set of initiatives focusing on consolidated technology and business purpose and priority, the first of which would be the inventory system. Mr. Wheeler further surprised Ryan by thanking his team in front of the executives for working diligently on the plan, a simple gesture that Ryan appreciated immensely.

Word had spread through the company about Project Focus, and the excitement intensified across every department, not because it was a mandated project, but because it actually made sense and would positively affect many employees. While some remained skeptical, Mr. Wheeler worked with the CEO to ensure the backing of this project came from his office. He knew that 70 percent of all IT projects fail due to lack of executive-level support. He therefore encouraged and cultivated the support from the CEO, and urged him to make a companywide statement about Project Focus.

Every department was asked to participate and provide input to their various portions of the project, and since the money was being made available, departments were lining up to get their needs and wants into the project. It was a huge win for the company and a political coup for Ryan, whose name had become synonymous with Project Focus. Now would come the hard part, keeping the momentum and navigating this ship safely to port.

Stacy's arrival compounded the excitement for Ryan. Having her on board gave him the comfort of having someone he trusted who could help him corral negative opinions. He also hoped that by adding her skills, the team would be better able to deliver a quality system. Her knowledge of the systems and the complexity of integration made her invaluable, but her prior experiences in integrating systems of this nature would be critical to the project. The one concern Ryan had was a potential standoff between Bill and Stacy. He believed that Bill would feel more threatened and attempt to sabotage Stacy, especially due to the new attention he was receiving regarding Project Focus.

At SportsCentral, colleagues were treating Stacy fairly, and her team was very happy to have her. She immediately developed rapport with her team, which consisted of three developers and two consultants. Ryan had designed this split to begin to erode Bill's power base. Each of the personnel assigned to Stacy came from Bill's staff. While Ryan knew this would be a sore point and could eventually lead to confrontation, he knew it was the most prudent course of action. It was his attempt to level the playing field in his group.

Stacy worked with her new team to understand who they were and what they enjoyed doing. It was very similar to the way Ryan managed at Paltz, and she used many of the lessons she learned there to gain their trust and confidence. Even though she worked almost ten to twelve hours a day for the first five weeks, she spent a good 20 percent of the time talking with her team to understand their strengths and weaknesses. This was important to her because she needed to know what their capabilities were to assign them appropriate-level tasks.

Bill noticed the way his former team was reacting positively to Stacy and he became agitated at how quickly they adopted Stacy as their new manager. The camaraderie they exhibited with her, which they never extended to him, irked him greatly. He became increasingly concerned that his former group might not protect him and his interests, and they might begin to divulge some of the internal discussions they'd had in the past, many of which included undisclosed details that he believed necessary to complete projects. He was concerned that these discussions might be taken out of context and lead to a perception of masking inefficiencies in his group or worse.

Ryan's problems with Bill were just beginning. Officially, Project Focus was underway, although the budget hadn't been released. During the next staff meeting, he unveiled to his team the order of the subprojects that they would develop and he needed to assign team leads. They would create a subgroup to handle the inventory system and have it in place within twelve months. This would be the cornerstone to Project Focus, and they needed to handle it with the utmost importance. A second and much smaller group would begin gathering requirements for the point of sale system and online system. Ryan made it perfectly clear that although it wasn't glamorous and exciting, the inventory system was the priority.

The team was expecting Bill to run the project since he was the most senior person in the room. Bill didn't think Stacy would be chosen since she wasn't as experienced in running projects, so he wasn't worried. In his mind, Bill thought that it could present a political problem for Ryan if he chose Stacy, especially due to her lack of project management experience.

Trying to avoid any favoritism, Ryan didn't consult Stacy on his ideas; however, he didn't have to consult her because he instinctively knew her reactions and she would understand his decisions. At least he hoped that would be the case. As he was explaining the major tasks of the inventory control system, he sensed the anxiety in the room over who was running the project.

Ryan told the team, "Major projects like this always go to the most qualified individual. Since this project doesn't clearly fall into any particular area of expertise, I need to decide who is the most qualified to run the project."

Bill interrupted him, "Ryan, you have my full support and you know I can get this done."

"I certainly know you do, and I appreciate your enthusiasm," Ryan said.

Bill forcefully continued, "I'll form my team immediately and get to work on development right away."

"Unfortunately, we may not develop the system," Ryan said.

"What?" Bill replied with a screech of disbelief.

"Why build, when these systems already exist? Personally, I've had bad experiences with purchased systems before, and I don't want to make the same mistake, but we must evaluate commercially available products, based on the business needs, and we must do it quickly. Furthermore, we must include the business; it must be a joint decision to build it or buy it," Ryan said.

"So we still may build it, if we can't find a suitable solution, right? Because, I'm pretty sure one doesn't exist out there for us," Bill said.

"That's exactly why you're not leading the project," Ryan said.

The room fell silent, waiting for a thunderous roar from Bill. Never before had he been told he wasn't leading a major initiative, and never so bluntly.

"Who can lead this? There is not a single person in this room who can match up to the experience I have," Bill said.

"That actually may be true. Maybe no single person in the room is capable of handling this project. That's why I need to do something a bit different."

Ryan now had everyone in the room at the edge of their seat. He deliberately stopped speaking and reviewed a few pages in his notes to create a bit more suspense to his decision. He was now feeding into the drama for effect.

"Rebecca, you are the project manager. I know you run the Project Management Office but this is too big not to have your direct involvement. Besides, you will need your team to handle the day-to-day task management and status reports with Stacy who will be the technical lead. Together you will be responsible for ensuring the stakeholders are involved and all phases of the project are delivered in a timely fashion."

Bill didn't utter a word but his face was filling with rage. Before anyone had a chance to say anything, Ryan continued, "Rebecca, I also want you implement the techniques you spoke about last month with me. Use this project to develop the template for which all projects will follow."

"You're insane," Bill said.

Rebecca was stunned; she was now part of a major project and had full authority to run her area. It wasn't about her technical inexperience; it was about her project management and leadership experience and capabilities. Stacy would provide the technical leadership and she would be her lieutenant to get it done. As the conversation between Bill and Ryan ensued, a smile slowly appeared on Rebecca's face as she kept her head in a downward fashion in an effort to contain her emotions. She was so grateful for the opportunity and could not help being slightly happy at Bill's misfortune.

Bill threw in a few quips trying to get Ryan to change his mind, saying that his inexperience was going to doom the project. Stacy, wise to keep out of it, began drafting her plan. She even moved closer to Rebecca and began to share some notes.

Ryan, who by now had lost his patience with Bill, asked him to step outside for a brief moment. They proceeded out of the conference room with Ryan leading the way. Bill closed the door behind him, but the tension was as thick as a fog on a fall evening in London.

"Bill, I don't appreciate the tone of voice or the comments you are making. My decision is final. You have a job to do, and I expect you to do it," he said calmly.

Bill wanted no part of this conversation and he stormed away from Ryan, saying. "Well, we will see about this."

Ryan wasn't sure exactly where he was going, but he had a pretty good idea. Ryan was astute enough to have shared his plan with Mr. Wheeler the day before, and although Mr. Wheeler had some initial reservations, he acquiesced because of how well Project Focus was conceived and with the conviction that Ryan showed in his organizational structure. It was risky for Ryan and Mr. Wheeler, but they both knew the only way they could achieve success was by taking manageable risks.

There was a noticeable uneasiness as Ryan reentered the conference room alone. Everyone in the room could hear their conversation through the thin walls. James asked Ryan where Bill had gone since he could see the silhouettes through the frosted glass panes and noticed Bill walk away from Ryan. He explained that they had a brief discussion and Bill had decided not to come back to the meeting. The displeasure on James's face was very noticeable. Ryan, trying to stay on course with the meeting agenda, proceeded with the objectives.

"This inventory system is the cornerstone and I need you to get it right. Stacy, you have the final call on decisions. I need a plan in a week," Ryan said.

"You will have a draft of the plan by next Friday," she replied, then turned to Rebecca and said, "Is that OK?"

Rebecca replied, "Absolutely, we will get that done."

It couldn't have been scripted any better. The atmosphere in the room completely changed, and Ryan was certain some may have believed the exchange between Stacy and Rebecca was staged. He hoped everyone would come to understand that he just managed his teams differently, and he expected the same of his team. Giving them a clear direction and the tools they needed to execute was the keystone of the leadership arch. Everything he did and everything they did would be dependent on their ability to understand the focus, agree, and be allowed to execute on the directive.

Although Ryan suspected that Bill went to Mr. Wheeler, he wasn't exactly sure. He hoped they could work out the situation, because Bill had valuable experience that could be leveraged and his inside knowledge would greatly benefit the team. However, if he chose to be disconnected from the project and the team, it would be better to keep him on the periphery so as not to interfere or even potentially sabotage the group.

Three days went by and oddly enough very little was seen of Bill. Ryan didn't actively go looking for him. He figured Bill needed his space and he was willing to give it to him for a few days. Bill would begrudgingly walk by and maybe ask a trivial sports question or political question, but something was amiss and the questions were almost forced and insincere.

Later in the afternoon on that third day, Mr. Wheeler asked Ryan to come to his office. There was no stated reason for the meeting, but Ryan casually made his way to Mr. Wheeler's office, not suspecting the discussion was anything terribly important. Upon his arrival, Mr.

Wheeler was primarily looking for a quick summary of a recently presented status report. He had some generic questions about the state of the project plan under way and he relayed some potential risks to the budget allocations.

Ryan indicated Rebecca and Stacy were working on the plan and that they would present their findings in a few days, including specifics about the composition of the team, the key high-level milestones and the required resources for the planning phase of the project. He explained how they would be researching the acquisition of the inventory system as an alternative to building the system.

Mr. Wheeler seemed pleased and confident in the selection of Rebecca and Stacy. He explained to Ryan that Rebecca was a talented individual who never really was afforded the opportunity to excel under the previous leadership and that working with a technically talented individual such as Stacy, would establish a formidable team. Ryan commented on Stacy's "take no prisoners attitude" and Rebecca's soft-spoken approach, which represented the yin and yang for the project. Mr. Wheeler, who had already experienced the forceful and direct commentary from Stacy laughed and agreed. While he thought Stacy could learn from a bit more seasoning, he believed that a personality of that type was essential in a successful team and he welcomed it.

Then, Mr. Wheeler discussed a developing situation that he wanted to make Ryan aware of. Bill had come to Mr. Wheeler's office three days prior directly after the Ryan's meeting and subsequent confrontation to express his disagreement with Ryan's handling of the project and the team. Mr. Wheeler understood that this was the first time Bill had not been chosen for a major project, however, he explained to Bill that he would not overturn Ryan's decision and usurp his authority. After fifteen minutes with Mr. Wheeler, Bill became more agitated, which was demonstrated in a more audible and forceful tone, and was borderline disrespectful. Mr. Wheeler demanded that Bill cease his outward objections and accept the decisions.

"Ryan, I have never had an employee do what he did in my office," Mr. Wheeler said.

"What happened?"

"Well, after I told him to accept it, he basically threatened me with his resignation."

"He resigned?" Ryan asked.

"Not exactly, he said he would resign if he was not leading the project. What you don't know is that he wasn't really resigning. He was threatening to resign because he wanted to use it as leverage against me."

"What leverage could he possibly have?" Ryan asked.

"He is the CEO's brother-in-law."

Ryan's expression turned from confidence to fear in a split second. He now feared retribution from the highest levels of the company, and began devising a way to salvage any damage Bill might be inflicting. Now he understood why Bill could wield so much power or at least strut around the office with the perception of impunity. Ryan was upset that Mr. Wheeler had never given him such a vital piece of information. He also wondered how many people had known and why no one on his team ever informed him.

Mr. Wheeler told Ryan that Bill went to speak to the CEO, which led to another meeting called by the CEO with Mr. Wheeler.

"So, you're telling me, I need to give the project to Bill?" Ryan asked, knowing it would kill Stacy and Rebecca's confidence. Ryan had finally been able to give them the opportunity they both long sought and now the rug would be pulled right from under their feet by something for which they had no control over. It seemed grossly unfair, and if he had been more informed of Bill's position, he might have handled the situation differently.

"Actually, no. Bill tendered his resignation today, which I accepted. He won't be coming back to the office."

Ryan said nothing, but Mr. Wheeler, knowing the obvious question said, "The CEO told him to tender his resignation for insubordination. He wanted no part of nepotism and that any hint of it damaged his reputation. He was infuriated that Bill thought he could walk into his office and make demands such as those."

Finally, Ryan found himself in a situation that had just worked out. The cards were stacked against him without his knowledge and by chance, the situation worked in his favor. His organizational problem was now gone and he could focus on completing his mission. Mr. Wheeler told him he would need to reshuffle his department and probably hire a replacement quickly. Mr. Wheeler concluded their brief meeting by saying to Ryan, "My guess is that you have your senior staff already available."

"Yes, sir," Ryan said as he walked out of Mr. Wheeler's office.

Ryan called an impromptu meeting with his management team. His e-mail request for the meeting listed the subject as "project update" so as not to arouse any speculation or concern prematurely, although he suspected Jim already knew. It was important for him to control as much of the information as possible and so only the five remaining reports were invited.

As everyone filed into the conference room for their meeting, they noticed Bill wasn't around as Ryan started the meeting. Jim asked Ryan if they should wait for Bill.

"Well, that's why I called the meeting. Mr. Wheeler called me up to his office earlier and he told me that Bill tendered his resignation this morning. I don't know the details of what happened but he tendered his resignation directly to Mr. Wheeler," Ryan said.

As they were absorbing the news, the disbelief engrossed everyone in the room except for Jim. He obviously knew more about the situation than he was displaying. Ryan expected Jim to favor Bill's position and be more sympathetic to Bill's situation, but he hoped Jim would come around, and at the very least he hoped Jim wouldn't subvert what Ryan was trying to accomplish.

Ryan brought a more positive focus back to the meeting and sought to keep the momentum he was building with the team. He reiterated his support and asked them to raise their level of effort to ensure they would collectively be successful. With the seemingly major obstacle and negative icon removed, they seemed energized, with the exception of Jim. Bill had been more of a distraction to the team even with his solid expertise and institutional knowledge. Ryan may have underestimated how much it really affected the team. With no other comments or questions from the team, Ryan dismissed the group.

As they left the meeting, Jim, who remained seated, asked Ryan to stay behind. Ryan came back to the table and sat back down closer to Jim and said, "Jim, I know you and Bill were close and had worked together for years, I'm sorry he decided to go."

Ryan was a bit concerned that Jim might have the perception that he had Bill terminated, but he decided not to broach that topic. Jim responded, "Ryan, you might think that I hold you responsible for Bill's departure, but I don't."

Ryan was very relieved at hearing Jim's comment but he made sure to remain collected. Jim continued, "Bill is a bit controlling, but he's really a nice guy. He undermined you, and it would have become worse if you had allowed things to progress."

The content of Jim's discussion wasn't an epiphany, but the discussion itself took Ryan completely by surprise. He had fully expected Jim to unleash a barrage of negative comments, which, although out of character for Jim, would not have come as a complete surprise given the circumstance.

"While I was skeptical at first, I think you're really trying your best to make things work and I commend you for it. However, I do disagree with the approach, and I strongly believe it's a recipe for disaster."

Ryan wanted to get a better understanding of why Jim thought the way he did, and was about to speak, when Jim interrupted him and said, "Since I disagree with the approach, and maybe it's because I am so old fashioned, I think I would be more of a liability than an asset."

"No you wouldn't, you are a valuable member of the team," Ryan said.

"Nice try, lad. I'm at the age, where I can just retire and let a new breed of managers come in, and I think, in light of the circumstances, I will tender my resignation as well and just retire."

"Are you sure about this? Maybe you want to think about it, and not make such a quick decision," Ryan replied.

"You still have a lot to learn. I've thought about this for a long while, and I just decided I would wait for the right opportunity, and retire for the right reason. Honestly, I think the right reason is because you have given this group a lot of hope, which they never had before. Keep it up, because it's really nice to see, and it's something I couldn't do."

Ryan expressed his deep gratitude to Jim for being candid and wished him the best of luck. Jim gave him six weeks' notice but if more time were needed he would gladly stick around a few more weeks. He wanted to give as much support as possible, while being afforded the opportunity to bow out gracefully.

Jim said, "One more thing. Don't let them change you. You change them." With that final comment, he stood up, patted Ryan on the back twice, and walked out of the conference room.

Jim caught Ryan off guard with his candor, support, and advice. Jim seemed very genuine in his comments and Ryan believed that he truly did want the team to be successful. It was odd though; since Jim would have been a critical player, he could have been a cornerstone to their success. Now they would need to hire a new person, but all that institutional knowledge would disappear. It was a very complex position; however, there was no time to analyze, and maybe at some point in the future things would be clearer.

During the course of the next five months, the project proceeded on time, but there were significant challenges. The difficulty in finding a replacement for Jim had led to confusion among the group looking to integrate the systems with the mainframe legacy applications. Jim's team was very strong technically, but the organization was run in an archaic fashion, whereby no decision could be made without him. In the absence of Jim, they were looking to a surrogate, which was usually Ryan.

Stacy and Rebecca, although they butted heads from time to time, were working well together. However, Ryan sensed that some micromanagement was occurring, based on the attitudes of their team. Most of the problem was rooted with Rebecca, who saw this opportunity as one to shine. Her conflicts with Stacy led to a few intense arguments, which were always resolved; however Ryan asked them both to tone down the rhetoric and argue away from the team, a warning that they heeded quickly.

Ryan had two major storms approaching. First, while he was confident the inventory system would be successfully delivered on time and under budget, he became increasingly concerned that modifications to the scope of the integration were compromising the long-term vision of Project Focus due to the pressure of meeting the stated delivery. This situation caused him some angst because a failure to delivery in a timely fashion would impede their ability to deliver the larger strategy in the projected time frame for which many promises were made. However, the changes in scope would clearly undermine the stated objectives and the vision of Project Focus to propel the company technologically. While he could always try to negotiate more time, that would work only so many times, if at all. In addition, he could demand that his team execute the vision exactly as specified, but that might compromise the time line and reduce the quality of the work.

During his review of the status report, Ryan became concerned regarding the delay in a decision on how the inventory system would be integrated with other systems. He noticed that the file exchange format, the method by which systems send data to each other, still had been undecided. It should have been an easy exercise for the team to come up with standard format for data integration, but it hadn't been completed, and he wasn't even sure whether or not it had been started. This was odd because he knew Stacy should have had her team propose the standard and put the issue to rest.

As he continued reading the status report, he further noticed that a significant number of key decision points were dependent on Stacy; however, there was no indication that any member of Stacy's team was either responsible or directly involved in those decisions. If his assessment was correct, Stacy was the bottleneck for the project. At no other time, in their history of working together, was she the bottleneck for any project. She had always managed her team effectively and delegated responsibilities accordingly, but now he needed to understand what was happening.

He called Stacy into his office and when she arrived, they began to discuss his review of the project plan. The concern in his voice took Stacy a bit by surprise, but she understood clearly his position. He realized that he may have been coming across a bit confrontational, and he subsequently toned down his inquisition. "I know you manage projects well, so I can't understand why you are listed as having the responsibility for almost all of the items," he said. "It looks as though you are the only one on the project."

Stacy responded, "I know it looks like that, but it's a bit more complicated. Can you call Rebecca in?"

He then called Rebecca, who immediately hurried into his office. After a quick update for Rebecca of what they were discussing, he explained his concerns about a majority of the project and key decisions being the Stacy's responsibility.

Rebecca stood up from her chair and proceeded to close the door, and said, "Ryan, we want to complete this project and we are doing everything in our power to do that. Unfortunately, the rest of the team seems to be taking awhile to catch up."

"What do you mean?" he asked.

"Well, Stacy is the key technologist on the project. Every time she assigns the work to someone, they usually keep asking her for guidance. It's not that they can't come up with solutions. The team has been so entrenched in their previous behavior that they always look for Stacy to provide the solution and no alternatives are ever discussed."

"Stacy, you haven't been able to encourage more free thinking?"

"No, I've tried everything and what's really slowing things down is not having people to bounce ideas off, or challenging positions. It's as though everyone is afraid, and no matter how many times I ask them or tell them, they are complacent," Stacy replied.

"Why haven't you said anything?"

Rebecca answered, "She was going to, but I convinced her to wait and allow us more time to keep trying, we can't come to you for everything. Unfortunately, we probably should have come to you sooner, or maybe I shouldn't have stopped her."

"Actually, you are probably right on all counts. We need to come up with another way to get them to perform."

"Honestly, Ryan," Stacy said, "I don't think they can make it. You may have to remove more than half of the team."

"That is an option, but we'll give it another try and maybe a few more months. These people have a lot of institutional knowledge that can be leveraged. We may end up removing people, or supplementing our team, but I think we can succeed at this."

He explained two key fundamentals for the group, which Stacy should have known from working with Ryan, although he never formally presented them to her. Stacy told Ryan she had no idea what he was talking about. Ryan laughed and said, "Stacy, you and I work in a certain manner and you instinctively know what to do and when. Well, what we never did was put down on paper exactly how teams are supposed to operate."

Ryan mentioned that he would set up an off-site meeting for the entire team. They would take the time to discuss what was going on and he would use the opportunity to more adequately present how he expected the team to operate. It wasn't going to be good enough to tell them what needed to happen; they had to believe it, experience it, and live it. In his opinion, the entire team would need to preach the gospel of this new dynamic of operating a team more effectively.

Chapter 8

STRATEGY

It was 7:30 a.m. on an unusually cold late October morning where Ryan had arrived very early at the SandBrook Hotel, about fifteen miles from the office, to prepare for the off-site meeting he had organized for his team. Many members of the team had never been at an off-site before, and never before had they been part of an off-site activity while working at SportsCentral. Mr. Tony Deagle, the previous head of the team, frowned upon off-site meetings and limited employees' time out of the office for conferences and training. However, Rebecca pointed out to Ryan in a conversation about two weeks prior that he never missed an opportunity to attend a conference himself. Some considered Tony's management style to be similar to a gulag, Stalinesque, which cultivated an atmosphere of discontent and trepidation.

This off-site meeting would be a watershed moment for Ryan and his management philosophy. He wanted his team to subscribe to a philosophy of management that required subordinates and superiors alike to be in tune with each other and not adversarial. The team needed to learn the foundation of success, which lay in working collectively by the clear understanding of aligned roles and responsibilities, while simultaneously understanding the negative effects of micromanagement. The purpose of the off-site meeting was to clearly articulate, without lecturing, how management style affects productivity and that through the effective application of management a leader can effect significant positive change with minimal effort.

Three weeks ago, Ryan had requested permission of Mr. Wheeler, to hold the off-site meeting. Although Ryan could attain permission rather easily, he wanted Mr. Wheeler's full support for such a broad and radical action. Mr. Wheeler had informed Ryan he would approve the off-site, but he also wanted a more detailed explanation of the topics they would cover and what Ryan believed would be the outcome. Unfortunately, he was under significant pressure from his senior management, who were wary about the progress of the inventory system, but he continued to remain confident about its progression. Even though, generally, all status reports showed the project to be on time and under or at budgetary levels, there were a few cautionary notes based on recent events. However, it was very clear the project was heading in a positive direction.

Ryan's meeting with Mr. Wheeler was late in the afternoon on a Friday, and suspecting the meeting might run very long, Ryan called Lisa and explained why he would be home late. After explaining the purpose of the meeting, Lisa wished him luck and told him she never fully understood his philosophy of management, but she was inspired and encouraged by his conviction. He appreciated her understanding, but it was hard for him to promote his management concepts when everyone around him seemed to feel otherwise or didn't demonstrate the same enthusiasm. Luckily, his research had demonstrated consistently that this philosophy was successful, if implemented properly. The real test for Ryan would be gaining the support he needed from the team, and effectively directing that support.

At 4:30 p.m. Ryan walked into the office of Mr. Wheeler, who was noticeably tired. He had been bombarded by a series of budget meetings with the CEO. These were grueling meetings of give and take, mostly take. When he saw Ryan, he welcomed him into his office and began discussing nonwork-related topics. It was a needed relief from the pressures of budgets and staffing considerations. He talked about his pending trip to North Carolina the next day to see his daughter play in the heated Duke–North Carolina rivalry and he was just glad to be getting the opportunity to see her. It was obvious that he sorely missed her and his other daughter, but his work schedule was so compressed it didn't afford him many opportunities for visits.

Mr. Wheeler asked, "So Ryan, tell me why you want to take twelve of your team off-site."

Ryan laughed and told Mr. Wheeler that before he provided the rationale for the off-site, he needed to explain the problem. The explanation would be more of a history lesson than an analysis of the current organization and its culture. He broke the problem down into two discrete but interconnected segments. The first segment was his direct reporting line consisting of the four managers. The second segment involved the organizational silos reporting into those managers.

The root of the problem was in the first segment, and Ryan needed to cure it as a priority. He defined for Mr. Wheeler the concept of human inertia, which he took from Sir Isaac Newton's principle on inertia. The principle states that a body in motion tends to stay in motion and a body at rest tends to stay at rest. It was this very principle that was at work within his first layer. There were three managers, who, out of the old habits from the previous management, operated with a degree of complacency with regard to decision making. They had been trained for years that the senior manager needed to make all the decisions, thus creating a bottleneck of immense proportions. Stacy, for example, whom Ryan believed would have never fallen into the trap, became like the old manager because she viewed the problem as a matter of either incompetence or incapability and therefore struggled to compensate for the inaction and indecisiveness of the group. Stacy, he explained, was performing the work of the manager as well as the technical leads, which he commended as noble but regarded as inefficient. While she could continue to operate in this manner for a short time, it wasn't a sustainable practice and she would need to push the work downward and across more effectively. He knew Stacy didn't normally subscribe to this level of management; however, the pressures of completing tasks sometimes blind individuals to the obviousness of problems that surround them.

The managers, he explained, that reported to him had previously always waited for Bill to make all the decisions even though he wasn't their direct boss. Apparently, as Ryan had discovered, his predecessor had all technical decisions directed to Bill for approval, which Ryan had since learned was done to mask his lack of technical expertise. It was unfortunate because Ryan knew that these managers had some good technical acumen; however, their old habits have completely overpowered them, rendering them unable to change their way of operating.

"So you believe you can change that perception at a single off-site?" Mr. Wheeler asked.

"No, but I do believe that if I can explain a few things, I can get them all to buy into a new philosophy that can serve as a foundation to be reinforced over and over and over, similar to tuning a piano. A piano is never just tuned once; the strings need to be tuned regularly to ensure the highest quality sound."

Mr. Wheeler understood what Ryan was stating since he had faced the same set of issues with his peers, who still clung to the old way of operating. He tried to have his peers look at new technologies, and be open to new ideas; however, it was difficult to change their mind-set, and would be impossible if the CEO never reinforced it.

Ryan then went on to explain the problem with the second segment, and while it was similar to the first with respect to human inertia, there were a few differences. First, the next group was very unclear as to what their roles were. The insulation provided by the upper level managers acted as a buffer during the tirades of Bill and the previous management team. However, the unintended consequence of these actions resulted in a lack of understanding of the goals and objectives of the organization as well as their roles within the group. They became cogs and automatons in a machine that wasn't operating anywhere near peak efficiency. If things were going to change, they must be given clarity as to their role and the road ahead.

Second, while this group was technically competent, they lacked the initiative to complete a major milestone without significant intervention from their management, which in the past always meant Bill. They allowed themselves to become complacent over time since there was no sense of reward or purpose to their respective positions and had no reason to become anything else. Ryan explained how unfortunate it was to have such qualified people working without a purpose every day and he likened it to running a marathon on an oval track.

Mr. Wheeler sympathized, but asked, "So exactly how will an off-site meeting help?"

"Simple, I'm asking you to approve something they have never done before. It shows commitment to a new methodology and it shows commitment to them. In addition, I will explain a few concepts to them that I have gathered along the way that work very well, and I will get them to buy into it."

"Ryan, we don't have a lot of time for theories, we can't fall behind on the project. I know it's not a lot of time out of the office. I'm just concerned with the perception," Mr. Wheeler said.

"I understand. Let me explain the concepts, and then you judge for yourself," Ryan replied.

They talked for almost ninety minutes with a very engaging debate on management style, philosophy, and its effect. They used examples from their previous lives, which solidified what Ryan was trying to explain, and after ninety minutes, they walked out of Mr. Wheeler's office together. Mr. Wheeler continued the discussion as they walked outside to their respective cars. While he never knew any particular name for what they were discussing, Mr. Wheeler had instinctively known that the management style Ryan was trying to project was needed to turn the organization around, and with the permission from Mr. Wheeler and full support, Ryan was very confident he could convince the team to look at their situation differently.

When Ryan announced to the team on the following Monday that he was conducting an off-site meeting, the team was surprised, their reactions muted. The continued thread of mistrust overpowered any sentiment of excitement they might have harbored. They respectfully questioned the motives for such an action, but Ryan rationalized the skepticism based on the old habits of the past.

For the three weeks leading up to the off-site meeting, he promoted the meeting as a treat for the team. They had earned a day out of the office and they could work collaboratively on making the department stronger. It would be their opportunity to voice their concerns and provide opinions in an uninhibited forum, or so he hoped.

The day before the off site occurred, Rebecca went into Ryan's office and asked, "What is your real agenda for the off site?"

Puzzled by the question, since he had been very explicit about his intentions, he replied, "Exactly what I have been saying, I want everyone to have some fun, and I want everyone to learn something about leadership, strategy, and each other."

Rebecca replied, "There is a lot of skepticism on the floor and I want you to know I don't share it. I am very confident this will be successful. I have learned a lot from you, especially over the past few months, and I am very optimistic and excited."

The irony in her reply demonstrated the enormity of the challenge Ryan was undertaking but he thanked her and he concurred with her statement.

The next morning, while in the parking lot of the SandBrook Hotel, a modest one hundred room hotel about a mile from the beach, Ryan was looking at his watch, which displayed 7:40 a.m. and he had been there for ten minutes waiting for Stacy. Then he noticed a white GMC hybrid Yukon pull into the parking lot, which he knew was Stacy's. Ryan didn't understand how one could buy a fully loaded SUV hybrid and be an "environmentalist" simply because the car was a hybrid. They always traded jabs about her environmentalist convictions, but he held the trump card on that particular portion of the debate, and Stacy knew it.

She walked up to the front of the hotel with three large bags of office supplies that Ryan requested she bring, and four boxes of assorted Munchkin donuts. Ryan asked, "Why did you get Munchkins? We paid for a breakfast at the hotel."

"I'm not passing up Munchkins, especially if I'm expensing them to you," she replied.

Ryan laughed and together they walked into the hotel and began setting up for the meeting. He asked Stacy to tape up large sheets of paper to the wall on both sides of the room and make sure that the permanent markers she brought were evenly spaced around the table. The room itself was shaped in a horseshoe style allowing the speaker to walk into the middle and engage the participants. There was a big whiteboard behind a moving screen, which was used for computer projection but he wouldn't be using that today. He took a blue marker and wrote three items on the whiteboard to the upper right side: Strategy, OODA, TIMA, the three agenda items he needed to discuss by the end of the day.

By eight o'clock, about three-fourths of the attendees had arrived and as expected proceeded right for the breakfast bar. Ryan saw a few cliques develop so he intermingled himself in between the groups and worked his conversation to mix groups together. It was critical to their success for him to break down the internal barriers among groups and cultivate new connections across the team.

At 8:30, he called for the meeting to begin. Everyone found seats and, as expected, they assembled themselves in small groups. Ryan would deal with that later, but first he needed to set the stage and begin the discussion portion, and in order to ensure maximum success, he wanted them to be comfortable.

He welcomed everyone to the off-site meeting and reiterated to them his understanding of the skepticism around the meeting. He had no hidden agendas, no surprise announcements. This was an opportunity to learn to discuss management philosophy and strategy and ensure his expectations were moving forward. It was an opportunity for them to speak up in a manner that they were not accustomed to, and he assured them, although he wasn't sure if they would fully believe it, that all conversations would be kept in confidence within the group.

"I want you to be open in your conversation and, I assure you, there will be no repercussions if you disagree with anything I or anyone else says. You have my word. I know that it may not be entirely comforting, but if you can't trust someone, how can you possibly work with them? I have no reason to doubt anyone in this room, and thus I trust each of you and respect your opinions."

Glancing around the room, the body language told him they were attentive and responsive, which was more than he could have hoped, for an opening statement. He needed to keep the momentum going and bring them along for the ride for this day to be a success. In the next ten minutes he gave a brief history lesson, describing his thoughts and his work history over the past ten years.

"Lastly, I hope you take away something from today that you can use daily because my goal is for us to walk away and become extremely successful together. It is together that we will be successful or together we will fail; surely, we stand no chance if we are divided."

Rebecca said, "Thank you, Abe," as she was the only history nut in the room that recognized the paraphrased reference to Abraham Lincoln.

The room, filled with tension and apprehension, was silent as he asked if anyone had any questions before they started. It would be critical to have engaging discussions and conversation among the group, and while he hoped for interactivity between him and the group, he hoped for more dialogue between each of them directly.

In an effort to gauge the perspective of the room, he asked for a show of hands of those who thought this meeting would be a waste of time. There were no takers. He then asked for a show of hands of those who thought they might get something useful and positive. Almost reluctantly three people raised their hands, Stacy, Rebecca, and Derek. He immediately thought to himself, this might be harder than he originally thought.

Derek worked for Stacy, had been at the company for three years, and had had a myriad of jobs since his arrival. When Ryan asked him what he thought he might garner from this meeting, he responded, "I don't actually know, but I have nothing to lose having an open mind. I haven't done anything productive since I arrived three years ago."

Peter, a peer of Derek's, who was generally very reserved in his comments at the office, opened his eyes and gazed over in Derek's direction, not realizing how noticeable he made known his astonishment. Ryan asked, Peter, "Why do you look concerned about what he said?"

"I'm not concerned at all," Peter replied in an almost defensive manner.

Ryan knew he had caught Peter off guard and immediately tried to ease any apprehension by not focusing on it anymore. He decided to move right onto the topics of the day so he turned and walked toward the blackboard with a hop in his step, and began to write the letters TIMA in a vertical manner toward the left of the white board. He turned around and said to the team, "TIMA! This is the way successful teams, organizations, and militaries have operated throughout history."

He wanted to get the team to understand that to solve the issues faced by the department they needed to focus their attention to how the team operated and not on the individuals of the team. It was very possible that certain members in the room would not subscribe to the ideas being presented, or that they simply had personal ulterior motives; however, he would not make that assumption. Instead, he would operate on the principle that everyone in the room was a highly capable individual who needed to simply be assigned to a role that fits.

The first letter was T and he began to write the word "trust," extending off of the letter T on the whiteboard. Trust was the foundation that would bind everyone in the room, and he had already alluded to this concept in his opening statement. He asked if anyone in the room had a mistrust of anyone else. No hands went up. Then a question again from Derek, "Do you mean, do I not trust anyone in the room to do their job, or do I not trust anyone in the room with my money or life?"

Ryan thought it was a very good question and replied, "Let's start small and focus on someone doing their job; however, while I won't say they have to take a bullet for you, at some point you need to trust the person to do no personal harm to you."

Then one by one, as if a wave had over taken the participants, six people raised their hands, in support of the response given to Derek. Ryan engaged in a spirited discussion for twenty minutes on the value of trust and reiterated that trust is earned; it is not something one automatically receives. However, the easiest way to earn another person's trust is to trust them first, even if it is in small doses. This initiation of trust will also break the cycle of mistrust. Ryan challenged everyone in the room to put down their barriers because if they didn't, they wouldn't succeed. He used the analogy of a fire company, where each member must trust the other members with their own lives or risk complete catastrophe. Each member in a fire department must trust that everyone else will work to the best of his or her abilities. It is this trust that saves their own lives and enables firefighters to save the lives and property of others in need.

By the time he had completed the concept of trust, he was already fifteen minutes behind schedule. It was 9:15 and he still had an enormous amount of material to cover. However, he would not compromise any opportunity for discussion with the group; it was the only way they would come to adopt the new philosophy.

He moved on to the second letter in the list, I, which stood for intuition. Intuition meant that each person in the room clearly knew what he or she needed to do, when to do it and how to do it. Job performance should be somewhat instinctual, enabling people to operate free of constraints for a greater purpose than the task itself. The premise was simple but very difficult to adopt, especially for managers grounded in the old ways. Micromanagers take exception to this rule because they believe strongly that their role is to tell people what to do, how to do it, and direct subordinates accordingly.

He asked the group, "Do you believe that a manager's role is to just be involved in every detail or would you say that a manager should let you do your job and be involved only when necessary?"

The question was somewhat rhetorical since he never expected anyone to truthfully answer the question. It was an obvious notion that people should be allowed to do their jobs, and anyone opposing that position could be considered a micromanager. Since people don't believe they are micromanagers it made the question rhetorical.

The consequences of micromanaging, he explained, are lack of trust, increased work by a select few, and inability to respond to issues. A micromanager will end up doing more work than necessary and increase the likelihood issues will go unresolved because managers will gather no input from sources that might be more knowledgeable about the current situation.

He explained to the group how intuition is critical to the success of any team faced with seemingly insurmountable problems. Police officers receive extensive training on responding to certain situations. Their training enables them to deal with situations that ordinary people would flee and provides officers with a sense of what other officers would do and how they would react, freeing their minds to focus on dealing with the situation at hand rather than worrying about another problem.

"Some of you in this room may have a strong intuition of what needs to be done, others may not. Ultimately, all of you should, at least in the areas you control."

"I completely disagree," said a voice from the right side of the room.

The voice came from John, a programmer who had been with the company for twelve years. He originally reported to James and didn't hide his feelings about the resignations of Bill and James. John went on to say, "You expect everyone in this room to just take responsibility for issues and resolve them. If they screw it up you just fire them. Not me, I want to come in, be told what to do, do it, and then leave."

Ryan was shocked because he knew some people do not like initiative due to the inherent risk; however, what John was saying implied that allowing the team to roam freely was a way to scapegoat personnel, and he needed to correct that perspective quickly.

"John, if I let people do their jobs, and they mess up, do you believe I will just fire them?" Ryan asked.

"Yes, as a way to protect yourself."

"Have I ever done that?"

A silence filled the room as they all waited for a response. John seemingly refused to answer and shrugged his shoulders as if to say, "I don't know."

Rebecca responded, "Well, you should at least answer him. You know he's never fired anyone, even though you believe that he had Bill fired."

"He hasn't been here long enough," John responded, then turned to Ryan and said, "What makes you different?"

Ryan didn't want this bombshell. It set off a string of conversations and arguments and immediately polarized the room. Some members of the team argued over Bill's effectiveness and it may have been a politically correct way to condemn or support Ryan's leadership. He could see alliances starting to develop as commentary supplemented more commentary. People were hurling examples of strengths and weaknesses of both approaches at each other like grenades.

Ryan looked and saw that the time was 10:00 a.m. He figured it was a bit early for a break but decided to send people out for a break and allow them time to cool down.

"Excuse me, everyone," Ryan said in the middle of a very audible discussion. When silence returned he said, "I love spirited discussion, but let's take a ten- to fifteen-minute break and stretch our legs. Let's return at 10:15 and we will pick this up when we return."

Immediately, his staff began to exit the room, unfortunately in small packs. Stacy stayed behind and said, "I hope you know what you're doing. I think things are getting worse."

He responded as if to question the motives, "So do I, but honestly, these opinions need to surface. I never realized how ingrained some of these perceptions were. So the situation may get worse before it gets better, but at least they are shouting to each other. In my opinion, silence would be worse."

"So what do we do now?" Stacy asked.

"We turn it up a notch. Go outside and make sure everyone is OK, when we come back let's see if we can't turn this ship around."

Ryan went to the board and wrote some new rules for the discussion. He would need to spend some time ensuring the discussion progressed in a manner that would yield positive results. He was only on the second letter of four in his discussion on leadership and they would run out of time, but it was important to enable people to speak their minds.

As everyone returned, they slowly gravitated to their seats as their attention was drawn to the whiteboard with four rules Ryan had placed on the board. He said to the team that these rules will help them participate in a more appropriate and productive discussion. His goal was to depersonalize the commentary and ensure progress utilizing the purpose of direction. The first point, "Limit the use of personal names," was designed to remove personal feelings both positive and negative, for Bill, James, Mr. Wheeler, or even Ryan, and he asked everyone to stick to pure facts. While they could relate examples to "previous management" or a "current manager," he respectfully asked that they refrain from using names.

The second point he made was to "enforce the golden rule" of treating each other with respect. He reiterated the importance of everyone's opinion, and disagreement to positions was equally important to a productive discussion.

The third point he requested was to "be forward looking while learning from the past." The past was only valuable in the lessons it taught; however, strict adherence to past principles and practices was no guarantee of success. It was vital that they be free to experiment with techniques and tactics that might yield more positive results.

Finally, the last point on the board was "no action or thought is useless." Every thought or action has a purpose, even if the purpose is to define actions that won't work. Everyone must be free to make mistakes and be cognizant that the greatest mistakes of the world have brought forth some of the greatest discoveries.

He summed up the points by saying, "I want us to complete this day in a better place than where we started. The only way we can do that is to respect each other's opinions and strive toward a common goal. Is there anyone here who thinks we cannot do that?"

Not a single hand went up, and after a pause of ten seconds and a deafening silence, Rebecca stood up and asked, "How many of you believe we *should* do this?"

Every person raised his or her hand almost simultaneously. There was no thought given to the question, it was almost instinctive for people to raise their hands, and in some cases, there were even smiles. Ryan wondered if this could have been the turning point. He was very surprised that Rebecca had addressed the room in such a forceful manner.

Stacy turned to the room and in a half-joking state, as if to get the room started on the right path, said, "My previous manager," she said as she smiled, " always wanted the best in everyone, and worked diligently to make sure I had what I needed. He gave me the tools to succeed and took responsibility for my shortcomings. I can honestly say, I try and will continue to try to live up to that example."

"Stacy," a voice said from the other end of the table, "I never trusted you." Tina, a business analyst who worked for Stacy, was the voice questioning Stacy. "The problem is I don't know why. Maybe it was because you came from—," she paused and said, "you came from another company with someone else."

Tina, having already violated one of the rules Ryan placed on the board, added, "I really should give you chance because I have no reason to do otherwise."

"Thank you," Stacy replied.

The atmosphere in the room had progressed from very contentious to cautionary. Rebecca and Stacy had continued to lead the discussion among the group with John supplementing the conversation with his opinions. However, the outbursts from before the break had ceased and there was more civility in the room.

Rebecca and Stacy had put themselves in front of the discussion for the betterment of the team and they were engaging each person in the room on the issue of trust. The conversation progressed from how much trust should be given or expected, and in what areas should they trust each other.

"OK, if we could have a minute, please," Ryan interrupted.

As the team quieted down, he reiterated the importance of the first two points, trust and intuition. It was obvious to the team that trust was a major component of success and without it, they couldn't be successful. While the trust may have been still lacking at every level, it was recognized as important and everyone in the room would need to work on reestablishing trust.

Ryan turned to the third point, M for mission, in an effort to get the meeting moving forward again. He added that without purpose and direction, there could be no cohesiveness or coordination of the group's actions. While it was important to have everyone instinctively know what to do and when, it was important that everyone is aligned to the mission at hand.

"Does everyone know what our mission is?" Ryan asked.

"Build the inventory system?" Tina responded.

"Actually that's more of a tactic, Tina," Ryan said. "It's important to understand the difference between strategy and tactics, and how they support a mission. The mission is our general objective. The strategy is like orchestra where every musician supports the symphony. Tactics would be individual musicians or even groups of musicians."

Strategy and tactics were consistently confused in many of the articles and conferences Ryan had read or attended. The word strategy was simply used as a buzzword to illustrate the importance of doing some task or project. He presented the concept that strategy is a continuous process of interrelating actions and objectives, a definition he adapted from the United States Marine Corps. In this manner, a specific action could never be a strategy or a specific project could never be strategic but the successful implementation of a project for a desired end would be strategic.

He added, "I believe our mission is to deliver applications that will enable the organization to become a premier sports retailer in both the physical space and the virtual space. We can accomplish this by ensuring our systems support customers through both channels with equal effect."

He picked up the dry erase marker and began drawing on the whiteboard. He drew three large circles interconnecting each other at their edges. Within each circle he wrote, inventory system, point of sale system, and e-commerce site. He then drew a square in a dotted line around all three boxes and explained how each of the systems currently in progress or under consideration, supports the strategy of dealing with the customer's needs from ensuring product availability to enabling the customer to purchase the product from the two most popular sales channels.

For the next thirty minutes, he and the team discussed the mission for the organization and how certain projects related to it. He also asked for input from the team about additional projects that might support the mission. As each minute progressed he received more input about how tasks individuals were working on could align or don't align. Some team members began to question whether their jobs were part of the mission. Ryan answered the question, "Everyone here is and must be part of the mission. If for some reason you're not or you believe you're not, we must work collectively to align your role to the mission."

The team continued discussing the mission and some even proposed changes to the wording to make it stronger. Ryan, Rebecca, and Stacy were writing down all of the input so that the entire team could review it later. Ryan was getting through to everyone; they were working together because they had accepted the common goal of becoming more efficient. He gave them two key components, which enabled them to accept this common goal. He was able to make them believe it was achievable and he provided them with the rationale.

He had now completed three of the four letters on the board for his discussion. The concept of mission was the glue that could bind and direct the team. The fourth letter would empower the team collectively or individually to execute and complete their assigned tasks in the most efficient manner possible.

"Now that we have completed the mission," Ryan said as he pointed to the whiteboard, "let's talk about the fourth word. The fourth word is agreement."

The meeting gradually progressed in such a positive manner that the team was more attentive and more receptive to the ideas Ryan presented. The group had seemingly embraced the concepts and appeared excited to learn more. The room fell quiet as they anticipated the explanation of the fourth word, agreement.

He explained how agreement empowers the group at an aggregate level or individual level with the drive to succeed, because they are in control of their own futures. It was necessary for each individual to understand that if they trusted the group and leadership, and if they instinctively knew their actions, and if they knew what the objective was, the final piece would be the authorization to execute.

However, this authorization needed to be in the form of a binding agreement between superior and subordinate.

"Agreement means that we will execute an implied contract. Your boss will tell you what needs to be done, but can never interfere with your means to accomplish it. Your superior will state the 'what,' and you will define and implement the 'how.'"

"Cool," said Michael, one of the younger members of the group. Michael followed up with a question, "Even for me? I don't have a lot of experience."

"Yes, even for you. You had enough experience to get the job; you should have a good handle on how to get it done. You are always free to ask for advice and consultation, but in the end you must take responsibility for its completion."

"What if we think it's wrong or we can't do it?" John asked. John at this point was very engaged in the conversations. He had turned the corner at some point in the last hour and his earlier resistance had now waned considerably. Some in the room viewed his question with a bit of skepticism, but Ryan knew it was not only a valid question but an extremely important one as well.

"If you don't believe you can do it, or have objections to its completion, then, as long as you inform your superior before you start, there can be no repercussions. Either you need to be convinced or someone else will need to be identified to handle that project. Again, you cannot be held in contempt for stating the truth. If you feel you cannot do it and I put you in charge, you have a higher probability of failure."

This was a hard concept to absorb. He was providing a way of operating that almost ran contrary to the traditional way of managing. It was predicated on the point that if people felt they couldn't achieve a task then they needed to communicate their opinions without fear of repercussion. The concept does have a fine line requiring leaders to observe at least initially for its abuse. However, if an individual is to be trusted, then the leader can trust that he or she would never cross the line because the person would share the same mission.

The team tacitly agreed with that principle because it was difficult concept to grasp since there was an obvious paradox. Ryan further explained how there were scenarios whereby if an individual never accepted a task he or she was probably in the wrong role or the superior was incompetent in delegating work. For example, asking a firefighter to handle riot control would not be the most prudent use of resources, and has a lower risk of success than delegating it to an experienced riot control officer.

The explanation helped to solidify Ryan's point. Tasks should go to the individuals with the capacity and the skills to accomplish them. Should the individual choose to reject the assignment, there was probably a valid reason that the superior should take into consideration. There are many reasons for subordinates to reject a request including lack of funding, inadequate resources, faulty equipment, no senior level support, misuse of resources in support of the mission, and even potential abuse; however, the authority to reject a superior's assignment can come about only with trust, intuition, and a complete understanding and acceptance of the mission. It is imperative that the superior and subordinate completely understand the responsibility that is placed on them. They must also be completely cognizant that they share success or failure because they have done their part and they are accountable to each other.

Ryan had glanced at his watch and noticed the time had now reached 12:10 p.m. There was a lot of material that people needed to digest, and he realized he was reaching a limit for their attentiveness. He decided now would be a good time to break for lunch.

"If there are no questions," Ryan said, "let's break for lunch. We have a bit more to go over this afternoon that I want to discuss in the final two hours before we leave our current list of projects."

Everyone was hungry, as was usually the case with off-site meetings. At the office, employees seemed to eat like rabbits, with small salads and some cottage cheese. However, these same people at off-site meetings order a six-inch high sandwich and somehow manage to eat the entire meal as if to make up for lost time. The anticipation of lunch predicated any desire to ask questions about the topic.

Ryan now believed everyone was starting to have some fun. He walked with some of his team down to lunch. They were talking about the responsibility factor and, while there was still some skepticism, a touch of optimism tempered it. There was no outright opposition, even from John, who had engaged Rebecca and Stacy in a conversation about trust.

Ryan approached John, put his hand on John's shoulder, and asked, "So are you having fun?"

John replied, "Actually, yes. I think I understand what you are trying to say a lot better. I would have probably changed the order of your presentation, because the first part left a lot of questions. Once you got to the end, things became much clearer for me."

"Thanks John, I'll take that into consideration. No one has given me that feedback before. I'm glad you're enjoying it."

In the cafeteria, the team occupied two large round tables. Ryan attempted to listen to parts of every conversation to get a feel for the mood of the group, which he determined was generally positive. He noticed Stacy staying at the other table, and she glanced in Ryan's direction a few times with a slight nod implying that the conversations were generally positive.

The lunch itself was ordinary but very boisterous and jovial. They all commented on the fun they had conversing and debating with each other, especially toward the latter half of the morning's session. No one had mentioned the tumultuous first half of the session, which was a good indication that the team now focused on creating a better reality for themselves. The quality of the food added to the general mood and the more they indulged themselves the more the conversation turned from strategy and tactics to food and party conversations.

Ryan wanted to return to the meeting room to prepare for the afternoon session. He excused himself from his table and told both tables that he would meet them back at the meeting room in about fifteen to twenty minutes. When he arrived at the room, he rearranged all the tables from the horseshoe setting into a chevron style; however, he moved individuals' seats so that now they were with new partners. He purposely put Tina at the front of one table and made sure Stacy was at the same table. John and Rebecca partnered up as well. Each table had no more than three members, with most having only two.

Stacy walked into the room ahead of the others, about ten minutes behind Ryan, and asked, "What are you doing now?"

"I am rearranging our seats. I want to create more trust," he replied.

"Let me guess, I'm with Tina, right?" she asked as she scanned the room. "Yep, I was right."

"Maybe you should run these sessions."

"You're just too predictable, at least to me."

"Or maybe you just know instinctively what to do and maybe you should run these sessions."

"Don't think I couldn't."

"I know you can," he said with a grin.

The team had started filing into the room and when they saw the seats rearranged some of them began to laugh, realizing the afternoon session was going to be very different. It seemed as if lunch had garnished a piece of optimism because the general mood of the team was very positive and excited, a far cry from the beginning of the morning session.

As they sat down, Ryan opened the afternoon with a brief recap of the importance of trust, intuition, mission, and agreement. He wanted to reinforce the concept since they were prerequisites for the remaining topics. The next hour would concentrate on operating more efficiently in a team environment and the importance of generating and maintaining momentum. After he presented these concepts, Ryan hoped they would begin developing a new way of working the minute they walked out of the meeting.

Tina, who earlier had expressed her distrust of Stacy, leaned over to her and said, "I'm actually excited about this, if we can pull it off."

Stacy leaned back and said, "We can and we will."

At the whiteboard, Ryan began to write down some boxes. There were four boxes, which Ryan had placed in a linear fashion from left to right. He intentionally left each box blank, but arrows connected boxes together. Ryan then asked, "If you were presented with a problem, what would you do?"

Three voices responded simultaneously, "Fix it!"

"Yes, of course," Ryan replied, "but how would you fix it?"

It seemed like a trick question, and no one was exactly sure how to answer it. John mentioned that he would get into the code and fix it where it was broken.

Ryan sensed that everyone was trained to fix problems as they arise but they weren't sure of how they actually decide to fix something. He asked, "When a problem arises, you examine the problem, right?"

Everyone agreed with that principle. There was no use in fixing a problem one didn't fully understand. Ryan went on to ask, "Don't you then prepare yourself with possible solutions and actions?"

Again, there was no disagreement from the group. He then asked, "Once you have a set of solutions, don't you choose which one or ones to do?"

No response came as he continued to speak, and concluded the thought by saying, "Finally, once you have a course of action, you execute on it, correct?"

"That seems very obvious, Ryan," said Michael, a junior-level manager who had now been positioned in the back of the room. "What's the point?"

"Well, if it was so obvious, how come no one said it? But let's ignore that for one minute." Ryan paused briefly and defined the scenario he was talking about as the decision cycle. The decision cycle was a concept by Col. John Boyd, who was relentless in his pursuit of understanding how one could gain an advantage in a conflict. The first area he examined focused on the reason American fighter pilots had great success in the Korean War. His research went on to explain that the American pilots were able to execute decision cycles faster than their Russian opponents because their planes allowed them to observe, orient, decide, and act, primarily due to hydraulics and a bubble canopy. The bubble canopy enabled the pilots to observe a larger area of the airspace in which to engage enemy fighters, and the hydraulics enabled the pilots to execute more movements, giving them a tactical advantage.

Using this concept of the decision cycle, he examined other conflicts around the world from superpower conflicts and wars to smaller conflicts including third world country revolutions and terrorist acts, and, in almost all cases, he ascertained that the side that could successfully execute decision cycles faster, regardless of numerical superiority or technical advantage, would be victorious.

Each component of the decision cycle must be executed quickly, and the faster it can be executed the more of an advantage one will have over an opponent. Relating the conversation back to the workplace, he described an opponent as potentially being internal opponents such as other departments or internal saboteurs, or external opponents such as competitors.

"Are you saying that our internal customers should be considered as opponents or enemies?" Rebecca asked.

"Yes they should be considered an enemy, if they are not an ally," he replied. "If a department is always looking to lay blame on you, then he or she is your enemy. If the person shares the same goal and works with you to come to resolution, then the person is your ally. There is no middle ground, just degrees of one or the other."

This was an abnormal concept for them because they had always learned to treat internal departments as customers, and that no matter what, they needed to deliver what was asked. Ryan countered that argument by using the old sales phrase "The customers are always right," however, he added to that "except when they are wrong."

He wanted them to understand that relationships with customers don't need to be adversarial but they need not be submissive. If other departments didn't share the same goal and the same mission, then they were adversaries. Some adversaries need to be considered more dangerous than others. He equated this to the issue of rogue employees within a department, and used the example of an employee who never did his or her work properly or who never worked collectively with the group. The room agreed any individual of that caliber should be removed.

Ryan countered, "If you don't run the company, you can't fire a whole department, can you? So therefore, you must treat the person as an adversary and work to get him or her to agree to your terms. It sounds unusual, but give it some thought."

The decision cycle was important because if any individual could provide answers and actions faster than an opponent, for example, in a meeting, the opponent may have no alternative but to cease any attacks for fear of looking naïve or incompetent. It was a tactic that Ryan had successfully employed many times and it was all about preparation and speed.

Ryan wanted the team to act using the decision cycle method and not be afraid to make mistakes. As he further described the concept of allowing people to make mistakes, he equated it to a game of chess. If two players are playing a game of chess and one person can make six moves for every one move his or her opponent makes, the advantage will go to first player making more moves, assuming the first player is seeking to win. Even if the first player makes a few mistakes, the quantity of moves will overpower any other player. Combine that with the power of observation and the ability to recall from experiences to provide the first player with a multitude of sound choices to minimize moves that are fruitless, and the odds of winning will go up dramatically.

It was important to understand that everything needed to work in concert. He went up to the board and filled in the first box with the word "observe." He explained how observation didn't mean simply looking at the problem, but rather, included an examination of the environment surrounding the problem, the implicit and explicit factors that may contribute to the problem, and the dynamic nature of personnel and organization that might be involved in the problem. He added that the observation portion of the OODA loop represents the collection of inputs from a variety of sources and as many sources as possible within a reasonable time frame in relation to the problem. He cautioned that too much observation without execution stunts the entire cycle and leads to analysis paralysis, which was a term common used in the industry, attached to individuals who focus on observing issues and problems in perpetuity and never achieving any meaningful resolution.

Then he moved on to the second box where he wrote the word "orient." Orienting meant the individual must use the observations and a collection of internalized traits and characteristics to prepare and place the individual in the best possible position to complete the assigned task, or resolve an issue. Haphazard decision making will yield ineffective and sometimes horrific results because the successful positioning and placement of the right resources at the right time did not happen. These internalized traits and characteristics included previous experiences, culture and traditions, genetic heritage, the analysis and synthesis of a combination of these, and the new information surfacing. There are two possible results from this stage, the first is a return to observation, in the case of more information being required, and the second result is to move to the third box of decision.

The third box now had the word "decide" written inside of it. At the third stage, enough information has been collected and the actors in the scenario are now positioned to decide what course of action to take. Decisions are made from the synthesis and analysis of all of the inputs from the previous stage. Once a leader or individual has decided on the course of action, the person moves to the fourth box, which is action.

The fourth box, act, completes the cycle, and acts as an input back to the first stage as quickly as possible. All of the results from the action stage must be returned back to the observation in as close to real time as possible, or in other words, as it happens. It is not prudent to wait for the completion of decisions and actions to return information back for observation.

"Why would you have to return information as it happens? I would think you would want to wait until you have decided what to do, and complete it first so you can then determine whether it worked," Tina said.

"When you make a decision, it is based on the information currently available to you, but no environment is static. Our environment is dynamic, which could potentially change our decision, although, it may not, and chances are in small intervals it won't. But, the longer the time interval from our action to our observation, the more likely it is that the situation and environment have changed," Ryan responded.

Stacy replied, "Actually that makes sense. We have all had the experience of getting requirements from our business units, and then a few months later, they change their minds. I think what we need is more frequent communication with the customers to act as inputs into our decision cycle."

"I agree," said John. "That's happened to me so many times. But I have improved the communication by meeting with my business users every two weeks or every month, and I still can't seem to get a good handle on it."

Rebecca responded, "Maybe you need to meet once a week or even three times a week. If you did that, your meetings would need to be shorter, but I think they would be by default."

Michael added from the back of the room, "Or maybe we should sit next to our business users in their departments."

The conversation continued interactively for the next forty-five minutes, and Ryan was very pleased at the solutions being proposed and, more importantly, how they were acting collectively. The conversation opened up among the tables making it almost impossible to hear anything that people said. It was fascinating how he hadn't received a single question on the OODA loop. The conversations seemed to take on lives of their own, and he hoped they had accepted the concept of the decision cycle, because if they had, as he suspected, they would be more apt to apply it back at the office.

Walking around the room and between tables, he listened to the conversations and examples team members discussed. He heard stories of how departments, such as the marketing department, a traditional adversary of theirs, would constantly change their minds on what they wanted accomplished. Unfortunately, they could never clearly articulate their requirements and, therefore, trying to complete projects for that department was similar to hitting a toy car traveling at a hundred miles per hour with a ballistic missile. The users in that department were never cooperative and always dismissive.

Tina, who had been an outspoken critic of the marketing department, suggested to Stacy that she move into that department to quell their concerns. She wanted to get into the fire, especially since she had been the target of many of their attacks. Prior to this conversation, and before Ryan had arrived, she had been relegated to simply attending the standard weekly meetings and was never empowered to rebuke comments made by them. Now she was requesting to own the process. The thought of treating them in a more adversarial manner was very appealing. She had always believed her career had been stunted by the requirement that she be a submissive party to the meetings.

John, in a separate conversation, also wanted more frequent communication directly with the users from the logistics and purchasing area. Although he believed he was better able to perform his duties in the IT area, he proposed an idea to have one of the logistics and purchasing people moved down to his group to act as a liaison. The recommendation received lukewarm support from the table, but Rebecca had agreed to research it a bit more and have the conversation with John and the head of the logistics department.

Ryan then asked the group, after thirty minutes of open discussion, to begin thinking about the major initiatives, which was to implement the inventory system and then subsequently handle the point of sale and e-commerce systems. The marketing department was adamant about the need for the point of sale and e-commerce systems and was disappointed in the time frame but reluctantly agreed to an extension of the time line due to the requirement of waiting for the inventory system.

He broke up the team into two parts, and asked them to review the proposals and identify problems or potential issues as well as ways to potentially speed up the process. He told them he would leave the room for an hour to alleviate any concerns they might have about discussing the projects in his presence but he would be available in the café near the lobby of the hotel. The real reason he wanted to exit the room was to afford himself some time to wind down. The day was grueling for him and he was exhausted.

He left the room and proceeded to the café where he began to recollect the events of the day. He wondered if the brief moment in the afternoon of camaraderie would last or if they would slip back into their old customs. It created an awesome impression to leave the room and see the group work its way toward goals greater than oneself, but if it didn't gain momentum would it have all been for naught? Tina, the quiet one, as she was known in the office, stood up to Stacy and stated her mistrust, which by itself it could have been no easy feat with the added weight of Stacy's personality and position in the company, emphatically demonstrated her courage and willingness to be an active participant. He hoped Stacy would recognize the importance of having an individual such as Tina on the team.

John was an enigma in the organization, a very bright individual, but very complacent. It was a pleasant surprise to see him potentially turn the corner, but Ryan was skeptical, especially because of John's very strong ties and relationships with James and Bill. John was a close associate of James's who had been his mentor. For Ryan, having James turn the corner would be remarkable progress.

Looking back at his own career, he knew that what he had just done was unique. Organizations are usually slaves to the corporate culture, which holds them like the binds that tie down ships in the harbor. Change of the magnitude he sought, requires determination, persistence, and patience, and cannot waver from its goal, which must be larger than personal gain. He realized throughout the day, that although his original intent was to be successful in turning around the team, there was another force working alongside of him. It was a genuine desire to improve the lives and careers of his team.

It wasn't important that they actually come up with ideas to radically change the state of the department or provide new innovations into the three projects on the slate. He genuinely wanted to create a different perspective on managing the group, which he knew would lead to better results. As opposed to treating subordinates like cattle, it was important to demonstrate that the traditional organization chart should be flipped, demonstrating the importance of those who are the last line of defense and thereby providing the rationale to allow the broader group to act somewhat, if not entirely, independently. If even some members of the team could believe in realizing their potential, then the entire team would benefit. The collective experiences shared among a group have an exponential effect on the ability of a group with an open mind, and it was this principle that became the driving force. The more freely people in the group shared information, the faster they would learn; the more experiences they would collectively have, the more information they would possess, leading to better decision making at a more granular level. Ryan realized in a simple phrase that he wanted everyone to benefit from everyone else and realize those benefits faster.

An hour had passed and there was no word from anyone inside the room. At this point, he'd had enough reflection and had become slightly impatient waiting to find out results from inside the room. He finished his second cup of coffee, left the table, and walked the long corridor to the meeting room. As he approached the room, he could hear the voices getting louder and louder. Nervousness set in as he began to have visions of screaming, yelling, and chairs being thrown across the room similar to scene from the *Jerry Springer Show.* He hesitated slightly as approached the door, and as he reached the door, he heard the room break out into laughter, which confused him even more.

He opened the door and stood in the doorway where John's voice greeted him and said, "Ryan, glad you could come back."

Ryan asked, "OK, what's going on and why do I feel I'm being set up?"

Rebecca replied, "Relax, you executive types are way too strung out. Have a seat; we are going to tell you what we want to do."

Stacy added her two cents' worth, "You better hold on to your seat."

Ryan became even more nervous. He wasn't sure if this was a Jekyll and Hyde moment since he didn't recognize this group at all. He approached his seat, grabbed a glass of water, and tried to prepare himself for what was coming.

Stacy stood at the front of the room and explained to Ryan, that although he had broken them into two groups, they decided after the first few minutes to change the approach. They collectively and unanimously agreed to get into one group and discuss everything; no single person would be left out. Second, she said that they established certain rules; no topic was off the table, from personnel, to tasks, to capabilities, to which everyone also agreed. However, in order to remain professional and courteous, they had established a couple of rules.

First, they appointed a "'Devil's advocate" whose sole purpose was to challenge every opinion, no matter what the discussion. This role was the most significant, because it was the great equalizer. Stacy mentioned that although she had some very strong opinions about the project, she had volunteered to be the Devil's advocate and the team agreed, at which point Ryan had a difficult time containing his laughter.

Second, they all agreed to set aside personal differences and evaluate every point from an objective view. Objectivity was very important in arriving at a sound conclusion, but it was always difficult to implement. In order to ensure more objectivity, if anyone was viewed as subjective they would immediately be challenged by someone in the group.

Finally, they collectively realized that their individual success depended on a group success, and while putting aside personal ambitions was difficult, there was more reason to believe that each person's personal ambitions would more likely be met if the group were successful.

John added that they based the reason for their unanimous agreement on the faith they had placed in Ryan. Without it, he said, there would have been no agreement. John illustrated his point by presenting examples of Ryan's leadership skills and his selfless efforts to create a more cohesive team. It was trust, above all else, that gave them confidence to forge ahead.

"I sincerely appreciate it, John, and to everyone here," Ryan said as he addressed the team. He was a bit embarrassed by the attention but very appreciative nonetheless. He took a deep breath and asked, "So, where did we end up? Do we have any epiphanies on this project?"

There was no expectation on his part for any major breakthroughs. They had been discussing for only an hour and it would be unfair for him to believe otherwise.

Rebecca answered, "We believe we have a major breakthrough for these projects."

"You do?" he asked, and then realized how bad that must have sounded.

Stacy, who now sat next to Ryan, laughed and nodded with a big smile on her face to express her acknowledgement. Ryan hadn't seen Stacy look this excited in a long while so, he thought, there must be some revelation coming.

Rebecca stepped up to the whiteboard, and began with a brief synopsis of their discussion. Each person in the room had various points to bring up and everyone was allowed to speak, and while they hadn't agreed on every minor detail, they did agree on some basic principles.

First, the completion of the inventory system was paramount; however, the team had pointed out that there was no provision for automatic ordering from suppliers, and no connection to logistics systems to track shipments to stores or customers. This was something that needed to be addressed immediately prior to implementation. Rebecca noted that two members of the team had experience necessary from another retailer and that they should be moved from supporting the older applications onto this project. In order to accomplish that, agreement would need to be reached to supplement their existing work with outside help.

"Done, I'll try to get that approved by Monday morning," Ryan said and then asked, "Who are the two?"

"Michael and Tina felt they would never have any real opportunities and therefore speaking up was futile. However," as Rebecca nodded in their direction, "they now feel they are a part of something bigger and want to immerse themselves quite a bit more."

Ryan was completely aghast, he never knew anything about Michael and Tina and he guessed neither did Rebecca or Stacy or anyone else from his management team. This was a major deficiency in his organization and in himself that he would note for the future.

Rebecca went on and said, "If we do that, we will have two extra bodies working on the inventory project and we should be able to add scope and finish on time since the responsibilities are somewhat overlapping with a few deficiencies we have in the group currently."

Stacy added, "This is exactly what we needed, most of the problems are centered on moving data from both internal and external systems. Michael and Tina would be expected to ensure the integration works and with their knowledge of what's needed for external systems, we can enhance the utilization."

At the whiteboard, Rebecca drew a box toward the left-hand side of the whiteboard and inside the box then wrote inventory system and drew two lines, one up and one down, connecting two more boxes that said logistics and suppliers. Then she prepared to drop the nuclear bomb. She told Ryan they wanted to ditch the point of sale system.

"Wait, we can't do that!" Ryan exclaimed.

Stacy was now laughing and hitting the table and said, "I knew he would react that way."

The rest of the team was laughing with her; apparently he had been set up and was now realizing they were playing a joke on him.

Rebecca asked, "Don't you trust us?"

"I get it. You guys are pulling my leg." Ryan chuckled knowing he overreacted.

Rebecca answered, "Actually, we aren't pulling your leg. We really don't think we should develop the point of sale system."

Ryan was thoroughly confused at this point and Stacy was now laughing uncontrollably along with a few other team members at Ryan's complete confusion.

Rebecca began an explanation of how the point of sale system and the e-commerce site are designed to ultimately service the customer. There was no difference in the base functionality for both systems. While everyone knew that there should be similarities between the two and that some of the functionality was the same, the team asked why they shouldn't they be identical, with the only difference being cash register functions for end-of-day tabulations, credit card scanner, and barcode reader for products. Essentially the team was building one application that had multiple uses.

Ryan looked at the proposal that Rebecca was drawing on the whiteboard and quietly turned to Stacy and said, "You agree with all of this?"

She quietly replied, "We all do, this was the Rosetta stone we were looking for. Everything was in front of us the whole time."

Rebecca explained a few more details, but added that she and Stacy would work on a presentation for senior management in coordination with key members of the team, and that they believed work should begin immediately with personnel rolling off the inventory system as functionality was put into production. She also requested that a few more personnel be hired to handle the maintenance on the inventory system to help alleviate any pressures on the development of the POS/e-commerce system.

"This is really amazing. I never put that together and it's brilliant. A tweak in a few directions and basically we could have it up and running six months ahead of schedule," said Ryan.

"We actually think we can complete this in four months, since the requirements have already been completed. We just need to rewrite them to align with this new strategy. The end result is we will be six months ahead of schedule but we think it could be as early as eight months ahead," Rebecca replied.

"Is there anything else?" Ryan asked.

"Yes, but we will hold that for another day. We would like to have more discussions over the next week or two in the office," she replied.

No one on the team realized the time was now 5:30 p.m. They had technically overextended their welcome at the hotel and needed to close out the session. Ryan concluded the meeting by thanking everyone and encouraging them to continue what they had started here. He made no promises for the future of the organization, but he did vow to work on everyone's behalf and continue his support for their success.

The team filed out in a much more jovial mood than when they had entered this morning. As participants walked out, they shook each other's hands, laughed and generally seemed very pleased with the day's events. Many of them went out of their way to personally thank Ryan for his efforts in bringing them together and inviting them in the first place; for some, it was an opportunity that had never been provided.

John, Rebecca, and Stacy stayed behind to talk to Ryan. John approached Ryan, thanked him, and said, "Now I know why you were hired, and I'm really glad."

Ryan thanked him for the unexpected reach of appreciation. They spoke for a few more minutes about the tasks that lay ahead in front of them. Ryan had no doubt John would be a major player, and John was appreciative of the chance. He apologized for ever seeming uncooperative, but Ryan thought nothing of it.

Rebecca followed John but before she could utter a word Ryan said, "I was really impressed with how you led the group, and from the way the last part of the session ran it looks like they have really seen you differently."

"I agree they have. I am a fast learner with a good teacher. I want you to know, however, there was no way I could have done this without Stacy. She is really the unsung leader of the group, I'm just following her lead," Rebecca said.

"Out, get out!" Stacy exclaimed. "No more of this." Stacy firmly grabbed Rebecca on the arm and dragged her out of the room laughing. Rebecca leaned her head back as she was being collegially pulled out of the room, "Thanks, Ryan, see you Monday." Her laughter could be heard down the hall

Ryan collected his things and thought how well Stacy and Rebecca had worked together. They had formed a professional bond, which, if continued, would make them an unstoppable force. He was happy Rebecca had finally gotten a chance to excel and he was even more ecstatic that Stacy, his protégé, was leading her down the path.

Stacy had continued to exceed his wildest expectations and he believed there was no limit to her capabilities.

As he exited the room about ten minutes later, he was startled by a figure. Stacy had been standing right outside the room waiting for him to exit. She laughed when he jumped in fright and said, "Do I scare you that much?"

They both laughed some more and as they walked to their cars, they discussed everything that happened. Ryan wanted to know more about the discussion that took place when he was out for the hour. Stacy kept the details to a minimum because she wanted to keep the conversation private within the team. She thought it appropriate to allow each person to have a say in the room without it getting back to Ryan. Although it would probably happen anyway, she didn't want to be the catalyst and she explained how she wanted to set the example. Stacy did, however, say that the discussions were very heated at the beginning and after allowing people to blow off some steam, the entire atmosphere in the room completely changed. Everyone understood that if we didn't succeed some people would be fired, and no one wanted to be the one fired. Stacy expressed her opinion to everyone that no one should feel safe. Playing it safe, she said, would lead to complacency and that would lead to defeat and failure.

Ryan couldn't believe what he was hearing. Stacy had become something he had never seen before. She was quoting leadership, analyzing situations, and not reacting and trying to get people to understand positions. He knew she was working on becoming a better leader, but it was apparent to him that she had become something worse.

"You're me!" Ryan said,

"I had a very good model."

"I'm really flattered, Stacy."

"Who said I was talking about you?" she said in a joking manner. "I've watched you deal with people and I have tried to absorb all the good points. I don't agree with everything, but I will learn and adapt."

Stacy and Ryan agreed on how well the day went and that it was beyond their expectations. Their biggest question was how to sustain the momentum. If they could sustain the momentum, they could accomplish anything. Ryan would brief Mr. Wheeler on Monday and hopefully, they would see the results shortly. Their big test would be the meeting to present their findings.

When they reached the car, Stacy said to Ryan, "I've learned a lot over the past few years, but today was really important."

"How so?"

"Because what I learned today was that strategy and management are about people. If you don't have the right people none of it matters."

Ryan continued that concept and recalled the time when he readjusted the department at their last job and gave Stacy a more prominent role. It was important to have the right people in the right place at the right time in order to be successful. He added, however, that if there isn't a team to share in success, then success is just a lonely mountaintop and he questioned if there was any good in that at all.

They chatted for thirty more minutes at their cars and reminisced about their past jobs and colleagues. It brought up memories of Tim, with whom they had lost contact, which upset them both greatly and they wondered if he would ever speak with them again. It was a bit painful to be on the verge of so much success and not have a key member of their team with them. However, Tim still hadn't reached out to them and had become more of a recluse.

Stacy then asked Ryan, "Can I ask a favor?"

"Of course," he replied.

"Would you mind filling out a letter of recommendation for my entrance into the MBA program?" she asked.

Ryan laughed, and was thrilled that she asked.

Chapter 9

WAR

Ryan prepared a briefing for Mr. Wheeler all weekend long. It was important for him to get the report right, and present the information concisely. Success of the meeting was predicated on quickly obtaining his agreement and acceptance of the team's recommendations, thereby preserving the momentum they had established. He was asking for three major changes in the department, all of which made perfect sense. At least in his mind they did.

He decided to forgo the formal presentation and simply create a single-page document with bullet points summarizing the new initiatives. Normally, when Ryan delivered important news, he would craft a presentation deck that contained the recommendations. This time the circumstances were different, and therefore, controlling the information flow was critical to gaining the appropriate level of consensus, and it allowed for dynamic modifications should they be required.

The Monday afternoon meeting generated high anxiety throughout the team, who waited to see how effective Ryan would be. Throughout the morning, the team reviewed what they learned the past Friday and discussed among themselves additional ways of making their jobs more effective. Overall, the feedback continued to remain positive and many on the team had hoped for another off-site in the future. Now, the result of the meeting was in Ryan's hands, as was his ability to convince Mr. Wheeler of the direction the team had decided.

Nervousness wasn't a common feeling for Ryan. He was usually a very cool character with a subtle demeanor. However, the pressure was immense. If he was unable to convince Mr. Wheeler of the proposal, would that mean that he was ineffective, or that Mr. Wheeler was simply not the leader he thought he was? Or could it simply mean that Ryan and his entire team were wrong? Although he didn't believe they were wrong, he couldn't assume that he was right. Maybe he had overlooked some detail, or maybe he didn't challenge the team enough. There were many questions swirling around his head and it created more confusion than clarity.

Regardless of his current perceptions, he had made his decision and he would stick to it. There was no sense in overanalyzing the situation. In fact, that was exactly what he advised against in the meeting on Friday. Over analysis is a dangerous trap that many leaders throughout history have fallen victim.

His resolve strengthened during the day, and he became more invigorated, which may have been a façade for increased nervousness. He knew the team was counting on him and he couldn't disappoint them. Mr. Wheeler would need to understand that their proposal was in the best interest of the company and was the most prudent course of action. The concept of developing a single system to handle both the e-commerce site and the point of sale system wasn't uncommon in the industry, but for this company it could be considered radical.

At 3:30 p.m., Ryan walked to Mr. Wheeler's office and knocked on the door. Mr. Wheeler was sitting at his desk, talking on the phone, facing the window. He obviously didn't hear Ryan knocking since he never turned around, so Ryan decided to just wait a few minutes until he finished his conversation. He turned to Mr. Wheeler's secretary, Julia, and asked how Mr. Wheeler was doing today.

"Not very good, he's been in meetings all day and I'm not sure they have gone very well," she responded.

"Ryan," Mr. Wheeler's voice bellowed from his office, "come on in."

With that, Ryan turned with a grin on his face, waved to Julia, and walked into Mr. Wheeler's office.

Ryan could see the frustration on Mr. Wheeler's face. After he sat down, Mr. Wheeler explained the issues currently facing the department, and how important it was to get things turned around quickly. The quarterly numbers had been posted and the outlook was not good. There might even be cutbacks across the board, which would severely diminish the department's capabilities to deliver on any major project.

After a brief pause, he asked Ryan what good news he was bringing. He couldn't help but notice the bit of sarcasm in Mr. Wheeler's voice, as if he was expecting more bad news. Ryan suspected that adding two new people to supplement Michael and Tina for the inventory system might not go over well immediately, so he decided to invert the order of the topics he was going to discuss. He would focus on the major positive to see if he could gain some consensus first, and he decided to phrase it as a question that he already knew the answer to.

"Well, how would you like to develop the POS System and e-commerce site in eight months?" Ryan asked.

Mr. Wheeler laughed and said, "Thanks for trying to cheer me up, but seriously."

"I am serious. At the off-site meeting, the team developed an option to develop both systems simultaneously, with no additional cost and in half the time, if not less."

Ryan discussed the debate that had taken place at the off-site, and how the team constructed a project to build both in an integrated manner. Instead of just trying to utilize the same programming logic, they would build one system, which would then identify whether it was a point of sale or e-commerce customer order.

The point of sale system would have additional features and interfaces for a barcode reader and cash register as well as a specified area for returns, but all other functionality would be shared. The added benefit would enable customers to have access to the same screens as employees. Additionally, modifications could be made in one area that would benefit both customers and customer service representatives, thereby minimizing the long-term maintenance costs of the systems.

Mr. Wheeler was awestruck. He immediately knew it was a stroke of genius to consider the two systems as one and his body language couldn't contain his excitement. Ryan added that additional features could be turned on or off based on the disposition of the system, and that it wouldn't be a major effort to do so and since they were still on time and budget with the inventory system, which was scheduled for delivery in less than three months, integration would be included as well.

"I need to soak this in a bit more. This is absolutely brilliant; your team came up with this at the off-site?" Mr. Wheeler asked.

"Yes and what I didn't know was that Michael and Tina have experience working on inventory systems and can provide assistance on some of the areas where we are struggling. I just need to replace them with two people to handle their day-to-day work."

Mr. Wheeler reached for the phone and, on speakerphone, called Julia and asked her to get Maureen on the phone as soon as possible. He asked Ryan if he had enough details about the proposal to speak to Maureen. Ryan thought it was a bit late to ask if he was ready, since the phone call to Maureen was already in progress, but he affirmed Mr. Wheeler's request. He knew this could be a defining moment for his team.

Julia shouted from her desk to Mr. Wheeler that Maureen was on line two, and with that, Mr. Wheeler brought her up on the speakerphone. The two exchanged some pleasantries and shared some anguish over the recent numbers. Maureen was still upbeat though as she was preparing to launch a new advertising campaign. Unfortunately, she wished she had an e-commerce site that could support a larger initiative.

Mr. Wheeler asked Maureen if she thought it acceptable to have a single system for the customer facing site as well as the point of sale system. He detailed some of the benefits and described how it might work and identified the similarities and differences. It could also be a great marketing campaign to include self-checkout, order from home with pickup at a store, among others features that their direct competition did not have.

Maureen became elated at the idea and wanted to know how quickly it could be done, and almost as quickly as the words came out, her voice became deflated and she said, "Or is this now going to take an extra year?"

Mr. Wheeler laughed, and said, "Well, let's talk about the time when we have more details, but we think it will be done much sooner than the original time estimates."

"That would be amazing because we really need something by the next holiday. Ideally, it would need to be up and running within a year for us to make the holiday season," she responded.

Mr. Wheeler promised a follow-up meeting at the end of the week with her and asked her to remain quiet and keep the information confidential until he had more time to sort out the details. Maureen graciously obliged and thanked him and his team for having some new hope, which was sorely needed at this point.

Mr. Wheeler hung up the phone and asked Ryan to provide a summary of everything needed to accomplish the goal of creating one system for order entry, and he agreed to get some contract workers to relieve Michael and Tina enabling them to work on the inventory system.

Ryan hoped there would be no strings attached to the agreement, but he would work with the team, get the summary, and reenergize the inventory system. He stood up and began to walk out when Mr. Wheeler stopped him and asked, "Ryan, your team really came up with that suggestion?"

"Yes, sir, they just needed to believe that they would be heard and not ignored. I was amazed myself. I really shouldn't be surprised, because I have a lot of faith in them, but I was dumfounded. I forgot the frontline troops usually know more about situations than the leadership in the back. If we empower them to make decisions, and we work on listening more we could be surprised by the result."

"Actually, I already am. Good show," Mr. Wheeler responded.

Ryan walked out and made his way back to his office. He had scored an enormous victory, and if the team followed through, it would certainly solidify his position with the company and give the team some well-deserved respect they sorely needed. His mind raced with different possibilities and angles to ensure he didn't miss anything. As he turned the corner toward his office, he noticed a small crowd gathered near his office down the hall. Apparently, they were all waiting for him to return from Mr. Wheeler's office in anticipation of the news. Ryan withheld a smile that was starting to emerge on his face and as he continued walking he could see the team was now fixated on his approach waiting for any sign from him.

Ryan slowed his gate, slightly increasing their torture as he pondered the best way to reveal the good news. The team's anxiousness was obviously starting to build as they began to walk toward him, when Ryan decided to reveal the news by lifting both arms in front of him and putting up his thumbs. With that simple expression, a bellow could be heard from each member of the team and Ryan's smile could no longer be contained.

After the gathering dispersed and the excitement tapered down, he asked Stacy to provide a summary document for the replacement of Michael and Tina and he wanted her and Rebecca to create a presentation deck by the end of the week on the single order entry system. She told him that they had already begun work on the deck, since they knew he would request it.

As they finished their conversation, Stacy said, "It went really well, didn't it?"

"Stace, it was unbelievable how well it went. We just need to get this horse across the finish line."

"We can, we already know how, we've been thinking about this all day, and it just seems like everything falls into place."

"Just remember one thing, account for the unexpected. You can't control everything that happens, so you need to be prepared to adjust quickly," he warned.

"OODA," she responded, "OODA."

Stacy and Rebecca worked all week on the presentation for the single order entry system. They had solicited help from almost everyone who was at the off-site and it made the presentation a real team effort. Stacy and Rebecca debated with each other over the use of certain words and phrases in the document, since they understood that success at these meetings hinged on almost every word stated or omitted. They left no stone unturned and wanted to make sure they pushed their point across quickly, succinctly, and effectively. Ryan asked for a few more changes to the document before it was ready for the meeting, but the document overall was excellent. It provided the rationale, the benefits, and the time line. Although aggressive in comparison to their last estimates with the previous design, it was well with their comfort range. Ryan didn't expect anything but complete approval of the recommendation from the senior leadership, and he hoped they would be excited by the new track.

At the meeting, the three of them walked in to the conference room, found their seats, and held their breath. The meeting lasted an hour and half, and the general mood of the group was very optimistic. Mr. Wheeler and Maureen had led the discussion as a new direction for the company. They were now going to be positioned as a multichannel store where the traditional lines for the customer would be merged into a single concept of providing for the customer in every channel, when they wanted, how they wanted, and in the manner of their choosing. It was a full 360-degree view of the store and its operations with the customer in the center rather than the corporation in the center. They were going to enable the customers to interact with business ubiquitously and it was all made possible by an idea conjured up in an off-site meeting with a group of technologists.

Ryan and his team had kindled a potential revolution for the company. They would now emerge into the twenty-first century abandoning their principles of strict channel management to a more fluid customer-centric view of the sales process. Stacy and Rebecca, who had been invited by Mr. Wheeler to attend the meeting, were merely observers, but they were elated that the ideas conjured up by their team were the source for this new brand of thinking. They felt part of something much bigger than themselves and much bigger than the project they supported. They were part of the revolution, they were the catalyst for the revolution, and their team would share the excitement. Senior management had given them permission and the mandate to proceed.

It was now time to get working on delivering the promises. Ryan asked Stacy and Rebecca to gather the team in the conference room, to deliver the news and get them started on this new direction. As the team gathered, they began to get bits and pieces of the news. They couldn't believe how much had changed in a short time but they also knew the real work was ahead of them. Stacy asked everyone to be quiet, and as the room silenced, she paused turned to Ryan and said, "Ryan, I think we all want to express our appreciation to you for believing in us and our ideas. Personally, I am more excited than I have been in a long while."

"Thanks, but you just needed to find your collective voice and have an ear to listen. We all did our jobs, and the result could be nothing less than perfect...so far. Now the real work begins, we must finish what we started, together. One word of caution, as we proceed on this path, we must be wary of events we cannot control and we must adapt quickly and decisively. If we don't, events will control us, instead of us controlling events."

The team took their time in celebrating their mini-victory, but they knew it would be a short one. The real battle was about to begin. They need to deliver on some very heavy promises and, while there was no guarantee it would really work, they all believed it would, and for now that was the most important asset they possessed. For now, they would enjoy the weekend, and a few of them at Stacy's request would head over to the local bar for a celebratory toast. Ryan would decline, which was unusual, but he had been exhausted and wanted to spend some downtime at home and return to work more rested and ready.

A month had progressed since the meeting, and work had begun on the single order entry system. The requirements were finalized and the developers had begun to code key components to the system. The inventory system, which was now being finalized, was scheduled to be in place in less than eight weeks, but errors had propped up during the testing phase, which was putting the entire time line in jeopardy. Michael and Tina had been great assets to the project and without them the project would be severely behind. Their collaboration turned into the critical component keeping the project close to schedule.

Tina had moved her desk to the logistics and procurement group. She had developed new relationships with the department, which helped her resolve some of the issues the users had in their requirements. She successfully negotiated an interpretation to a requirement that stated that when inventory levels reach certain levels, an automatic reordering process occurs. The problem she discovered was that static ordering of inventory, or ordering of items at a set quantity, wouldn't work at certain times of the year, at least not quick enough.

The intended requirement was to keep inventory levels at the pace of the demand, so she worked with Michael to develop a method by which the demand would be forecast using previous year's numbers and projected numbers. Jim, who always maintained that all reordering be approved by an individual, gave cautionary approval for this methodology. While he liked the idea of the system placing the orders, he wanted someone reviewing the orders regularly, due to his mistrust of the automation. He acquiesced that in the future he might relinquish that demand, but for now he wanted the manual approval process to remain. Tina's recognition of the potential problem could save the procurement department hundreds of hours of work and during the busy season of the fourth quarter, it could mean the difference between a profitable and an unprofitable year.

This was exactly the type of initiative Ryan sought from his team. If the team was to be successful, they must look to solve problems before they arise and seek consensus as much as possible, but aggressively pursue a track they believed was in the best interest of the company. The team responded very well to this new direction and aggressively searched for efficiencies. In addition, they streamlined the process by limiting the items requiring Ryan's approval.

Ryan granted them authority to make changes they sought with the approval of the business owner. It was risky for him, but the caveat was that the team was communicating internally very well and therefore, there should have been no surprises to anyone, including him, since he regularly reviewed the status reports. His job now was to make sure everything proceeded according to plan and provide periodic direction to align to the strategy.

Stacy and Rebecca now became the two critical players in Ryan's department. Each had her own staff and together they were working very well. Of course, they did have some very heated arguments, but because they respected each other's positions, their debates were productive and usually resulted in added benefits to the project. Whenever they could not agree on a particular topic, instead of isolating the discussion, they opened it up to the team. They brought in more opinions instead of closing it off and this had a profound effect on results and morale. It demonstrated their willingness and desire to be open to all suggestion and reiterated their commitment to the value of each member on the team.

Six weeks later, the inventory system, now only two weeks away from implementation, was running through its final phases of User Acceptance Testing, where the business users provided the final validation. It would be a critical two weeks requiring a coordinated approach to populating the data. The system was scheduled to be in place for three months, running in parallel with the old system. It was a very fortuitous schedule since the previous holiday season recently closed without incident, and the new system would run in parallel during the least busy time for the retailer, the end of the first quarter. It would also give them a good six months to work out any issues in the system in time for the next holiday season.

Jim was very excited to have his new inventory system. During the final meeting before the system would go into production, he remarked how impressed he was with the team's professionalism and dedication to the project. He mentioned a conversation he had recently with Mr. Wheeler, where he remarked how the team's knowledge of inventory and logistics made them prime candidates for hire within his organization. He was originally skeptical about the team's ability to deliver such a robust application, because traditionally they viewed projects as technical in nature. He appreciated their focus on the business aspects of the project and delivered a special thank-you to Tina and Michael for being so adamant in their demands on various requirements including automatic reordering.

The team soaked in the compliments like sunbathers on a beach in Brazil. Never before had they been complimented in such a fashion and their faces gleamed with pride at both the system and their work, and it just felt great. Stacy warned the team about being overconfident since the system wasn't in production yet; however, all indications were that the system was going in on time and under budget in less than two weeks. They would monitor the system and compare results with the current system for two months, and if all went well the old system would be retired and the new system would be standing without a crutch. She was very cautious not to dampen their spirit and simply urged restraint for the time being.

Monday evening, less than six days to the implementation of the inventory system, Ryan received a call at 2:30 a.m. on his BlackBerry. It was very unusual for him to get a call on his BlackBerry since he wasn't responsible for operations. It was the primary reason he stayed away from infrastructure operations. He hated to wake up in the middle of the night for petty issues like a backup not working or a server being down. He could barely get out of bed in the mornings, so answering a phone call in the middle of the night was not his strength.

He picked up the phone and saw it was Mr. Wheeler's cell phone. He knew it must be urgent, but what could possibly be going on that Mr. Wheeler was calling him at 2:30 in the morning?

"Hello?" he answered.

"Ryan, I need you in the office at 5:30 a.m. There's been a fire at the warehouse in Indiana. The entire warehouse burned including the merchandise. We are putting the business recovery plan into effect immediately."

"Oh my God! Was anyone hurt?"

"No, thankfully. The security guards managed to get to safety. They believe there was an electrical fire and it just consumed the entire building too rapidly. Also, we believe the fire safety system may have failed. I'll brief you shortly."

"I'll be there," Ryan said, and then hung up the phone.

Lisa, who had overheard the conversation, asked what had happened. Ryan told her what he knew. He was a bit worried because this was the worst-case scenario for a retailer, losing the inventory. They were covered by insurance, but insurance doesn't help lost customers and lost business, not to mention the long-term effects of customers shifting to a competitor.

He went to the kitchen to make himself a cup of coffee since he couldn't sleep anymore. The severity of the situation was overwhelming and he wondered what the long-term effect would be on the company. As he stood in the kitchen watching the pot of coffee brew, he grabbed a napkin and began sketching a few notes. On the paper he wrote, inventory, receivables, and shipping. These were the three things that would pose a problem to the organization. He started to conjure up ideas on how to get inventory and where could they put it.

He decided he needed to call Stacy and let her know what was happening, he really didn't want to wake her up, but he wanted her in the office at 5:30 in the morning with him.

"Hello? Ryan?" Stacy answered.

"Yeah, Stace, it's me."

"What's up? Everything OK?" she responded.

"Not exactly, the warehouse in Indiana is destroyed. A fire or explosion destroyed it. I just received a call from Mr. Wheeler."

"Oh my, anyone hurt?" she asked.

"No. But I have to be at the office at 5:30 for a meeting. Can you join me in the office? I'm not sure what you could do, but I'd like to have a skeleton crew on hand in case I need help."

"Sure, I'll call Rebecca, Michel, and Tina. I'll make it optional for Michael and Tina but ask them to at least come a bit early."

"Thanks. See you there."

He finished his cup of coffee and looked at the clock, which now said 3:15 in the morning. He figured he would just get dressed and go to the office. Mr. Wheeler would probably be there in forty-five minutes if he wasn't there already. If he could just get some information before the meeting he could try to find ways to help the situation, but he really wasn't sure there was anything he could do.

Without inventory, the stores couldn't be replenished and items would go on backorder. If that happened, customers might buy elsewhere, especially online, and since the online system wasn't ready, this was sure to be a disaster. Without integration to the inventory system, customers would be purchasing online never knowing if their order was filled. Jim had warned about this perfect storm, and it led to the acquisition of the new inventory system. They weren't ready with anything and now this situation could set them back a year.

At the office, Ryan noticed quite a few more cars in the parking lot. Mr. Wheeler's car was already in the lot as he suspected and he could see the light on in his office. He even noticed some of the executives like Maureen walking into the building. It was a sure sign that this was probably the most serious event the company had ever faced. As he contemplated the situation at hand, he remembered his old coach, from his college days, saying, "You can do everything prefect, you just can't control everything."

It was as true now as it was then. All Ryan could think about was how well things were progressing and in a flash the company was turned on its head. He was optimistic they could handle it, but the consequences were unknown, it was a part of life and he knew it. He needed to be energetic, positive, and resolute. He couldn't control what was happening, but he could be part of the solution. What the solution was he had no idea.

He walked directly to Mr. Wheeler's office instead of putting his stuff down. The scheduled 5:30 a.m. meeting Mr. Wheeler had asked for was now an impromptu 4:05 a.m. meeting. Ryan greeted Mr. Wheeler with a smile, but saw that he was noticeably tired. He asked Mr. Wheeler how he was doing. Mr. Wheeler, with a tired response, acknowledged he was very tired but there was too much to do right now and they needed to come up with a plan.

"Should I get some marshmallows?" Ryan asked.

Mr. Wheeler was puzzled at the comment and after a few seconds, burst out in laughter. Ryan apologized for a bad joke, but he couldn't resist, especially since no one was hurt. Mr. Wheeler needed a laugh and he thanked Ryan for coming in so early. It demonstrated Ryan's commitment to him, not his job, which he recognized. It was something he had come to appreciate from Ryan although he never made mention of it.

"Where do we start?" Ryan asked.

Mr. Wheeler explained there were a few problems. First inventory levels at the stores would be OK for most stores at least for a day or two. They needed a way to get products to the stores on a regular schedule as soon as possible. However, in order to do that, they needed to replenish their inventory, which would take at best ten days if everything went perfectly. However, the reorder process was manual so they would need to hire temps and train them to get all the ordering done in a timely fashion. Furthermore, with all the new hires and inexperienced personnel, the error rate would go up, which would further erode their profits, but that might be a risk they needed to take. Finally, there was no place to store the inventory. Even if they could, the old inventory system was so archaic he didn't know how long it would take to program a new facility into the system.

Ryan listened intently to the problem. The real bottleneck appeared to be the ordering process, even if they could get a new facility, they couldn't properly get product to the new facility. A thought ran through his head. He asked Mr. Wheeler to excuse him while he made a phone call on his cell. He called Stacy on her cell phone.

"Hey, Ryan," Stacy answered.

"Stace, quick question for you. Mr. Wheeler told me that one of the biggest problems they face is the old system not being able to choose a new facility and the fact that the process for ordering is heavily manual. Can you give me some options?"

"Yeah, ditch the system."

"Stace, no time for jokes, please." Ryan responded.

"I'm not joking. Ryan, we programmed the system to do automatic ordering without manual intervention and location isn't a problem."

"I thought Jim didn't want that feature."

"He didn't, but we knew it was an important feature and it might be useful in the future so we coded it anyway and just turned it off. It will take a little bit of time to turn it on and test it properly, less than a day, but we ran through our own tests, and it worked pretty well. I'll be there in ten minutes. Shall I meet you at my desk?"

"No come to Mr. Wheeler's office. Thanks."

He told Mr. Wheeler that the manual intervention problem may not be a problem after all and he explained what Stacy told him. Mr. Wheeler was impressed, and wondered what other functionality was put in the system that he didn't know about. They both waited anxiously for Stacy's arrival and, while they waited, Mr. Wheeler called Jim to ask him about the facility location. Jim, who was for obvious reasons very busy and curt on the phone, explained to Mr. Wheeler that his primary concern was the inventory levels and notification of an alternate facility to suppliers, because they had a deal in place to use space in another warehouse for just such an emergency; however, the problem had always been the inventory.

Upon hearing that news, Mr. Wheeler told Jim he was heading to his office to explain how that might not be a problem. Unfortunately, Jim would have to make the decision to use the new system six days early and lose the luxury of running the system in parallel or focus his efforts on the manual reordering process and the acquisition of temporary personnel to accomplish the task. Mr. Wheeler would need to explain the pros and cons of such a direction and right now, there was no solid proof this would work, except for Stacy's word. Mr. Wheeler, as he headed out of his office, told Ryan to wait for Stacy and then come right to Jim's office when she arrived.

Ryan waited for another ten minutes and Stacy walked in with her cup of coffee in her hand and another one for him. She brought one for him figuring he had no time for a cup. He thanked her for it since he was in desperate need of another cup; it was just one of those mornings. Before they headed to Jim's office, he asked her how much work was done on the automatic reordering process. She explained that Jim didn't want it, he wanted to stick to the manual ordering process; however, the team coded and configured the system to eventually include it. The problem was that there was only limited testing, so she wasn't sure if it would pass a quality assurance cycle. Since the functionality was off, there was no requirement to rigorously test it. Stacy also mentioned that while they could order the entire inventory automatically with orders being sent to the suppliers, any new suppliers in the last two weeks would not be in the system already and the inventory levels would need to be populated manually.

As they walked to Jim's office, Ryan began to think about how to structure the team to help manage the issue for the next few days. He asked Stacy if Rebecca should be in charge of the effort. While she wanted control of the effort for the challenge it posed, she agreed Rebecca was best suited, along with Tina and Michael.

When they arrived at Jim's office, he said to come inside, and they made their way to a seat at Jim's conference table. Mr. Wheeler had already briefed Jim and they were contemplating the risks of such an action. The benefits, as Mr. Wheeler explained to Jim, would be that once the system sent out the inventory orders, inventory could begin flowing in within twenty-four hours and it was estimated that the entire stock of inventory would be repopulated within a week unless the suppliers had no more in stock. In addition, a significant number of staff would not have to be diverted from other areas of the company, nor would temporary staff need to place orders for thousands of products with the vendors, which could take approximately three to four weeks to complete the entire process.

Jim would ultimately be the person who would have to decide which route to go. He was very skeptical of the system being able to place all the orders, although he suspected, in this case, it was the right way to go. It was just a high level of uncertainty for Jim who had been an old school logistics manager and liked things done his way using a managed process that had been in place for the last twenty-five years.

Ryan, seizing an opportunity to discuss his thoughts, said, "I understand your apprehension, but I think I have a way to mitigate the risk for you."

He explained that the programming team still had work to complete in order to accomplish this task. First, since the functionality never went through quality assurance, it would be a good idea to get the director in charge of testing involved to perform some base level quality checks. Second, they would need to code the new warehouse into the system; while it was one of the weakest parts of the system, it was simpler to make the change in the new system over the old system. Finally, they would need to populate the current inventory levels of each product instead of ordering a full load of every product; this would require an export of the current system to the new system.

Since this process could take twenty-four hours, he told Jim that he could begin his preparations to adjust staff and bring on additional help, but that if he allowed for twenty-four hours, they should be able to complete all the tasks and start reordering by tomorrow morning. If they couldn't, or they ran into a situation, they would let him know immediately and he could institute plan B, and the most they would lose is twenty-four hours.

Jim reluctantly agreed; he knew the twenty-four hours was worth the time savings of two to three weeks in inventory. He hoped they could pull it off, although he still wasn't entirely convinced. Mr. Wheeler also agreed but he had a lot more faith in his team and he would provide them the support they needed. With the agreement to pursue this approach, Ryan and Stacy left the room and Jim and Mr. Wheeler proceeded to the CEO's office to explain their course of action. There was no turning back at this point.

On the way back to their desks, Stacy said to Ryan, "Ryan, I think we will need more time than twenty-four hours, the load of the data itself maybe a problem. Remember that system is very slow."

"I know, but Jim needed a comfort level that we were going to be aggressive. This is too important to be apprehensive. You know the solution will work. Get everyone together. Start calling them in, it's now 5:15 a.m. See if you can get everyone in here by 7:30."

By 7:00 a.m., all the key players had arrived at the office. They all began to filter directly into the conference room and Stacy and Rebecca, who had arrived at 6:00 a.m., began to brief everyone on the situation and on the plan of action. Michael and Tina would begin immediately on ensuring the logic for the automatic ordering was in place and working, ready for official testing. Michael expected this to be completed in the early afternoon along with the programming for the location of the warehouse. John offered to work on the data transfer since he knew the system pretty well and he had a few tricks up his sleeve to get the data over faster. However, he believed that the data wouldn't be ready until the early evening at the earliest. Finally, Ryan would work with the director of quality assurance to get the system up and running and tested as quickly as possible. Unfortunately, that would be the last mile and it was the last mile that would be the hardest.

Understanding their assignments, everyone began to attack their problems. It would be a very grueling day. Ryan would keep tabs on the executives and keep them briefed on the progress. Stacy would get briefed every four hours from the team and provide Ryan with the update. They wanted to stay out of everyone's way as much as possible but they also wanted to ensure proper communication with the senior staff. Rebecca would be the critical point of contact, coordinating all of the efforts between each of the sub teams.

There was an enormous amount of pressure being placed on them, not by senior management but by themselves. They had undertaken the responsibility of trying to save the company by accelerating the recovery effort with a system that wasn't officially ready for production. The team could have sat on the sidelines and allowed the logistics team to struggle with the existing system and the intensive manual labor required for the reordering process; however, Ryan understood two critical points. First, if they were successful, it would be a great win for the team. It would be comparable to a cavalry charge coming to save a brigade under heavy fire. By itself, that could propel the team's status within the organization. Secondly, he understood that his team and the logistics team, while sometimes at odds with each other, shared the same goal, which was the continued success of the corporation, and right now his team could provide a better solution. It was a win-win scenario in the midst of a pending disaster, if they were successful. If they weren't, he would take responsibility and probably take a hit on his credibility, and worst-case scenario would be a perceived ineffectiveness of the inventory system, leading to more concerns and doubts, which could lead to the project's demise, but that was very unlikely.

Ryan's team didn't need much coaxing to take on the responsibility. Everyone was called in and they willingly showed up earlier than requested. They accepted their assignments and began to work immediately in spite of the seemingly overwhelming tasks. It was a testament to how far they had come in a short amount of time. They began to trust each other and they had faith in each other to accomplish their respective tasks. No one complained, no one argued, they embraced the adversity and they did so collectively. Now Ryan would wait and see the result.

By midday, he could see the team was struggling even though they tried not to show it. Michael and Tina seemed to have a handle on the modifications, but it was progressing much slower than they had anticipated. Tina, who had been monitoring the progress, now estimated that they would be two hours behind schedule, but what made matters worse was the fact that she wasn't sure. At every turn, they found a few new issues impeding their progress, which needed to be reconciled.

John had worked up an optimal way to retrieve the information; however, the system was performing slower than it ever had and he could provide no explanation for the poor performance. His original estimate was right, that the information wouldn't be available until early in the evening, but now it could slip even further. Unfortunately, once they had extracted the information in the proper format, they still needed to get it into the new system. Since the new system was built using better equipment, he hoped the process to import the information would be significantly faster. John's frustration continued to build as he watched the progress move at an agonizing pace.

Across the organization, tensions were running at a very high level. At 1:00 p.m., Mr. Wheeler called Ryan and Stacy into his office. Mr. Wheeler didn't indicate why he summoned them, but Ryan knew it couldn't be very good since he had just provided the status update less than an hour ago. He bellowed over to Stacy's cubicle to walk with him to Mr. Wheeler's office. When she met up with him in the aisle, she asked if everything was all right. He told her he wasn't sure, but they were to go to Mr. Wheeler's office immediately.

As the two walked to his office, they could hear Maureen's voice emanating from Mr. Wheeler's office. Her voice carried through the aisles, especially when she was angry. They couldn't make out exactly what she was talking about, but they did hear her mention Paltz, which was very peculiar. Stacy and Ryan looked at each other with Stacy mouthing the word "Paltz," to which Ryan simply shrugged his shoulders.

When they entered the office, Maureen exclaimed, "It's about time!"

Ryan, perplexed, responded, "Excuse me?"

Mr. Wheeler responded, "Maureen, this will not get us anywhere, you need to calm down a bit. Please sit down."

Maureen reluctantly sat down; however, she did realize her jab was unwarranted. Ryan and Stacy now knew they needed to be wary of an attack, although they weren't sure exactly what the attack would be. Stacy was not very happy to be in the office; she had more pressing items to attend to than to be jabbed at for some political show.

Ryan asked Mr. Wheeler, "So what can we do for you?"

Mr. Wheeler was about to respond, when Maureen, whose patience had been worn completely out throughout the day, interjected. "Ryan, we are in big trouble. I know the inventory is down, and it's a priority but we need to do something about the Web site or we will lose customers."

"I don't understand," Ryan responded.

Earlier in the day, Paltz had announced a 20 percent discount on all merchandise, and while their Web site indicated that it was the end of winter blowout sale, she had learned that the supposed sale was simply a ruse. Paltz believed that SportsCentral couldn't fill orders due to the inventory issue and they were trying to capitalize on it. In fact, Paltz was guaranteeing shipment in twenty-four hours.

"They can't do that," responded Ryan.

"Why not?" Maureen asked.

"Because their inventory system doesn't work efficiently enough," Stacy responded.

"I don't understand," Maureen said.

"Well, Ryan and I used to work there; I was there up until about a year ago. Their systems were never set up to handle shipment in twenty-four hours. It takes forty-eight hours for the systems to go through their nightly cycles and get the orders to the warehouse, so they really can't ship product for seventy-two. It's very inefficient," Stacy responded.

"Couldn't they have fixed the problem since you left?" Maureen asked.

"Doubtful. Inventory systems are very intricate and have a tremendous number of moving parts. While it is possible, there would be so much risk that it can't be done in a year's time but even with that time frame, I know they weren't working on it when I left," she answered.

"Also, the management team there never focused on the logistics issues. They were very headstrong, and still are. When I was there, they never produced what the business wanted or really needed because it wasn't glamorous. I know that hasn't changed," Ryan added.

The exchange did little to ease Maureen's nervousness but the four of them continued their discussion. If Ryan and Stacy were right, then Paltz would have a problem if customers began ordering and expecting shipments to come in early. Plus, Ryan knew that Paltz had no way of determining exactly what was in stock, which meant customers could order items that would ultimately be on back order. Paltz was making a bold statement, which Ryan and Stacy believed was doomed to fail, but no one in the room knew for certain if anything had changed at Paltz that might make them successful.

Mr. Wheeler then briefed Maureen on the progress of the inventory replenishment. While the time line was tight and the team was running into issues, they were still somewhat on track. Maureen listened intently to Mr. Wheeler's description of what the team was doing, although she really didn't understand. The one thing she did understand was that they were trying to reorder the entire inventory in a matter of hours as opposed to a matter of weeks.

Maureen knew the importance of their work because it meant they could resume normal operations faster than previously thought. Unfortunately, she needed to figure out a way to neutralize Paltz's campaign, which was clearly designed to take business away from them. She thanked the team and then excused herself from the room and said she would look for ways to minimize the impact of the Paltz campaign, and she agreed that right now the best course of action was continuing exactly what they were doing.

Stacy and Ryan were about to leave the office when Mr. Wheeler asked Ryan to stay behind. Stacy continued her exit while Ryan returned to his seat. Mr. Wheeler said to Ryan, "We really are counting on you to do this. This is very critical."

"I know it is. We will get it done. Everyone on the team is aggressively tackling the problem."

"Actually, I don't think you understand. We have been having meetings over the past few months. Our financial numbers aren't that great and an incident like this is something we may never recover from. If Paltz is successful in luring customers, they may never come back and we might be in very serious trouble."

"We are doing the best we can, and I am confident we will get it working. Remember the system was working—we are just modifying it from the original spec."

Their conversation continued for a few more minutes before Ryan left the office. His impression was that the company was in worse shape than Mr. Wheeler stated. His expressions of concern were out of character for the usually composed man. Ryan knew the concerns about the reordering problem, but he had addressed them very early on when he arrived. It was like pulling teeth to get management to listen. Something so obvious and simple should have been a trivial discussion but unfortunately it wasn't and the consequence could have been worse had the team not had the foresight to implement it anyway. He wasn't laying blame on Mr. Wheeler; rather, he knew that the other managers were resolute on their deep-rooted business processes. Therefore, they were susceptible to complacency and were hesitant to change, which explained why they had so much difficulty with some of the newer requirements.

At the 6:00 p.m. status meeting, the team gathered around Stacy's cubicle. There was no time, nor was there any need for a conference room. Everyone just grabbed a chair from a cube and moved it to the aisle. As they all sat down, Michael and Tina said they had completed their tasks, and the system was working to the new reorder specification. The quality assurance representative concurred with the assessment and gave it a go for deployment.

Ryan knew now that the lone dependency was the data load from the old system to the new system. The hope was that they would complete the system by the morning in order to begin placing orders. If they could accomplish that, then inventory could begin flowing into the warehouse by Wednesday and orders could be fulfilled by Thursday.

John, whose task was to complete loading the data, said to Ryan, "Remember when I said it would take awhile to complete the data load because of the slowness of the system? Well, I was thinking earlier today and I came up with a way to expedite it. Instead of waiting for all the data to be exported, then convert all the data, then import all the data, I wrote a small program that would do all of that as each record was ready."

"Great idea, so when do you expect the data to be loaded into the new system?" Stacy asked.

"Well, actually, I asked a favor about thirty minutes ago from someone on the logistics team to just take a look and spot-check some of the data. They were going to get back to me at 6:30. If he says were good to go. We are good to go."

"That's great, why didn't you say anything earlier?" Stacy asked.

"Well, I knew it would work, but I spent every bit of my time watching the process and spot-checking as the data went into the new system. I hadn't left my desk since one o'clock. While I was confident it would work, I wanted to absolutely sure. We would really have only one shot at this."

Ryan was grateful for his dedication; it was a testament to how far he had come. It also vindicated Ryan's belief in the team and their ability to adapt to the new style. John was given the assignment, which he accepted, allowed to do his job uninhibited, and the result was better than expected. While John could have just sat back and allowed his task to run into the late hours of the day, he understood the mission as prescribed, modified his tactics accordingly when he saw an opportunity to do so, and he did it without permission or fear of retribution.

Tina provided the status report for her and Michael, since he was preoccupied at his desk. She mentioned that Michael had begun importing the data into the new system as John was completing his checks. They had decided there was no use in waiting for John to run through his complete checks before importing the data into the new system. She said the worst-case scenario would have been that the data was wrong and they would have to start over again; if that were the case though, John would have to start over, which meant the clock would restart anyway. By using the time to begin the importing, the result would be faster and if there were any problems they would be, in effect, testing their import process.

Tina said, "In that way there would be no wasted action. If we just sat around waiting for John, we would be completely idle. Right now, since John had completed his tests and was satisfied with the data, we are in a position to be completely ready for ordering in the next hour to hour and a half."

"Mr. Wheeler and the executive team are going to be very impressed, I know I am," Ryan said. "You guys have done an excellent job."

Rebecca added, "Now we need to put together a plan to monitor this thing over the next few days as the orders are placed and as product arrives at the warehouse. I also suggest we move the official implementation date of the entire system to this evening, and forgo the parallel runs since the older system is currently idle."

Ryan agreed with the approach, but he needed Jim and Mr. Wheeler's approval. Normally, he would never agree with a proposal of this sort, but it made perfect sense in light of the circumstances. While the approach was risky, Rebecca was correct regarding the increased risk of moving the information to the old system at this point. In addition, keeping the old system running might be more of a nightmare with all the orders that would be coming in over the next few days.

As the meeting ended, they subtly congratulated each other, since they knew they had accomplished their mission. However, the next few days and especially the next twenty-four hours would be critical and would ultimately prove how successful their efforts had been. While the orders appeared to have been placed correctly and the anticipated inventory levels in the new system were established, the orders needed to arrive. If the suppliers didn't receive the orders correctly or if the orders were mismatched, the result would be incorrect orders and quantities, resulting in more chaos on arriving inventory.

Ryan had called Mr. Wheeler and asked him to bring Jim for an update. He told Mr. Wheeler they had completed assignment; however, he wanted both of them to be certain of the risk and take appropriate measures as needed. Mr. Wheeler agreed and had decided to include Maureen as well, who was still in the office. All the senior executives would be giving an update to the CEO in less than an hour so he wanted to make sure they spoke with a united voice to avoid any surprises.

When they had all assembled in Mr. Wheeler's office, the mood was upbeat. Jim started the updates by informing the team of the progress on establishing the warehouse floor at the backup site. They would be ready before noon to begin receiving shipments and the timing coincided perfectly with the work the IT department was performing. He had received regular and detailed updates from his staff and Tina, who had become an integral point of contact between logistics and IT. In fact, Jim commented how he actually believed for a time that Tina worked for his group until someone told him differently. After Jim updated the group, he had given his approval to proceed with the use of the system for the ordering.

Ryan couldn't help but feel a sense of pride in his team as Jim continued his accolades. Jim even commented that the work would probably save the company from a disastrous quarter, assuming, of course, there were no surprises. Once the executive team reviewed the report from Jim and his approval was received, there was no objection to proceeding forward. It was at that point that Ryan decided to bring up Rebecca's proposal.

Addressing Mr. Wheeler directly, he said, "I want to discuss the option of putting the entire system into production tonight one week ahead of schedule, instead of running it from the test area."

Mr. Wheeler responded, "I don't see any issue with that. Things have progressed very well and, in light of the results, I think it's a reasonable request."

Jim concurred with the assessment but then Ryan added, "Thank you, but I don't think I am being very clear. I would like to move the system in production and run it as the primary system from this point forward and not run it in parallel as originally proposed."

Mr. Wheeler said, "That wasn't our original plan and that puts the organization at risk. Ryan, you know we run major systems in parallel to avoid any potential issues."

Jim was very concerned that Ryan would even want to consider making the system the primary system. In fact, he mentioned that the company couldn't afford to take on added risk. He added that the focus should be just receiving the inventory and getting back to business as usual as quickly as possible.

Ryan paused and told them that his team had weighed the options, and in fact, had concluded that the risk of maintaining two systems during this time was a greater risk than implementing the new system. Furthermore, both the IT teams and logistics teams would be required to do double work to ensure the systems were in sync for the duration of the parallel run and this would be precious time that could be devoted to getting the company back to business as usual as quickly as possible. Ryan deliberately used Jim's words exactly to make sure his message came through very clearly. He knew this was the right approach and he needed to get their consensus; failure to do so could severely damage both teams.

After fifteen minutes of deliberation among Jim, Maureen, and Mr. Wheeler, they really hadn't reached an agreement. Although they agreed that maintaining the two systems could be more of a problem. Mr. Wheeler looked at his watch and said we had to be in the CEO's office in five minutes. "What's our verdict?" he asked.

Jim paused, knowing that his voice was really the vote that counted. He would need to give the approval for such an action. He looked at Ryan's face and the determination in his expression. He knew that Ryan believed this was the right move. He asked Ryan, "Your team believes this will work and that this is the best approach? Including Tina?"

Ryan never realized how much respect Jim had for Tina, until now. He implied that Tina understood his department well and trusted that she would never put him and his department at risk. Once again, she had made herself a member of their department and as such had gained their trust. He responded affirmatively to Jim. After another brief pause, Jim finally concluded, "Your team has performed admirably over the past few months and the work in the last twenty-four hours is a testament to your group, and as such I would be remiss if I didn't give you the respect you have earned."

Jim turned to Mr. Wheeler and said, "I approve of the proposal, but I want you know I will take full responsibility if this doesn't work. I want to be clear that I need to take responsibility for a decision of this magnitude."

Mr. Wheeler replied, "We will do so jointly, although I don't think we will have to worry."

"Somehow, neither do I," Jim said.

They walked out with Maureen and headed toward the CEO's office where they would make the recommendations. Maureen was fully on board because if everything worked right, her marketing plan could prove a substantial blow to the Paltz campaign to try to lure customers. She was a fighter and she wanted to make Paltz regret attempting to take advantage of the situation. Her plan was to provide next-day shipping for many of their products, those under a predefined weight, in the hopes that Paltz would try to do the same. Since she knew they couldn't deliver next day, customers would become angered, and hopefully they would be lured to SportsCentral, as she and the internal communications director created press releases indicating that despite the fire, they were committed to getting customers their product in a timely fashion. This was the exact reason why Maureen was a highly sought-after marketing executive. Like a tigress on the prowl, she looked for ways to exploit weaknesses of her competition and pounce on her prey with lightning efficiency. Ryan's intelligence from Paltz, coupled with his team's success in recovering from the disaster, gave her the elements of a perfect storm with which she would strike at Paltz. It would be a very interesting few weeks as she implemented her plan.

Ryan headed back to his team with the positive news, and upon learning of the decision, they immediately went to work to ensure everything went smoothly. They pulled all the implementation documentation, and began the preparation for moving the system into full production. Orders would begin flowing out in less than thirty minutes and suppliers whose cutoff time was 8:00 p.m. would be able to get orders on trucks later this evening and some of the inventory would arrive before noon.

Ryan split his core team of six into two groups. The first group of Ryan, Rebecca, and Michael would stay the night and review the orders as they left the system. They would diligently spot-check orders as they left and acknowledgements as they arrived to look for any anomalies. The second group, Stacy, John, and Tina, would arrive back at 6:00 a.m. and work with the logistics team monitoring the orders as they arrived and ensuring inventory levels were up to date. The second group would be more process focused which is why Tina was placed in that group. She, once again, would be the key point for communications with the logistics team.

The night proved to be long and uneventful for Ryan and his team. He spent the time talking to Rebecca and Michael, and understanding their careers in more detail. They expressed their gratitude to Ryan for the opportunities never before afforded them. Michael at one point said he had learned more in the year and half since Ryan arrived than from the time he was hired to then. Rebecca expressed similar feelings; however, her appreciation was more rooted in Ryan's ability to break the old boys' club, which had suppressed her as well as others who had tried to express opinions.

While the discussions went on, they did notice a few minor problems with orders. Most of them were corrected and resubmitted. Some, however, required more manual intervention and were recorded for the logistics team to handle in the morning upon their return. Ryan and the team would brief Stacy and her team upon their arrival before heading home.

At 6:00 a.m., Stacy's team had arrived and she briefed them on the status of all the orders and the issues that were encountered throughout the night. The three overnighters were very tired and couldn't wait to rest their eyes, although they had agreed to return by 3:00 p.m., and, therefore, it would be a fairly short rest. Stacy told Ryan when he arrived that she would bring him up to speed and that she would be in contact with Mr. Wheeler, who spent the better part of the evening in the office and didn't leave until midnight, when he arrived. Ryan told Stacy not to expect Mr. Wheeler before 11:00 a.m. but that Tina should attend Jim's 8:00 a.m. status meeting. He also told her if there were any issues to call him and he would come back to the office.

In only the way Stacy could, she said, "Ryan, if I need you, you know I will call. I'll only call you if Mr. Wheeler is not around and I need a high-level decision. You get some rest; we'll handle it from here."

Ryan felt very comfortable leaving the situation in Stacy's hands and without hesitation he waved and headed out of the building to get some sleep. He didn't dwell on any issues that had arisen over the evening; his main focus was keeping his heavy eyes on the road as he drove home. When he finally arrived home, he noticed Lisa sitting at the coffee table getting their son ready for school and herself ready for work. There wasn't much in the way of conversation since Lisa and A. J. could see the exhaustion on his face. However, when Lisa asked how everything went, he replied, "Better than I could have ever hoped for," and then he went to the bedroom and fell asleep.

When Ryan arrived back at the office, Stacy greeted him and asked if he had rested well. He became a bit nervous at the question and asked, "Why? Yes, I did. Why?"

Stacy laughed and said, "Boy, you're a bit cynical this afternoon, aren't you?"

She sat down in his office and began her update, which was positive. They had one major problem receiving acknowledgments from one supplier; however, the cause was determined to be inability of the supplier's system to change warehouse locations overnight. They usually required twenty-four hours' notice for orders, since the delivery location needed to be modified the night before.

Stacy spoke to Jim and Mr. Wheeler twice during the day, and they were both pleased at the progress. Orders had begun to arrive from local suppliers at around 11:00 a.m. and other orders were confirmed on shipping trucks. The biggest challenge they were now facing was the lack of training on the new system. Everyone in the logistics department had only a minimal amount of training on the new system, and Tina was spending all of her time showing them how to navigate the system. Michael, who had called Tina at 12:00 for an update, arrived at 1:00 p.m., after learning of Tina's predicament, to lend a hand training the users.

The entire operation moved with clocklike precision. The new warehouse was receiving orders and the systems were responding as designed. Although some of the features in the system were new, the situation had left no room for criticism and the teams just progressed as best they could. The entire organization worked together to ensure everything worked. This behavior, Ryan knew, was a classical behavior found when adversity suddenly strikes a group of people or an organization. During times of need, the group will set aside their differences for the common good and execute their responsibilities willingly and without hesitation. Ryan also noted the intense feelings of animosity toward Paltz for trying to take advantage of the situation. While everyone understood it was a part of business to take advantage of the competition, they channeled their energy to ensure that Paltz would fail in its endeavor to take customers away.

The situation reminded him of the attack on Pearl Harbor. Even though the attack occurred thousands of miles away, the horror and surprise of the attack was a blow to the entire nation, which resolved to defeat an enemy with all resources available. Although not to the same scale, the feeling and intensity were similar. There was no mistaking the resolve of the employees who had vowed to get the company back up and running as quickly as possible.

At 5:00 p.m., no more issues had been reported and the operation continued very smoothly. Stacy walked in to Ryan's office once again to discuss an idea she had. Ryan wasn't leaving the office for another few hours so there was no urgency in discussing the idea. They had a relaxed chat about what happened over the past few days and they shared a few laughs but mostly they were gleaming with pride about how the team responded. There was no doubt that after this incident; this team would be changed for the better, permanently.

Stacy asked Ryan, "Would you consider a radical idea right now?"

"You mean everything we have done over the past few days was by the book?" he joked.

"Actually, when you hear my idea, you will probably scream."

"OK. What is it?"

Stacy realized during the day that the major obstacle to releasing a new Web site was the inventory system. Since the system would no longer be running in parallel, they could accelerate the time to delivery by at least three months. He agreed; however, it was an obvious assessment that probably would have been uncovered over the next few days when the situation normalized.

Stacy then said, "I think we should release a new version of the Web site in three weeks."

Now she had Ryan's attention. She explained how in about three weeks' time, Paltz would be struggling with customer complaints due to their shipping guarantee. If they could release a new version of the Web site, it would put more pressure on Paltz while giving existing customers and new customers a secure sense of SportsCentral's situation. She laid out her plan by separating the core components that were already completed and currently in the testing phase. These components included customer reviews, more enhanced cross-selling and up-selling opportunities, and videos of products, to name a few. Some other components that weren't finished could be completed in the four weeks after. This would effectively move the production date for the new Web site four months ahead of schedule. The point of sale system additions, including the barcode system, credit card scanning, and store closing modules, would be completed twelve to sixteen weeks thereafter. However, Stacy reiterated that the timing for the Web site implementation was more important now because of the opportunity it presented.

Ryan loved the idea. He grilled Stacy to make sure all the risks were reviewed; he wanted to be sure they were thorough in their discussion. Rebecca had joined in the middle of the conversation and upon hearing of the plan concurred with the assessment. Collectively they believed they could do it and should do it.

Unexpectedly, Mr. Wheeler and Maureen had walked by Ryan's office. Ryan called to them and asked them for a moment of their time. They stood in the doorway of the office as Ryan began to explain the idea. Maureen quickly moved in to the office, sat down in the last open chair, and with intensity began asking questions. Rebecca and Stacy, along with Ryan, answered all of her questions. Mr. Wheeler seemed to agree with the logic proposed. He reiterated to Maureen what Ryan had said in months ago, when they agreed to postpone the Web site and point of sale system—that the inventory system was the keystone to the entire operation.

Mr. Wheeler, sensing that the team had already discussed the pros and cons of the approach and granting them a large degree of latitude based on their recent performance, asked Maureen, "Do you want to proceed with this approach?"

"Absolutely!" she yelled with an excitement that no one in the room had ever heard before. She turned to Stacy and said, "Are you sure you aren't a marketing person?"

"No, I just learned about observations and recognizing opportunities," she replied as she looked in Ryan's direction.

Maureen left the office with Mr. Wheeler in great excitement. Mr. Wheeler, who lagged behind her, leaned back into the doorway and gave the team a big thumbs-up. Ryan and the team would now have to go to work to accomplish this new mission. Stacy would pull the team together in the morning and reshuffle the plan accordingly. Rebecca would need to remain with the inventory system for the next few weeks to ensure continuity, but she would return to the project after the first implementation. It would be a rough couple of weeks to make sure everything worked to perfection and, with the die having been cast with Maureen and the executive team, Ryan was gambling their recently gained political capital, but he knew this was a pretty good bet. He remembered Virgil's quote that "Fortune favors the brave!"

Over the next two weeks, Stacy and her team aggressively worked through the problems they encountered with the new Web system. Many of the functions worked as designed; however, there were some sporadic problems with the checkout process. Stacy was concerned about all the changes the marketing team had been making to the layout and navigation. While they didn't necessarily affect functionality, it was taking away valuable resources from fixing functionality issues. Stacy and her team spent many long nights during this period correcting and adjusting, testing and retesting the new versions of the code.

Stacy had engaged in numerous intense arguments with Dave Texiera, the marketing lead who reported to Maureen. He had been responsible for the numerous changes to design and navigation; however, he had not seriously documented his changes. With only two weeks left before implementation, Dave had requested another major change to the design. Making matters worse, he told Maureen that he had requested it from Stacy months ago, and she deliberately misled him and his team about its completion.

Enraged upon hearing this, Stacy stormed in to Ryan's office and demanded a meeting with the entire team. Ryan, who had been kept informed of the situation, asked Stacy to calm down. Ryan remembered that asking Stacy to calm down was akin to asking a lion not to eat its prey after it hadn't eaten in three days. He told Stacy he would call the meeting but only with Dave, Maureen, Stacy, and himself.

Stacy was adamant that she wanted everyone from both teams in the meeting. She felt Dave was smearing her name and she wanted to put him in his place and demand an apology. She felt very strongly that an opportunistic player was sabotaging her reputation and that his motives were less than honorable.

Ryan asked her to remember that she was fighting a war, referring to the conflict with Dave, and no longer engaged in the conflict with Paltz. He stressed that the conflict with Paltz was more important than her conflict with Dave and in the end that would be the event that would determine her reputation. However, he did empathize with the need to act, and as such he wanted to keep the damage localized, meaning they would take care of Dave in front of Maureen and let her deal with the problem. He arranged for the meeting later in the afternoon, but he asked for the meeting in his office and not Maureen's. He wanted to have the psychological effect of home territory and he wanted to make sure he controlled the display on his terminal, which he would use to show the Web site to Maureen. Stacy, although still very angry, trusted Ryan and deferred to his approach; however, she added, "If this doesn't work, I will take that little shit outside and drop him."

Stacy turned and started to walk out of the office when she turned back to Ryan with a sarcastic smile and said, "And then I'm coming for you."

Ryan laughed and said, "Get out of here."

Later in the afternoon, Maureen, who had agreed to come to Ryan's office for the meeting, arrived fifteen minutes early. She told him she understood there were some problems with the Web site and she wouldn't tolerate the date being moved. He understood the necessity of the time line and sympathized with her. He listened to her five-minute rant and, using a technique he had learned in leadership class, he said, "Maureen, I understand and share your concern about the time line. We share the same goal right now and I don't want anything to get in the way of your success."

Ryan was sympathizing with Maureen and ensuring that she knew he understood her predicament. Furthermore, he used a term that *she* would find favorable, "your success." She continued discussing the importance of the requested changes, but suddenly, after another few minutes, she stopped. It was apparent she was thinking about something. He hoped it wasn't another change. Fortunately, for him, it was.

"You know as I listen to myself talk, I think maybe we do have too many changes," she said, and then asked him to bring up the site on his screen. She navigated through a couple of pages and scenarios with him and concluded that the site needed no more changes. At that very moment, Dave walked in, followed closely by Stacy, who had approached the office from the opposite direction.

Maureen turned to Dave after he sat down and said, "I just reviewed the site with Ryan. We're done. No more changes, any new changes will have to wait."

Dave responded, "I agree, I think it looks good the way it is."

Stacy's face turned a pale white, uncertain of exactly what had just happened. She came in ready for a gun battle, but none ensued. She wasted her entire preparation on an anticlimactic episode of agreement. Dave, who had been in her face for the past week about more changes, now suddenly capitulated based on Maureen's recommendation, without so much as a word of rebuttal.

Dave turned to Stacy and said, "I think we are ready to sign off on the site moving into production, I'll prepare the paperwork."

Dave then proceeded out of the office. Stacy was still silent unsure of how to react or what to do. Ryan actually thought this was a colossal moment. The woman, who was never short on words and never silent, was stunned, motionless, and speechless. He wanted to laugh but since Maureen was still in his office, he thought better of it. However, he wouldn't be silent later.

Maureen moved closer to Ryan to lower her voice and said, "You know, he's bugged me for the last week that more changes were needed and he didn't even flinch when I said it was OK. That's a problem."

Ryan responded in a similarly low voice, "It's important to have dissenting opinions; otherwise, why have people reporting to you?"

Maureen nodded, turned, and said good-bye to Stacy, but before she left she said, "Stacy, you should be proud of the work you did. It's fantastic."

A smile blossomed on her face as Maureen left the room. Stacy got up from her chair, closed the door turned and said, "What the hell did you do? He said nothing. *Nothing*. That weasel!"

Stacy had a lot to say, but they didn't need to dwell on the meeting when they had plenty of work to do. He explained everything briefly, but summarized his approach and said, "I just wanted Maureen to realize that we sympathize with her and we understand the importance of the project to her. She saw everything herself, and because it was her idea and her success at risk, she came to a very reasonable conclusion."

"OK, you need to show me that sometime. Right now I have to get ready for a production move." Stacy left the office and began gathering her team to prepare the new Web site, which would now be live in less than three days.

Three days later, the Web site moved into production flawlessly and the marketing campaign to attract new customers was fully engaged. The team noticed the Web site traffic jump, and it was obvious that the new site was making an impact on sales. The simplicity of ordering and the quality of the information delivered, including the quantity available, shipping date, and enhanced product images and video made the site very appealing to the customers. The marketing department even noticed an increase in sales in the previously poor cross-sell opportunities. It was a great hit for the customers, and for the company as a whole.

During the last eight weeks the team had successfully implemented the new inventory system in the middle of a disaster, saved the company hundreds of thousands of dollars, thwarted an attack by its enemy Paltz, and counterattacked with the new enhanced Web site. Everyone was energized and took an immense amount of pride in what had been accomplished. They had snatched victory out of the mouth of defeat and had accomplished their herculean tasks with utmost efficiency.

Ryan was very pleased and proud of his team, for it was only a short while before, when he worried about garnering their confidence and trust, and now it seemed like a distant memory. They could have done nothing more, and there was nothing they could have done better. It was a team effort and he needed to ensure that Mr. Wheeler and the rest of the executive team knew it. They fought two adversaries successfully, Paltz, an external enemy, and the two departments that had given them a problem in the past, logistics and marketing. Right now, they were on his side, but that could change quickly and he needed to ensure the momentum didn't cease. The major challenge ahead was winning the peace in the aftermath of winning the war.

Two months later, Mr. Wheeler unexpectedly called Ryan into his office. Ryan had been given no indication about the purpose of the meeting and he was a little distressed at being called into his office at 5:00 p.m. in the afternoon. Mr. Wheeler was always very conscious about people's time and rarely called a meeting for the late afternoon, unless it was very important, but he always communicated the reason for any meeting. He was lucky that he had no plans for the evening, and it really wasn't a big deal, so he trotted up to the office.

Upon arriving at Mr. Wheeler's office, Ryan received a warm greeting and Mr. Wheeler asked him to sit down. Mr. Wheeler had just arrived back from a long board meeting where the senior executives lauded the IT department's handling of the inventory system and the Web site. Jim and Maureen had given stellar reviews about the department's professionalism and results. The CEO congratulated Mr. Wheeler and his team for a job well done, and it was for that reason Mr. Wheeler asked Ryan to come up to his office.

Ryan was ecstatic at hearing the news and his face once again beamed with pride, only this time he couldn't contain himself. He could remember the day when he hoped to just survive through the day without being sabotaged and now his team was receiving accolades for its exemplary teamwork. He couldn't have asked for anything more.

Mr. Wheeler had continued to tell him that for the first time, SportsCentral sales had exceeded Paltz's sales, and it was primarily due to the sales on the Web site, which completely surpassed Paltz's capabilities. There were many customers who indicated in their online surveys that they tried SportsCentral after failing to receive their products from Paltz at the guaranteed time. Ryan and Stacy had been correct; Paltz had never been able to solve their inventory problem. Their marketing campaign to guarantee delivery in an effort to lure customers away, coupled with the successful counterattack of free next-day shipping, resulted in a major coup for SportsCentral who now was poised to significantly increase sales for the latter half of the fiscal year and well positioned for a record holiday season.

Mr. Wheeler said to Ryan, "If you don't mind, I'd like to buy you a drink. You deserve it and I want to congratulate you."

Ryan said, "Thank you, sir, but I would much rather celebrate with the team since it was their work and their ideas that enabled us to be successful."

"Ryan, I don't think you understand. I know your team is responsible and I know you would have it no other way. That's not why I want to buy you a drink and congratulate you."

"Then why, sir?"

"I want to congratulate you on your outstanding leadership. You pulled the team together and gave them the motivation and the tools to succeed. You deserve all the credit for that. Shall we go?"

Ryan smiled, thanked him, stood up, and followed him out of the office. All he could remember was "outstanding leadership." Ryan had arrived at a destination he had long sought.

Chapter 10

PEACE

The restaurant Lisa had chosen, E. B. Elliot's, for their fifteenth wedding anniversary was one of their favorite spots and had significant sentimental value for the two of them. It had a very romantic ambiance since it was located at the edge of the canal where one could see the fishing boats, pleasure cruises, and casino boats moving in and out regularly. At night, during the summer, the entire strip alongside the canal would light up with life, as couples would walk the streets holding hands in the warm, refreshing ocean air. The second floor of the restaurant gave diners the best view of the area and provided picturesque scenes that one couldn't easily forget.

It was here on the second floor at the very edge of the water, where Ryan proposed to Lisa and where, two years later, she surprised him with news that she was pregnant. They shared many happy moments at this place and it was a point of refuge during very troubled times for them both. They needed a place to get away from the rest of the world and laugh and talk as couples often do.

Lisa wanted to get Ryan away, for no particular reason though. All she wanted to do was to give him some time to reflect and tell him how proud she was of his accomplishments over the past two years. It had been three years since he had arrived at SportsCentral and the impact he was having couldn't be appropriately measured. Stacy, who spoke to Lisa often, would tell her more than Ryan would about what was happening at the office. Although that wasn't very unusual, because Ryan lived the experience daily, so the thought of coming home and regurgitating everything was not appealing.

Stacy mentioned how well she and Rebecca were doing at SportsCentral and how they both appreciated Ryan's support. It would have never been possible without him, Stacy told her. However, she also told her that she was a bit worried about Ryan, because he had become slightly disengaged over the past few months, not in a bad way, but rather, it was as though he was thinking of something different. She wondered if he was creating a new plan and wasn't telling anybody or seeking any input for anyone. If that were true it would be completely out of character for Ryan and she thought it was important for Lisa to know.

Lisa had told Stacy she wasn't worried, because Ryan didn't seem any different at home, but that she would inquire to see if anything was bothering him. This was the real purpose of their escapade to the restaurant, and what better place to stir up emotions than their favorite home away from home. The truth of the matter was Lisa already knew what was bothering Ryan, but this was one time she didn't divulge her knowledge to Stacy.

During dinner, Ryan said, "I love this steak. Not as much as I love you, but close."

Lisa smiled and replied, "Great, so I'm just a bit better than a steak."

"Hey, the steak has butter on it, not much could be better."

She wholeheartedly agreed, then asked after a few minutes, "Is everything OK at work?"

Ryan explained that everything was fine, and that since the new Web site went into production over a year ago, things couldn't have been better there. However, he was concerned that he needed to maintain the momentum, and that was proving to be a far more difficult task, one that he originally thought would be easy. He used the analogy of a runner who wins the first marathon and then a second and then asks, is wining a third that important?

They discussed Stacy and Rebecca at length on how they had grown over the past two years, and Lisa reminded him that Rebecca and especially Stacy would never have been able to succeed in that environment unless he had given them the opportunity and the support. She also mentioned that it was Ryan's patience, persistence, and perseverance that enabled his team to succeed.

He really appreciated her words and said, "When things go wrong everyone looks to you, but when things go well everyone looks elsewhere. Don't get me wrong, I've been thanked for the work I've done, but it sometimes feels like a very lonely road; however, it is very rewarding. It's really hard for me to explain."

"I know, I can see it on your face, but as far as the lonely road goes, there is always only one leader."

It was an obvious fact that he seemed to overlook. There was only one leader, so no matter what it would be a lonely road. Even in the presence of multiple managers, there was only one leader.

Although Stacy and Rebecca may not have felt their management capabilities were up to par, he was very confident in their abilities. . Unfortunately, there was still the nagging though of a missing piece.

At the end of dinner, as they drank their cordials and coffee, he told Lisa that he believed something was missing, but he wasn't able to identify it. It was just a feeling, as though something was left incomplete among all the success he had experienced in the last few years. He struggled to get his organization in order, he identified the key resources and empowered them to succeed, he developed a mission and strategy that his team could follow, and he allowed them to execute with almost perfect precision. Even with the adversity, the accomplishments were substantial, yet he felt empty as if a void needed to be filled.

Lisa asked him if he felt fulfilled with his job, and his response came quickly with a resounding "No." She told him the lack of fulfillment was a symptom of a larger problem that he needed to resolve. It would take a lot of personal introspection to identify it, but Ryan should be open minded and not dwell on it, since he was very successful and he should take enormous pride in what he had been able to accomplish in a relatively short time.

Ryan smiled, kissed her hand, and said, "Thank you." He refused to talk about work for the duration of the night and once they left, they decided to take a nice long walk down the strip just absorb the atmosphere with each other.

Back in the office, Ryan continued his work, but he couldn't shake Lisa's comment about fulfillment. He thought she hit the problem right on the head but he needed to figure out what would fulfill him. This was now a new journey for him, and he was determined to find out what was missing. He wasn't sure how long it would take, but it became a new personal mission for him to undertake.

Stacy, who happened to be passing by Ryan's office, entered Ryan's office unannounced and noticed Ryan sitting in his chair with his back to the office door staring out the window thinking. She said to him, "Uh oh. You're thinking again, this is very dangerous."

He laughed and said, "What do you want, Stacy?"

"Actually, nothing, I just was walking by and saw you staring outside your window. Everything OK?"

"Yeah, things are great."

He paused for a moment, and asked Stacy the same question Lisa had asked him. He asked her if she felt fulfilled at work. She told him her work was very fulfilling and the people she worked with were a part of it. She wouldn't trade anything for it. She rambled on about how bad things were at Paltz once Ryan left, and how nervous she was coming here. The nervousness and the struggles she had coming here were all worth it and it proved to be the greatest experience she ever had.

He agreed with her that it was the greatest experience for him because he learned how to construct the organization and get it to succeed, but none of it resolved his ultimate question. He asked her if there was anything she would do differently, and she replied, "Not a thing."

Getting up from his chair, he walked around the desk, passed her, and closed the door. Then he told her about his conversation with Lisa. He explained how he thought something was missing and that's why he asked the question. It wasn't as though he was going to leave his job—he loved working here—but he explained that nagging feeling of the void he felt since they had completed their assignment last year with the Web site and inventory system. Granted, there was more than enough work to keep everyone busy and the work was challenging, but none of it really mattered. It was almost as if he was succeeding at every step but he was now just going through the motions.

Stacy reminded him of a conversation they had years ago in which he told her, the important part of leadership isn't the technology, it's about the people, and everything he just mentioned was more tactical and technology oriented. She added that maybe he was looking in the wrong spot, and then she got up and said, "I'm sorry, Ryan, but I'm a bit late for a meeting. Maybe we can chat after work."

In the afternoon, Mr. Wheeler contacted Ryan and asked him to come up to his office for some very good news. When he arrived, Mr. Wheeler got up from his chair, walked around his desk, stretched his hand out, and said, "Congratulations, Ryan."

"For what?" Ryan asked.

"We just won an award from the most prestigious trade magazine for our work on the Web site and inventory system. Our customers have been raving about it so we submitted the experience to their editorial council and, upon review, we won."

"That's great, but why are you congratulating me?" he asked.

"It was your work and your team who did it, under your leadership, and we, the entire management team, want you to represent us and speak at the conference."

Ryan was amazed. The award was handed out to the company that faced adversity and persevered. The editorial council of the magazine reviewed the submissions and researched the submitted claims. It was no small feat to be honored with the award, and he was much honored that his management recognized his work by giving him the privilege of accepting the award and speaking at the conference. He asked if Rebecca and Stacy could go with him since they were instrumental in the success. He agreed to send them along with him, there would be some minor details to work out with HR, but he didn't foresee it as a problem.

Ryan told Stacy and Rebecca the news and they in turn told the team. Everyone was ecstatic at the thought of just being nominated as a finalist, but to win was priceless. It made it more special that the senior management of the organization would elect to send a representative, instead of using it as a soapbox to promote and enhance their personal images.

He spent the next month with Stacy and Rebecca preparing the presentation for the conference. They wanted the presentation to focus more on the organization's handling of the event rather than just the problem and the resolution. They felt it was more important to discuss how they arrived at their decisions rather than the arrival itself. In addition, they believed that the conference participants would gain the most benefit from recounting their experiences.

The final presentation format included three main parts. The first part provided an overview of the restructured organizational structure and its importance to the success of the team. They wanted to demonstrate how the changes to the structure optimized the group's efficiency, since a strong organizational foundation is the key to success. By providing the rationale for personnel movement and the ensuring key positions were filled with the appropriate skilled personnel, its effectiveness and ultimately its benefits during the crisis could clearly be shown.

The next part focused on the operating principles of the group. This section would be a summary of the principles of trust, intuition, mission, and agreement that Ryan established with his team and positioned the team and management to excel and deal with the crisis. The presentation would provide specific examples during the crisis of how they successfully employed the principles.

Finally, they would discuss the crisis. It would lead with the fire at the warehouse, the early morning meetings, and progress through the technological decisions they made, along with some of the mistakes they encountered. It would stress the importance of long-term planning and integration of systems to ensure redundancy and coordination across the entire enterprise.

Ryan would then summarize the presentation by reiterating the importance of having the right people within the organization, empowering the people by listening to their ideas, giving them the tools to succeed, and implementing the technology afterward. He would add that many technologists and other managers believe that technology is their greatest asset and most important aspect of their companies. He would stress that it was the people within his organization, their preparation, and empowerment that led them to success in implementing the right technologies during the crisis.

Ryan was a bit nervous about accepting the award and giving a presentation. He wasn't a great fan of public speaking, but it was a skill that he had spent some time cultivating. His goal was to keep his audience engaged and answer questions that might be wandering in their heads. Using himself as a model, he repeatedly asked what lessons a participant like himself would want to hear from his speech. He reviewed the presentation and made edits, changing words and sentences, never really deviating from the structure he originally set. The day before the team flew out, he decided to leave it alone, and not make any more changes.

On the plane to San Diego, he had some quiet time to think. It was a night flight and the plane was very quiet except for the noise of the engines. Stacy had flown out with him, but she was gradually dozing in the window seat next to him. Rebecca and Mr. Wheeler were taking separate flights out, and would meet them at the conference.

In the darkness of the cabin with only the overhead light shining directly on his tray table, he continued to ponder the question that Lisa had asked him, "Do you feel fulfilled at your job?" He kept wondering what would make him fulfilled, especially in light of everything he had accomplished. There was more to the question though. If he was simply task oriented, then accomplishments should be more than satisfactory; however, because he focused on being a leader, he would have to focus on more than just tasks such as creating a team and empowering them to succeed in the same way an army successfully marches on an enemy.

His answer was too simplistic. Anyone could have built a team, and there was always a distinct probability that it could succeed. Putting the two together though and repeating the success would be a more substantial accomplishment, but it still lacked meaning. Meaning, he thought, was the root of the answer to the question he was looking for. He knew there had to be a distinct meaning that was bigger than himself. He remembered the previous managers he had who were so focused on ego gratification that they failed to see solutions directly in front of them, which caused them to alienate their subordinates and peers alike.

One thing he knew was that since the crisis had occurred, his team had focused on maintaining the strong relationships built—the essence of winning the peace that he had been advocating. It was important that old adversaries continued to find common ground at almost every turn, and use the past to strengthen their bonds when weakness becomes evident. The team practiced humility from a position of strength, which attracted positive sentiments from their old internal rivals. The company newsletter noted that the IT department "had been transformed from a group of techies to valued business partners in which their insight into the industry was valued." His team had eroded the traditional line between business and technology to form a new nameless entity that worked instinctively and efficiently.

Ryan began to think he was overanalyzing the situation, and that he should just stop. He wasn't getting anywhere, and it wouldn't come to him through the endless doodling of notes on the page. He needed to accept what he had done and move on to the next challenge. The conference would start the next day and Ryan's speech would be one of the first in the morning. He scribbled his final thoughts on the piece of paper and decided to just relax and enjoy the rest of the flight.

The conference attendance was the largest it had been in the last three years. Many IT executives used it as a way to network and converse about various projects, budgets, and, of course, look for time to escape, play golf, and enjoy expensive dinners. The vendors all lined up in the exhibition hall to peddle their software, hardware, and services, making connections and sales pitches in the twenty to thirty seconds they had to capture people's attention. It was fun for all of the attendees, including Stacy and Rebecca, who couldn't contain their enthusiasm. Mr. Wheeler commented to Ryan as they were walking, that the excitement on their faces was a pleasure to see and he wondered if he could work out a rotating schedule to send people to more conferences. He had grown so accustomed to these that he overlooked how others in his department might respond to them. Ryan added that it's a nice reward to give to people and a fantastic incentive, for those who deserve it. Mr. Wheeler agreed and asked Ryan to remind him, upon their return, to examine how it could be implemented throughout the department.

Ryan separated from Mr. Wheeler around forty-five minutes prior to his speech to prepare and set up for his speech and presentation. Doug Carance, the editor of the magazine, and Jim Greene, the president of the Information Technology Society, met him as he entered the grand ballroom where the awards presentation was schedule to take place. Doug dressed in a business casual manner with a white collar shirt, tie and his trademark blue jeans. His powerful handshake took Ryan by surprise even though Ryan could tell by his very large arms that he lifted weights regularly. Jim seemed to be the typical Information Technology professional, with two blackberry phones on his belt, dressed in an off color brown jacket and brown pants. Jim, who stood next to Doug as they approached Ryan, stood a foot taller than Doug and the two seemed a very odd pair appearancewise.

The two greeted him warmly and they expressed their appreciation for his attendance. Ryan was thankful to be the representative for SportsCentral and expressed his gratitude to them for selecting his company.

"The entire selection committee unanimously selected your company, and we applaud your work during that challenging time. I thoroughly enjoyed writing the story for the magazine chronicling your adventure," Doug said.

"When you have a solid organization behind you, dealing with adversity becomes much more manageable," he responded.

The three continued to talk about the award as they proceeded to the stage. Ryan received the layout of the stage, which showed where he would present, and where the projection screen was in relation to his position on the stage. As they walked around the stage, getting Ryan acclimated to his surroundings, a sound technician followed them to fit Ryan with a wireless microphone. A few sound checks where completed to ensure his voice carried well throughout the room without the annoying feedback that comes from the sensitive equipment. When everything was ready, they headed back stage and opened the doors to allow the attendees into the ballroom hall.

Just before it was time to give the speech, Ryan peeked out from behind the curtain. He noticed the room was filled to capacity, and must have had almost five hundred people. Ryan began to get a bit nervous and he adjusted his collar with his index finger. Luckily, he had grabbed a few paper towels from the bathroom, which he now used to wipe the sweat from his forehead and back of his neck. He wasn't sure if it was nerves or the heat of lights on the stage. Either way he was sure it wasn't a very pleasant sight. A voice suddenly came from behind him and said, "You're not nervous, are you, Ryan?"

Ryan turned and saw a calming familiar face, "No, Mr. Wheeler, thank you."

"You'll do just fine. When you're done, we will meet you near the rear of the room. It's going to get very crowded toward the front," Mr. Wheeler said.

Ryan laughed and thanked Mr. Wheeler as he walked away, and almost simultaneously, he heard the announcements to begin the award ceremony. After twenty minutes of announcements and introductions of the editorial staff and panel, the emcee announced the presentation of the award. SportsCentral was flattered with a grand introduction of a company aggressive in its pursuit of excellence with a strong propensity to use technology as a driving force. Ryan wasn't so sure that it was a very accurate statement, but he understood the need for creative license as a means to generate enthusiasm. After the announcer described the problem and summarized the outcome, Ryan heard over the speakers, "Here to accept the award for the Technology Department of the Year, and to present the results of their labor, from SportsCentral, Ryan Sheridan."

The loud applause filled the room, with a bellowing thunder unlike anything Ryan had ever experienced and they were all clapping for him. He walked out very nervous and made his way to the podium, which was at the other end of the stage. They had asked him to walk across the stage to give the audience time for applause. As he reached the other end of the stage, Doug and Jim greeted him and presented him with the award. Ryan hadn't seen the award prior to his receiving it, and he was a bit disappointed at its appearance. It was a standard size plaque no bigger than a normal piece of paper, with a cherry wood border and an engraved glossy black face.

Ryan accepted the award graciously and thanked the committee for his company's selection. The nomination alone was an honor to the team. Winning the award was the pinnacle of a successful road, which was laden with obstacles, he told the crowd. His lead in to the presentation was a statement he prepared, which summarized the sentiment of the team and the experience they shared.

"Everyone expects technology to save the day during times of crisis; however, many companies and organizations fail to see the greatest asset they posses. The people in their organizations can move mountains, if properly guided and unequivocally empowered."

There was an odd silence in the crowd as they were expecting a discussion of the technologies employed; however, it was readily apparent to the audience that this discussion was going to take an entirely different approach. As Ryan delved further into his speech, he emphasized the importance of putting the right people in the right position; providing details of previous ignored personnel, who rose to the occasion and offered valued and successful solutions. He passionately spoke about empowerment and trust, but the further he moved on, the more he sensed some members of the crowd disengaging. In fact, he noticed a few people stand up and leave the room, at various points of his discussion.

By the end of his speech, he received a round of applause from the remaining group of attendees, although about ten percent of original group had left. Ryan wasn't discouraged, he knew many of them probably had other things to do, or wanted to be elsewhere. It was a shame, he thought, that they wouldn't benefit from his experience. It was his hope that his speech would ignite some of them to reevaluate their management methods and embark on a new direction.

As the applause tapered, he exited the stage, and proceeded down the center aisle where he had hoped to meet up with his team in the lobby. On his way out he received a number of congratulatory remarks from audience members still around. Once in the lobby, he found his party who congratulated him on a wonderful performance. Mr. Wheeler added, "You made us proud, great job."

Ryan was relieved it was over, and as he was speaking with his team he was tapped on the shoulder by a few of the attendees who had some questions for him. For a few minutes, Ryan answered their questions about trust and empowerment. He was enjoying the questions and felt invigorated by the audience that had circled him. He relished the conversation and began to describe in more detail the importance of his team and the qualities that enabled them to be successful He added, "It's not easy to give up the control, but the more people try to control situations, the more control they lose."

It was a concept this group seemed to embrace. Without realizing it, he had now been separated from his colleagues, who were now about 30 feet away. As he continued to speak, he heard another familiar voice in sarcastic tone say, "Congratulations on your award."

He recognized the voice but couldn't place the face. As he turned and scanned the area where he thought the voice originated, his eyes finally fixated on the person behind the statement. It was Eric, his former boss at Paltz, who attended at the conference and apparently heard his speech. Ryan now faced his nemesis, and he wasn't prepared. He briefly forgot that he should respond to Eric and hesitantly thanked him, although now the two stared at each other like two rams about to battle for territory. He noticed that three other people from Paltz were standing next to Eric on either side and one of them was Phil. Phil had the stupid grin on his face that Ryan could never forget.

"You know everyone in the audience knows you really didn't do everything you said you did. It's all a bunch of fluff."

The comment was loud enough that Stacy and Mr. Wheeler could hear it from their position ten feet away. Stacy, who had her back turned to Ryan, turned and immediately recognized Eric. She fully turned her body and watched intently as Eric engaged him in a conversation. She began to feel a bit queasy at the site of Eric and she would have loved nothing more than to deck him but she just watched, for now, with Ryan unaware that she, Rebecca, and Mr. Wheeler were watching.

In addition to Eric's group of three, there were about five other attendees standing in the vicinity, who heard Eric. They were intrigued as to why this man had decided to expend effort to challenge the speaker who had just won an award for his company. They turned their attention in the same manner that drivers on a highway slow down to look at a wreck on the other side of the median.

Eric turned to his colleagues from Paltz and said, "This guy used to work for me, I had to fire him for incompetence."

Ryan, angered by Eric's bold assault, volleyed back and said, "You have your facts wrong once again, Eric. I resigned and I found a better opportunity that enabled me to win this award."

"Look, winning the award is no big deal, companies always embellish what happens and someone gets paid off to win an award for their company since its great publicity. It doesn't mean anything."

Eric began a standing lecture of how inventory systems are supposed to work. His organization was in the middle of a massive overhaul of the inventory system that would enable them to handle same-day shipping for orders placed before 4:00 p.m. With the addition of scanning machines and barcode readers throughout the conveyer line, which carried the packages from their storage area to the loading docks, they could move packages at a faster rate. He continued addressing the group trying to draw attention. Ryan, insulted by Eric's remarks, stood by patiently for a minute or two, and actually began to feel sympathy for Eric because of his insecurity and need for attention.

But Ryan couldn't resist the urge to ask, "So if you had this great plan, why haven't you done it already?"

Eric responded, "Listen, we are almost complete."

"If I recall correctly, you've been at this for years."

"We would have buried you guys during your downtime if we didn't run into a few minor hiccups."

Eric then challenged Ryan on the points of his presentation with his belief that having the right technology is more important than the right people. Anyone can learn how to push a button in a system and it brings the cost down as well. He also sarcastically quoted the presentation by saying if a manager needs to explain the goal to a team, then you need a new manager and then new staff. Eric further belittled Ryan's presentation by comparing employees to children, whereby managers must constantly provide oversight or nothing will ever get done.

Stacy, who was gleaming with pride as she talked of the award with Mr. Wheeler and Rebecca, had turned and noticed Eric and Ryan speaking. Her demeanor changed immediately upon seeing Eric with Ryan. Stacy moved closer to the conversation along with Mr. Wheeler and Rebecca. She became very angry with Eric as she overheard the conversation, and became incensed with Ryan for not arguing with him.

She looked at Mr. Wheeler, expecting a response, but he was watching with great intensity to see how Ryan would continue to react. However, Stacy couldn't take anymore, she was being insulted just as much as Ryan was and she wanted to retort Eric. She took one step to engage in the conversation, when she was grabbed gently, but forcefully, by the arm. She turned her head and saw Mr. Wheeler holding her arm. As she looked at him, he said, "This is his."

She stopped and he released her arm and, although she couldn't admit it, she knew he was right. She wanted Ryan to fight back, but he would have to handle it the way he saw fit. If she engaged Eric, it would probably make things worse.

Ryan paused for a moment after Eric stopped and realized that engaging in a debate with Eric was not only futile but a complete waste of his time. Eric's need to pretend to be of a superior intellect matched his inept capabilities. He decided that he wouldn't engage the conversation anymore, but at that same moment he decided to say one last thing before he left.

"Eric, I know you believe the presentation was useless and you derided it as much as you could, and while I respect your opinion, I don't agree. I am also very certain that no one in my company paid to receive the award and I think the editorial committee would be very distressed to hear anyone talk of any sort of impropriety."

Eric was not going to allow Ryan to say anything and so he continued to identify points of Ryan's presentation that were, as he called them, naïve and childish, to the laughter of Eric's counterparts. There were others in the gathering intently watching Ryan, who was oblivious to the small group that gathered around.

Ryan abruptly interrupted him and said, "I know you have some objections to my presentation, and you have deeply rooted misgivings about my employment with you. However, I have moved on and I have learned much in that time. I would like to thank you, however, for your time in listening to my entire presentation; it appears as though you have remembered it very well from the way you are talking about it. I sincerely hope you learn something from it."

Eric became enraged at the audacity of Ryan's comment. He was appalled that all Ryan could say was that he remembered everything from Ryan's presentation and so he turned and stormed away saying, "This guy will never get it, it's a waste of time. There was nothing worthwhile in it to remember."

Ryan couldn't help but snicker at Eric's tantrum, which was something he hadn't seen since his son was about five or six years old. He had scored a fatal blow to Eric's ego, by not engaging the conversation.

Ryan thought it was a complete waste of talent for people to be so petty, as to preoccupy themselves with attempts to belittle others in an effort to self-promote. Managers should spend more time focusing on their teams and individuals on their teams rather than themselves.

Three of the men, who had gathered behind Eric and had witnessed the exchange, approached Ryan once Eric had walked away, and congratulated him on a remarkable presentation. They were especially complimentary about the way he referred to leadership as a function beyond technology. He appreciated their comments and was surprised at their enthusiasm. As he conversed, he noticed the conference badges hanging around their necks, which provided their names, companies, and titles. He was surprised that each one of them was a C-level executive of their respective companies, and he was honored to be speaking with them, let alone giving them information.

A few minutes into their conversation, a man by the name of Brian, which was the only name he could clearly see on any of the badges, glanced over Ryan's left shoulder and motioned with his hand as if to get someone's attention. He then, in what could have been considered a rude manner by speaking over Ryan's conversation, loudly said, "A. W.!"

Brian Sewell was the chief executive officer of a mid-sized financial institution in San Francisco. He had known Mr. Wheeler for over thirty years. The two had actually worked together and were instrumental in transforming the company that Brian currently ran. Although Mr. Wheeler had left almost 12 years ago, the two had a very close friendship.

Ryan, curious as to who was being summoned turned over his shoulder and saw Mr. Wheeler moving toward them with Stacy and Rebecca behind him. He realized the "A. W." was for A. Wheeler. To Ryan's knowledge, Mr. Wheeler never divulged his first name. Although he was certain that others in the office knew his real name, it was a very well-kept secret. Many people in the office speculated as to what his first name was, however, there was a rumor that he never liked his given first name.

As Mr. Wheeler stepped closer to the group, Brian, who had summoned him, said, "He's your guy, right?"

"Yes, he works for me, and we are very proud to have him."

"August, you hit the jackpot with this guy."

Ryan's eyes opened wide, completely ignoring the fantastic compliments about him, as he thought to himself, "August?"

Rebecca and Stacy had a difficult time containing themselves upon hearing his real name. Mr. Wheeler was a sophisticated, always well-dressed and well-framed professional, who walked with an elegant gate and whose first name, spoken aloud, had somehow now humanized him. Mr. Wheeler, noticing his team's obvious attempts to contain their amazement upon hearing his first name, said to all of them in a half-joking manner, "OK, now you know. Let's keep it to ourselves, I never liked the name." Mr. Wheeler then turned back to Brian and sarcastically said, "Thanks, Brian."

"Anytime," he responded.

Apparently, Brian had a habit of informing people of A. W.'s first name. He was a practical joker, and never missed an opportunity to poke fun at him. The group of executives who were speaking with Ryan had been good friends of Mr. Wheeler, either from college days or from prior work experience. Mr. Wheeler had explained to the team that he had known most of the group for over thirty years, and they had learned much from each other. He valued their opinions and they collectively relied on each other for advice and counsel on many issues.

As they spoke, they continued to compliment Ryan on his ability to get his team to perform in very adverse circumstances, adding that one of their greatest difficulties as executives was exactly that. In many cases, teams consist of individuals, and having them act collectively for a common purpose was the greatest challenge. They knew the value of loyalty and getting the right people together, however, it seemed more difficult at times. They never attached a label to it, but Ryan's explanation gave them a structure by which they could try to demonstrate to their teams the value of trust, intuition, and mission.

Ryan added, "Don't forget the agreement, without it, everything will fail, it is the glue to the whole process."

Brian, who had been the impressed the most with Ryan, said, "Ever thought about coming out west? I can have a position ready for you anytime."

"Easy does it, Brian," Mr. Wheeler said, hoping Ryan wouldn't take him seriously.

"Thank you for the offer, but I am very happy where I am; besides my wife doesn't quite like the shaking of the ground out there."

"Diplomatic too, I like that. August, you let him go, and I'll snap him up."

Mr. Wheeler grumbled as Rebecca and Stacy laughed, and said, "OK, we are done here," as he gathered the team and guided them to begin walking away. As he did, he said to Brian and the group, "We will meet tonight at the restaurant; add three more to the reservation. Think you can handle a phone, Brian?"

"Will do, see you all there," Brian responded.

Later that evening, the dinner, held at the best steakhouse in San Diego, certainly lived up to expectations. The steak was tender and savory with a béarnaise sauce that made one's mouth water. Brian, the obvious ringleader of the bunch, had ordered three relatively expensive $250 bottles of wine, and used the opportunity to conduct numerous toasts to anything, in order to continue imbibing. The drinking added to the atmosphere of camaraderie as they shared memories of their prior experiences, poking fun at the moronic nature of some of those who worked for them and for whom they worked. One could easily have surmised based on the similarities of the stories that they were talking about the same person or group of people, but this wasn't the case.

Rebecca at one point asked why the people generally behaved the same way, adding that she could name a handful of people she had previously worked with who exhibited the same traits. Stacy concurred with Rebecca who couldn't believe how pervasive the problem seemed to be in corporate cultures and she was even more puzzled as to why the behavior appeared to be condoned by management.

Mr. Wheeler responded, "Because they don't know any other way. It is a trait learned very early on in one's career, and when one achieves some level of success, by luck or otherwise, they stick with it. You very rarely find people who are looking for new ways of solving problems and are looking to better themselves and others."

Brian added that many managers tended to be more dictatorial; however, strong leaders were able to get their people to think independently for a common cause and in those cases, success was guaranteed and enduring and that it applied to militaries, governments, and companies. Brain was attempting to convey the importance of team-oriented focus and empowerment as an axiom to leadership, but since this approach ceases to be self serving, it is ignored by many managers. Finally he added, that what Ryan, who had been very quiet through most of the discussion, had done was an exemplary model of leadership that should serve as a lesson to those who want to learn, but would most likely be ignored by over 95 percent of the people with whom any of them would come into contact.

Ryan was absorbing all of the information provided, and he listened intently to the conversation. He added, "It's a shame more people aren't truly focused on the success of the mission as opposed to themselves. While many managers stress the ultimate goal, their actions are purely self serving and the irony is, if they change this perspective, they would probably be more successful."

Mr. Wheeler said, "That's absolutely true, but it takes a great amount of faith and courage to do it."

The dinner concluded with a cordial and dessert, which was as exquisite and as rich as the dinner had been. It was a fantastic conclusion to a great dinner, and they laughed as Brian, who was inebriated, continued to speak unstoppably. The table, with the exception of the newcomers, knew he had a tendency to drink, which was exactly the reason he was not allowed to drive to the restaurant. However, the night was coming to close and they all bid each other a fond farewell.

As they walked in the parking lot, Mr. Wheeler and Michael McMullen, the CIO of a law firm in Los Angeles and another long time friend of both Mr. Wheeler and Brian, guided Brian to their car. They both put him in the car and Michael drove away to their hotel. Stacy and Rebecca decided to walk back to their hotel, which was only a short fifteen minute walk. Mr. Wheeler asked Ryan to stick around for a few minutes before they would do the same

Mr. Wheeler and Ryan also walked back to the same hotel. They slowly walked along the water's edge toward the hotel admiring the scene of the city across the bay. It was a great night for a walk, with the seasonal average temperature of sixty-seven degrees, and not a cloud in the sky. The air was clean and there was a gentle breeze from the water. Mr. Wheeler said to Ryan as they walked, "You couldn't have performed any better, Ryan."

"Thank you, sir, but you already complimented me on my handling of the situation."

"I'm not referring to the situation at the warehouse. I'm talking about what you did today. You handled Eric's tirade with the skill of a seasoned professional. I was very impressed by your demeanor and your answers."

"Truthfully, I was really angry."

"I know. We watched the whole thing, but you handled it very well," Mr. Wheeler said.

Brian had expressed his admiration for Ryan's handling of the situation to Mr. Wheeler. Mr. Wheeler explained that Brian looks for professionals of all types because he realizes the value of skilled people, and that his job offer wasn't actually a joke. Brian also mentioned to Mr. Wheeler that it was the first presentation in quite a long time in which he learned something of tremendous value, which, coming from Brian, was the ultimate compliment.

Ryan was humbled by what Mr. Wheeler was saying, and didn't know how to respond, and Mr. Wheeler could sense it. After a pause in the conversation, with the hotel entrance now in sight, Ryan asked Mr. Wheeler, "Are you satisfied with your job? If so, how do you know?"

The question continued to nag him, and he was hoping Mr. Wheeler might have an answer. Mr. Wheeler, puzzled by the question, responded by asking, "Aren't you satisfied with your performance?"

"I think I have performed to the best of my ability, but I feel there is something missing and I can't tell what it is. I listened to the entire conversation tonight trying to see if I might get an idea."

"Well, you may be trying too hard. I can tell you this; if you feel you need something more, it may have nothing to do with your job. I know that for me, I always look back at what I have done and see if I left things in a better state then when I got them, regardless of what other people think of the end result."

They walked into the hotel, chatted for a few more minutes, and then proceeded to their respective rooms. Ryan didn't think he received the answer for which he was searching. It was frustrating because he was receiving all of these accolades from his colleagues and strangers yet he continued to feel as though something was missing. He also began to feel guilty and somewhat selfish at his own attitude. Once again, he would resolve to put it aside.

On his flight back home three days later, his resolve would fail, and now he was determined to solve this mystery. Stacy, who was on the flight sat next to him and as she did on the way she was falling asleep. However, she glanced at him because the reading light above his head was one of the few lights turned on in the darkness of the inside of the plane. She gazed at his paper for a few minutes and said, "You're still haunted by the question you asked me weeks ago, aren't you?"

"I wouldn't use the word haunted, but it does still irk me," he responded.

"You are a bit obsessed with it, but if you weren't, you wouldn't be you."

Ryan smirked at her feeble attempt at humor, but in a way, she wasn't kidding. She began a very brief history lesson going back to their previous employer, how Ryan was so focused on the members of his team and their well-being, adding that it was his encouragement that led to her pursuit of her MBA, but more importantly that was merely an effect of his empowerment and belief in her. She added that his attitudes toward her weren't unique but that she had witnessed firsthand Ryan acting in the same manner with people like Rebecca and Jim.

She wanted him to know that he empowered, believed in, and mentored many of the people he came in contact with and not just with words but with actions, and that he did so without prejudice to the people with which he was associated. He treated everyone as equally as possible, while understanding and leveraging each person's independent needs. He masterfully handled this amazing and difficult balance.

She finished her statement by saying that he had learned much over the past years and that he had made many mistakes, but unlike others in the same position, he learned from the mistakes and was able to avoid repeating them.

"What makes you so special, Ryan, is that I know it's been a very difficult journey, and you've handled it masterfully, although you would probably disagree."

He nodded in agreement and thus she continued, "You have a great amount of humility, which I know has been cultivated well over the years. Above all, everywhere you have been, and every life you have touched has changed immeasurably for the positive, or at least they had the opportunity. Above all, that is what you should be most proud of."

With that final comment, she turned toward the window next to her seat, closed her eyes, and began to fall asleep. Ryan immediately began to feel a sense of relief because he knew somewhere in what Stacy had said there was an answer to his question, but he needed to identify it clearly.

On his notes where he had been scribbling thoughts since the beginning of the flight, he wrote comments from Mr. Wheeler and Brian. He added Stacy's thoughts and reviewed them, intently looking for the answer. Each time there had been a recurring theme, he had done a good job, and they had learned from the experience. His spirits were lifted by the thought that each of them would be appreciative of his actions and comments.

He recognized a pattern between his feelings and the accomplishments that had been attributed to him and thus the characteristics required of a leader. Taking his piece of paper, he turned it over to the blank side and wrote down the word "self," to which he noted the attributes of self-learning, self-introspection, and behavior. Personal growth was what was important, which included constant learning and constant improvement in all areas. The individual must operate with the highest level of integrity and honor in order to be a true leader.

Next, he scribed the word "others." As simple as the word was, he attributed the empowerment of individuals to do their best and give them the right tools to succeed. This meant the development of communication skills and listening skills and having the ability to discern needs without needlessly pandering to demands. This required a balance of compassion with discipline and it was no easy task.

The third item he noted was "team," which meant that a leader needed to organize the individuals into a cohesive unit, leveraging their abilities for the betterment of the group or organization. They also needed to be provided with a clear direction in order to perform at the most optimal level and they must be left to their own devices except when necessary. He knew this was the essence of the trust, intuition, mission, and agreement concept he had provided to his team, which enabled them to successfully navigate the challenges they faced. So long as they shared the same goal, it was relatively easy to get them to perform successfully.

Finally, he closed his eyes and remembered what Stacy had mentioned earlier. He noted that each of the items he had written down all occurred at some point in time; once the time was over so was the event. While the event may remembered it didn't necessarily mean that he would be remembered. His success hadn't been the fact that he navigated the almost disastrous events of the warehouse, but rather, his entire handling of the situation with a team that once viewed him with skepticism and now viewed him as a valued leader.

All of the discussions centered on how he pulled everything together and how effectively the team performed. Each of the players involved garnered some internal benefit and clearly expressed the benefits of the experience. The lessons learned continued to blossom for all of the participants and each of them had grown immeasurably; ultimately, this was exactly what Mr. Wheeler and Stacy had attempted to convey. Ryan had come to a situation that was fragmented and uncoordinated and he turned the team into a high morale cohesive unit that knew exactly how to operate. It was currently in a better state than when he received it.

He had been searching for the answer that was in front of him the entire time, but no one could clearly articulate it. It was the satisfying feeling of leaving a positive legacy that made everything worthwhile, and he had accomplished that splendidly. For Ryan, knowing that he could leave his current job in a better state should have been good enough, however, it wasn't.

He had a new drive and a new mission. He wanted more for his team, not for himself, so he noted a vision for the next two years that included all members of his team. Assuming it aligned with their own personal wishes and interests, he would use the opportunities provided to help mentor them to achieve their goals and, hopefully, lead teams of their own. His new mission, he hoped, would be his legacy.

Chapter 11

LEGACY

It had been almost two and half years since the confrontation with Eric at the conference in San Diego and it couldn't have been any further from Ryan's mind. Since that day, he never looked back with disdain at any of his prior experiences, but rather, he embraced all of the struggles and battles in which he had engaged. Without adversity, he never would have achieved his accomplishments, nor would he have grown as an individual and it was that understanding that made him grateful. While he joked many times about having an easier road to travel, at this point in his life he wouldn't trade his experiences for anything.

He was particularly pleased at how Rebecca and Stacy had progressed in their careers. Together with John, whom Ryan had promoted in the last year, they formed the core of his leadership team, and they continued to perform admirably. They continued to think independently while working collectively toward common goals and they reiterated that approach with every member of their team. Ryan's job became easier as his tenure continued and it gave him more time to search for more opportunities for improving the organization as well as himself, and develop strategies that were more ambitious for the company.

He had set out over two years ago to leave a lasting impression on the organization, and he executed his plan with diligence. His single goal for the organization, for which all actions would be aligned, was very simple; he needed to ensure the organization was in a much better place than when he received it. His core group ran the organization like a machine with very little involvement from him, except as needed.

Stacy had come up with many new creative ideas on managing her team, some worked while others didn't, but she wasn't afraid to try. Her belief in a metrics-based organization never waned and she successfully implemented a series of indexes, which were a great barometer for how her team was performing. It took her the better part of two years to perfect, but she now had a consolidated view of the performance of her group with nine key performance indicators, and not only had there been no resistance from her team, they were very keen and supportive of having a clear and unbiased understanding of their performance.

Her leadership never again came into question and she earned the admiration of her subordinates, peers, and colleagues throughout the organization. Others referred to her as the bulldog of the organization that could raze the most arduous challenges, while never compromising her attention to detail and process, and she did so without ever raising her voice in anger. Her personality, Ryan noticed, really hadn't changed, even though she was a bit mellower from her earlier years. In fact, her personality simply matured, but she was the same old Stacy he respected and admired.

Stacy had recently completed her MBA, and she became one of the biggest advocates for the company's tuition reimbursement plan. She encouraged every member of her team to go back to school if they were able to do so and she proactively worked with their schedules to help them meet the demands of school and work. It had become her belief that it was the challenges of school, rather than school itself, that helped her team become more productive.

Ryan was surprised by the leaps that John had made in his transformation from a lead developer to a leader of his group. In a short period since the warehouse incident, he had gained the trust and admiration of his team, and reluctantly, he assumed the post of running the mainframe development team, the position previously held by James, who had resigned after the confrontation between Bill and Ryan.

John was somewhat of the reluctant leader. He never saw himself in a position of authority and he never really liked telling people what to do, which was ironic since he originally advocated the position of getting direct orders at the off-site. However, his previous beliefs may have explained his reluctance to lead a group, since in his mind it was easier to just take an order and do it, rather than be responsible for giving it.

John's transformation was a work in progress, but his technical capabilities were very strong and he was a likeable character. He struggled with the concept of allowing people to do the work and it was difficult for him to avoid the temptation of stepping in on occasion and performing the work himself. However, he had two very strong characters in Stacy and Rebecca to guide him along the way. John would probably be content for the next few years in his role, but only time would tell exactly where he would take it. Ryan wasn't completely sure how he might turn out in a few years, but he had confidence in

John's ability. John was given the tools to succeed, and it would be up to him to choose his own path.

Finally, there was Rebecca, the person who rose from obscurity in the organization to a position of prominence. Rebecca had changed the way the group handled projects and her unyielding commitment to gathering requirements and proper planning. She received the nickname "The Quiet Storm," because of her ability to listen intently, gather all the information, and then unleash a barrage of questions she knew no one had the answers to. It was a technique that served her very well, ensuring that every member of her team and each business user were well prepared. Little got by her line of questioning and if it did pass, there was a good chance of success.

Rebecca had been empowered by Ryan to change the processes for incoming requests as she saw fit. She always ran it by Ryan, mostly as a formality, but she relied on a second opinion for her ideas. She always sought feedback from wherever she could get it, and her colleagues admired her for it because she did so with sincerity and respect.

Unfortunately, for Rebecca the past two years weren't as smooth as she would have hoped. She faced two major challenges in the past two years, which affected her more than she would care to admit. The first was the passing of her father, with whom she shared a very special bond. He was her moral compass, her guide, and sounding board. They had enjoyed that special relationship between a father and daughter, and they spoke about everything including family, friends, and her career. She credited him with many of the ideas she brought to action. In reality, he served as the devil's advocate for her concepts and he merely helped her strengthen her own thoughts.

As a testament to her reputation in the company, almost every senior executive, except those who were out of town attended the funeral. The entire IT department created a special set of shifts to allow every team member to attend services. Nearly three hundred people showed their support for Rebecca, for which she would be grateful, but she never knew how to express it.

She spent many days mourning her loss, but Stacy, who had been through the experience before, consistently consoled her with numerous evenings at the local tavern where they drank and toasted their fathers together. They formed a bond that would probably last them into their old age.

The other challenge for Rebecca came about six months later, when an employee accused her of harassment. The employee who had made the accusations was disgruntled regarding his review and he felt the pressure he was placing on him was unnecessary and unwarranted. He directly accused Rebecca of withholding promotions and salary increases, saying that his performance was equal to or better than his fellow employees who had received larger raises.

HR took up the issue and involved Ryan and ultimately Mr. Wheeler. After a thorough review and investigation, it was discovered that the employee's performance was subpar, according to the metrics being produced, and that he never once questioned the results except during this review period. They assessed that he had ample time to raise the issue of his performance since the policy in the department was a quarterly review of performance against the metrics, but that he failed to do so in a timely fashion and therefore implicitly agreed to his performance throughout the year. They also discovered during the course of the investigation that the employee, who had been with the company two years, had a history of making similar charges against two of his previous employers. Upon learning this news, the HR department, along with Mr. Wheeler, offered the employee a termination package in exchange for his resignation. The employee, motivated by greed, accepted the nominal sum and gladly resigned from the company with no further action.

Rebecca was very disheartened and distraught by the accusations. It took a number of discussions with Ryan and Mr. Wheeler to help her out of it. Her father's recent passing increased her uneasiness about the situation and prolonged her distress. Ryan knew it was a moments like these that she relied on her father who was a strong source of guidance, but he hoped that his words along with Mr. Wheeler's could serve as an adequate substitute. In time, Rebecca did come to realize that she was not at fault for the employee's actions, and she knew the support network helping her was the lifeline she needed. She eventually returned to her old self, and Ryan knew she had completely recovered when he overheard someone say, "The storm is coming back—be prepared," an obvious reference to Rebecca's imminent approach.

Ryan had assembled and cultivated a great team, and had worked diligently on developing a legacy. He realized slowly that in order to have a legacy he must hand something down. This meant one thing for Ryan. He must leave a legacy to someone. Therefore, if he were to have a legacy he would have to leave the company. It was a thought that he had struggled with over the past few months. He knew he had done much to further his organization, and he wasn't sure he could do more. It would soon be time to leave.

As luck would have it, he began having discussions with EduCARE, a nonprofit organization dedicated to educating youths in underprivileged communities across the country. They were in sore need of a new technology strategy and someone to help them create one and implement it. The prospect was exciting, because he could start from scratch and build a new team. He knew the organization very well and could easily support its mission. Unfortunately, it would pay him about ten percent less and he would have fewer staff members to run the organization since their budget was very tight.

After speaking with Lisa, who fully supported him, he decided to have a final conversation with the CEO of EduCARE, Arthur Kenneth. Mr. Kenneth, had become the CEO two years ago, and had struggled to bring EduCARE out of its struggles. He had to cope with a failing technology department, lack of resources for marketing and an overall poor strategy to promote the message and expand its reach. He had successfully over his tenure managed to mitigate many of the issues except the technology piece and he desperately needed an individual who could develop and implement a technology strategy that was in line with his overall mission for the organization.

During Ryan's interview with Mr. Kenneth, he explained his thoughts on leadership and the concepts he had brought to SportsCentral. He mentioned that if he joined he would want to build the team that would have a long-lasting effect, and he wanted the CEO to understand that he might last only three years; once he set the course and he was confident the organization could run efficiently without him, he might decide to pursue other opportunities.

"If you get us on the right track in three years, I'll be glad just to have had you for those three years. We are in need of help and this organization cannot survive if we can't implement a technology strategy. This organization is too important to me and its cause is important to the children we serve," said Arthur with a slight southern accent.

Arthur had mentioned he would consult the board and the other interviewers but he felt very strongly that they would make him an offer. Ryan was very satisfied with the way the conversation went and indicated he would be willing to accept an offer, but would need some time to contemplate.

Ryan waited to hear back from EduCARE, and he became concerned when he didn't hear for two weeks. He really wasn't concerned that he hadn't received an offer, but he was upset they didn't at least have the courtesy to call or e-mail him, stating the decision was still pending. It may have been a warning that he should consider it carefully.

The next day, a call came in to Ryan's cell phone from Arthur.

"Ryan, I am very sorry you haven't received notification from us. We decided to extend an offer and we sent it via e-mail; however, our e-mail system has been intermittent at best and we have been trying to get our federal and state grants completed before their respective deadlines. All of our efforts have been engaged in those grants. Please accept my personal apology for not contacting you sooner. As I mentioned, we are in dire need of someone like you to help us. I certainly hope you will give our offer consideration."

Ryan listened as Arthur detailed the terms of the offer. He would be receiving a 10 percent increase in his current salary and five weeks' paid vacation, since they couldn't give a bonus. It was a great and thoughtful offer, since they had come in way above their intended pay scale and they considered alternatives to a performance-based bonus. Based on his current position they would also wait three months for him to join if a longer transition period was needed, although they expressed their desire for him to join as soon as possible.

Once again, Ryan consulted Lisa and they talked for an hour at their kitchen table about the new position. Ryan was a bit nervous about leaving the stability of SportsCentral, but he knew this was an exciting opportunity. He would run the entire IT organization for EduCARE, a major step for his career. Unfortunately, he would leave behind many of the people he helped grow and who helped him grow, and this was very distressing. Would they perceive him as having abandoned them? How would they react to his departure, and could they survive without him?

Lisa listened intently to his concerns and said, "You always said you wanted to leave a legacy there, right?"

"Right," he responded.

"Well then, how will you know if you don't leave?"

He knew that was right, because he himself had said the very same thing. It was harder than he thought though. He thought it would be easy to just pick up and walk away and not worry about anything, and that everything would run smoothly, but he slowly began to get cold feet until Lisa said once again, "Think of the other people who could benefit, if you repeat your success, and think of the other lives you will touch. It will grow exponentially."

That was it—she had given him the answer and he turned to her and said, "You're absolutely right, I love you. Thank you."

"I'm always right, remember that," she said as she rose from the table and walked away.

Once again, as always, she needed to get that last word in. He laughed as she walked away and he began preparing to tell Mr. Wheeler, but his most pressing problem would be who should take over the department. He had many things to consider and a lot of work to finish, but he was confident he could handle it, and he was very confident whoever he recommended could handle it as well. But there was an additional piece of unfinished business that he needed to address.

The next morning he went to the office and reviewed some paperwork regarding open requisitions that needed filling. The most recently approved requisition was the one he was looking for. It was for a manager's position in the development group. It had just been approved and posted two weeks ago and would report to Stacy. He called Stacy into his office.

When Stacy arrived, he asked if she remembered her request last quarter to create a position for manager of development. She acknowledged the request and asked if it was approved. He told her the position was recently approved and had been posted for internal consideration. Stacy was a bit disconcerted that Ryan didn't let her know immediately when it was approved, but he had been so inundated with other tasks that it completely slipped his mind. He asked her if she knew anyone for the position. She told him there was no one she could think of, but she hoped a candidate would apply soon to help with the workload.

"Why don't you call Tim?" he asked.

"Tim! That's a great idea!" she said. "He absolutely could do this job. He is working already but he isn't in development anymore."

Tim had struggled with his cancer, but it had gone into remission. He had opened a dialogue first with Stacy and then with Ryan, and ultimately they had reestablished their friendship. He had placed the blame squarely on Ryan and Stacy, and it took some counseling for Tim to deal with the psychological stress he had endured during that time.

Unable to find work, he finally found a job as a customer service manager, but had a new appreciation for life and much more positive attitude about everything, especially his family. Gina had mentioned to Stacy that in some way it was an odd blessing, because as much as he adored his family, he now truly lived life to the fullest and they have never been happier.

Stacy asked Ryan, "Do you think HR will have an issue that he hasn't been in IT for a while?"

"You and I can make the case for him. Why don't you get in touch with him and see if he is interested, and if not, let's get him interested."

She ran out of the office quickly, excited to once again work with Tim. She hoped he would not have a problem reporting into her, but she was confident she could help him succeed and Ryan knew they would not let each other down.

The more pressing question for Ryan was whom he should recommend to run the department once he left. He knew there was a strong likelihood that his recommendation would receive great consideration, especially since Rebecca and Stacy had both performed admirably.

They each had unique qualities that made them successful in different ways. Stacy was a longtime advisor for him and had taken on a unique circumstance, being new to the company and performing very well. Rebecca, who had significant institutional knowledge, was an asset to the corporation and had learned how to be a leader in a very short time.

He spent the better part of the morning contemplating whom he should recommend. He never considered bringing in an outside individual because he believed they had both earned the right of consideration. As he was gazing out his window, thinking of the qualities each had and who would be best for the department, he heard a knock on his door. He turned around to see Rebecca standing in the doorway.

"Come in, Rebecca. What can I do for you?" he asked.

"Well, I have a unique favor to ask, and I really don't know exactly how to ask it," she replied.

"Sure, anything, what is it?"

She proceeded to tell him, that she wasn't sure how to come in and ask, but she trusted Ryan implicitly and felt she could ask him for an enormous favor. He was her mentor, he had helped a lot through some very difficult times, and she was very grateful and didn't want to come across as unappreciative.

"About a month ago, I was approached by a headhunter who was looking for a person to head a development group."

Rebecca had been offered the opportunity to run a development team and project management office for a children's media company. Her passion had always been working with children, as was evidenced by her tremendous community involvement. She active in the Big Sister program and was the treasurer of her local Kiwanis chapter. The prospect of working for a company that serviced children appealed to her in a way no other job could and with expanded responsibilities, there was no way she could pass up an opportunity of this nature.

"You're leaving?" Ryan asked

She shuddered at his question and replied, "No, I would never…Not exactly. I haven't accepted…Actually, they haven't offered me…," she stopped, and her face began to redden and her breathing was shallower.

"It's OK, Rebecca, anyone who could get you would be very lucky."

"What?"

"If they haven't made you an offer yet, I think they are pretty dumb," he said.

"You're not angry?" she asked.

"Why would I be angry? You've done a tremendous amount of work here. If you feel you can do more elsewhere or if it's better for your career, I support you 100 percent. What was the favor?"

"Well, that's exactly it, I'm a leading candidate, but I was hoping I could get a reference from you."

"Of course, call them up and tell them to call me right away. I'm at my desk, and I'll speak to anyone. Give them my cell, just in case."

"Thank you Ryan, I really wanted this job because it's a great move for my career. I love it here and I don't want you to think I'm ungrateful. I love the people, Stacy and Mr. Wheeler. You've all been so wonderful to me."

"Rebecca, stop. We're not dead. We will still be around. We are professionals, although I know not everyone is. But we most certainly would understand if something is better for your career and this sounds very much like it is. I would be very sad to see you go, but very happy for you at the same time."

Rebecca was elated but Ryan asked one more question, "Are you sure there is nothing we can do to make you stay?"

"Actually, no, I want to go into another industry and broaden my experience."

"If I left and recommended you for my job, would you accept?" he asked.

"Thank you, but I would decline. First, I think Stacy should run this department and second, I really want to move to another industry. I love media and it's an opportunity I can't pass up."

"Then don't think twice about it. I'll wait for the call."

She left the room with a tear in her eye, still unable to fight the feeling that she was abandoning them, but simultaneously very happy for the privilege of working this group. Ryan was genuinely happy for her, because she deserved the chance to run a group and she would do marvelously. He had received the same break years ago when he came to SportsCentral.

Rebecca would get the job offer twenty four hours after Ryan's recommendation. His recommendation and stellar reference was the differentiator. She had decided to take the offer and would begin in three weeks. Therefore, she was respectfully tendering her resignation. He couldn't have been happier for her and he told her to never hesitate to contact him if she needed anything. Ryan asked if Stacy knew the news, and whether he could tell her. She said, "Of course she knew, who do you think told me to come and ask you for a reference?"

"The Stace strikes again!" he said, adding, "I'm always the last to know."

Now Ryan's decision was much easier. He could go to Mr. Wheeler and recommend that Stacy take over his spot. Ryan hoped he would agree with the decision. Unfortunately, he would have to go in with a double blow—Rebecca's resignation and his resignation.

Ryan went up in the early afternoon to see Mr. Wheeler. It was a slow day, and he had been doing some online planning of a cruise he intended to take next quarter. He was looking for a weeklong luxury cruise up the West Coast to Alaska where he could breathe the fresh air and gaze at the snowcapped mountaintops to the east. He motioned to Ryan to come into the office and have a seat.

"What can I do for you, sir?" asked Mr. Wheeler.

Ryan had noticed some subtle changes in Mr. Wheeler over the past two years and his calling him "sir" was one of them. He had achieved a very high level of respect, so that even in cordial settings, Mr.

Wheeler would sometimes use the term sir, which was a singular honor for him.

"Well, I have some potentially bad news."

Mr. Wheeler didn't like the sound of it and it was almost as if he knew what was coming. As an executive, he had been in this situation many times before and was rarely caught off guard, but this time he thought, might be a rare exception.

"Rebecca has tendered her resignation effective three weeks from today. She is going to be running an entire development team and it's a great opportunity for her career."

"I'm very sad to see her go, but if she thinks it's great for her career, I will wish her all the best of luck. Is there anything we can do to keep her?"

"No, she pretty much made up her mind. It has nothing to do with money or the situation here. She is really looking for the challenge this new position presents."

"Well, if she is happy, I am happy for her."

Mr. Wheeler was saddened but relieved at the same time. He remembered how she languished under Bill years ago and through Ryan's mentoring, she had become a critical asset to the organization, and she would now become an asset to someone else and most likely mentor her group in the same way Ryan had his.

"One more thing," Ryan said.

After a brief pause, he said, "I am leaving as well. I'm sorry you have two at the same time, but Rebecca just informed me about an hour ago, and I had only decided to accept the presented offer earlier this week."

"That was the one I was afraid of. I'll ask the same question, even though I already know the answer. Is there anything we can do to keep you?"

"I don't think so. I will be running the entire IT department for EduCARE, and they are in desperate need of help. I like the challenge they pose and I especially like the organization's mission."

Mr. Wheeler said to Ryan he wouldn't try to convince him but he did need time to get a suitable replacement and he asked if he had anyone in mind. Ryan immediately recommended Stacy for the position. Mr. Wheeler agreed to the recommendation, saying he couldn't think of a better person. She was the best candidate and she deserved the opportunity. He did ask Ryan not to tell Stacy, since he wanted to be the one to tell her. Ryan loved the thought of keeping

Stacy in the dark for once. He knew she would be very upset that he didn't tell her first.

Ryan would stay for the next two months, long enough for Mr. Wheeler to take his well-deserved cruise and enough time for Stacy to get accustomed to her new role. He decided to act as an observer for the last month and let Stacy make the decisions, and only intervene if she asked. The group would be hers and he wanted to leave her with the department that was hers, not his.

A few days before his final days at the office Stacy, John, and Mr. Wheeler took Ryan out to dinner as a farewell. John thanked Ryan for his patience and confidence with him and he said he would try to continue to exhibit those same qualities. Stacy, who would undoubtedly continue to badger Ryan till his old age, told Ryan that even though he was leaving the company he could never get rid of her and that Lisa would see to that. She also praised Ryan for his mentoring and his confidence in her and the trust he placed in her. He believed in her when no one else did, and even when she did not. She would always remember that.

Finally, Mr. Wheeler said Ryan was leaving the company in a better state than when he received it. He recounted stories of how Jay had recommended Ryan for the job and reminisced about how Bill attempted to sabotage Ryan, who skillfully handled the situation. He compared that situation with the confrontation at the conference.

He summarized the sentiment at the table and said, "Ryan, you handled every situation you could with professionalism and courtesy, even when you were angry and harmed. You never lost sight of your focus on your team, their well-being, and the mission; it is that dedication and spirit, I hope, at the very least everyone learns. You leave us a wonderful legacy."

The table agreed with the sentiment and raised their glasses to Ryan in a toast. Ryan reflected on the sentiment of the table and realized he was satisfied. He was very satisfied at the job he had worked so diligently to accomplish. He was leaving the organization in very capable hands, and she would put her own mark on the group and establish her own legacy. He could accomplish nothing more here. As much as he hated the prospect of leaving his friends and colleagues, he would have an opportunity to meet new friends and establish a new legacy.

Ryan went home that evening and decided to make an entry into his journal that he had started a year ago. He remembered all the times he tried to write down the meaning of being a leader, and the attributes of leadership. He decided to write an entry for his last day at SportsCentral. He picked up his pencil and began to write down the comments John, Stacy, and Mr. Wheeler had ascribed to him so that he wouldn't forget. Then he wrote down the same heading he had done years before, which had remained indelibly in his head, "Thoughts on Leadership."

He wrote down as many words as he could in no particular order and listed them vertically including: integrity, trust, intuition, clarity, direction, agreement, empowerment, speed, decisiveness, selflessness, and legacy. Every single one of these words seemed to be attributes that a leader must possess in order to be successful. While many good leaders may have had many of these attributes, only the best leaders would have possessed every single one. He recounted the exercise he once tried to complete of examining leaders that possessed the key characteristics across every industry.

He looked at the list one more time and recalled one characteristic whose omission was glaringly obvious. He tried to condense it to the single word, "control," but it failed to convey the meaning he wished to convey. He wrote it down in a line by itself:

"The more control you try to exert, the less control you actually have."

This sentiment conveyed the principle of patience, faith, and adaptability that many micromanagers fail to exhibit and that many great leaders overcome with skill. By writing it down, he remembered an old saying that he had long forgotten that somehow resurfaced in his head. It was the Serenity Prayer from St. Francis of Assisi and he wrote it on the last three lines of the page, because he thought it summarized one of the most critical aspects of leadership.

"Grant me the strength to change what can be changed, the patience to deal with what cannot be changed, and the wisdom to know the difference."

Great leadership, he thought, comes from knowing one's own ability and the ability of the team. Proper employment of one's resources at the right time is critical to success, and a great leader must have patience to know when to effect change. Only through wisdom can one hope to achieve such mastery of leadership.

Everything became very clear in an instant, even though it was a decade long journey from his first scribbling on a napkin and his intense belief that he might find a magic bullet. He hadn't found the magic bullet, but he certainly had found *the right ammunition*.

The next day, Ryan was excited to see his son's high school championship baseball game. It was a great break from thinking about leadership and work. He returned to his true passion of baseball. He had seen his son, A. J. grow into a very good baseball player in which he took immense pride. A. J., now a sophomore in high school, had made the varsity squad earlier in the year and he had become one of the leading hitters on the team. The coaches were a very fine crew and they diligently worked with A. J. to develop his talent.

The game was against last year's champions, the Cougars, who were looking for their third title in a row and everyone suspected it would be a battle since both teams had their star pitchers on the mound. It was a fantastic cool early June day and the sun was high in the sky with no clouds around. The field was a well-manicured municipal field and the crowd numbered around a hundred for the game, a scene that could have been the subject of a Norman Rockwell painting.

The game lived up to its expectations with each team scratching out two runs apiece with base hits and bunts. There were only two extra base hits in the game and the teams played superb defense. Ryan watched as A. J., who had played the outfield, made a wonderful inning-ending diving catch in the outfield in the fifth inning with the bases loaded, which easily saved three runs and allowed the game to remain tied. Ryan was the loudest person in the stands, cheering to the slight embarrassment of A. J. Secretly, though A. J. loved the fact that his father was so into the game, but being the sophomore on the team, he didn't want to his teammates to know.

In the top of the seventh inning, the Cougars scored the go ahead run on three straight singles, but A. J.'s team managed to keep the damage to only one run, and with the heart of the order coming up, the team was confident they would get the run back. In the bottom of the inning, the first batter hit the first pitch for a single up the middle that ignited a cheer from the stands. Both teams were standing up and every fan in the stands was standing up cheering for their respective teams. The next batter followed the first with a double in the gap, which the center fielder played well, and which could have probably scored the tying run but traditional baseball wisdom told the coach not to send the runner. They were going to play by the book and they were executing their plan perfectly. Unfortunately, the next two batters struck out and they were unable to score the tying run from third base.

A. J. was the next batter, and for a moment, Ryan thought the coach might pull him out for a senior on the bench, but the coach knew he needed contact and that a strikeout would be the worst possible result. A. J. had the fewest strikeouts on the team and he had the best intuition of the strike zone the coach had ever seen, having only struck out three times all year.

A. J. stepped up to the plate and all Ryan could do was close his eyes and pray, "Please hit the ball. Please hit the ball." Ryan was a nervous wreck, but A. J. seemed very cool and collected at the plate with an unmatched confidence. He had been waiting for a moment like this all year.

The first pitch came over the plate for a strike. A. J. liked to take the first pitch in order to time the pitcher and get a feel for his velocity. The pitcher threw the next two pitches outside of the strike zone. There was a moment when the opposing coach thought of intentionally walking him, but because he knew A. J. was a sophomore, he decided to pitch to him. The next pitch came over and A. J. pulled the ball foul down the third base line. With two strikes, the third baseman would now back up about three steps behind third base to prevent an extra base hit.

A. J. stepped into the box and waited for the pitch. He was looking for a fastball, figuring the pitcher wanted to blow him away. The pitcher went into the wind up and A. J. picked up the pitch immediately as a fastball. He stepped in and swung perfectly. A. J. made great contact and the bat made the perfect sound of the cracking bat, which is exactly what happened. The bat shattered into three pieces and the ball rolled behind the pitcher to the shortstop, who threw A. J. out by two steps at first base.

A. J. fell down to the ground after he reached first base and pounded the ground with his fist as he was hunched over. The coach went over to him, patted him on the back, and walked him back to the dugout as the Cougars celebrated their third consecutive championship. A. J.'s coach congratulated the team after they shook hands and spoke to them for five minutes in the dugout praising their effort. Ryan was near the dugout listening in to what the coach was saying. He could see the immense disappointment on A. J.'s face and couldn't help but sympathize with him.

When the coach released the team, A. J., who was very disappointed, came around to his father and said, "What bum luck. I did everything right. I was patient, I knew the pitch, and I stepped in and swung perfectly."

Ryan replied, "You did the best you could. Sometimes you can do everything perfectly, but the result may be less than perfect. One day you will understand, the more control you try to exert, the less control you actually have. You did your best, honorably, and that's all anyone can ask."

8196859R0

Made in the USA
Lexington, KY
18 January 2011